MODERNITY'S CORRUPTION

MODERNITY'S CORRUPTION

EMPIRE AND MORALITY IN THE MAKING OF BRITISH INDIA

NICHOLAS HOOVER WILSON

Columbia University Press *New York*

Columbia University Press
Publishers Since 1893
New York   Chichester, West Sussex
cup.columbia.edu

Copyright © 2023 Columbia University Press
All rights reserved

Library of Congress Cataloging-in-Publication Data
Names: Wilson, Nicholas Hoover, author.
Title: Modernity's corruption : empire and morality in the
making of British India / Nicholas Hoover Wilson.
Description: New York, NY : Columbia University Press, [2023] |
Includes bibliographical references and index.
Identifiers: LCCN 2022043086 | ISBN 9780231192187 (hardback) |
ISBN 9780231192194 (trade paperback) |
ISBN 9780231549707 (ebook)
Subjects: LCSH: East India Company—History. |
East India Company—Corrupt practices. East India Company—
Officials and employees. | Great Britain—Moral conditions—
Case studies. | Great Britain—Colonies—India—Administration. |
Public administration—India—Corrupt practices. | Corruption—
History—18th century. | Corruption—History—19th century.
Classification: LCC DS465 .W743 2023 |
DDC 954.03/1—dc23/eng/20221223
LC record available at https://lccn.loc.gov/2022043086

Cover design: Noah Arlow
Cover image: New Government House, Calcutta
(view South East), engraving by James Moffat (1775–1815).
Courtesy of the British Library.

MODERNITY'S CORRUPTION

EMPIRE AND MORALITY IN THE MAKING OF BRITISH INDIA

NICHOLAS HOOVER WILSON

Columbia University Press *New York*

Columbia University Press
Publishers Since 1893
New York   Chichester, West Sussex
cup.columbia.edu

Copyright © 2023 Columbia University Press
All rights reserved

Library of Congress Cataloging-in-Publication Data
Names: Wilson, Nicholas Hoover, author.
Title: Modernity's corruption : empire and morality in the
making of British India / Nicholas Hoover Wilson.
Description: New York, NY : Columbia University Press, [2023] |
Includes bibliographical references and index.
Identifiers: LCCN 2022043086 | ISBN 9780231192187 (hardback) |
ISBN 9780231192194 (trade paperback) |
ISBN 9780231549707 (ebook)
Subjects: LCSH: East India Company—History. |
East India Company—Corrupt practices. East India Company—
Officials and employees. | Great Britain—Moral conditions—
Case studies. | Great Britain—Colonies—India—Administration. |
Public administration—India—Corrupt practices. | Corruption—
History—18th century. | Corruption—History—19th century.
Classification: LCC DS465 .W743 2023 |
DDC 954.03/1—dc23/eng/20221223
LC record available at https://lccn.loc.gov/2022043086

Cover design: Noah Arlow
Cover image: New Government House, Calcutta
(view South East), engraving by James Moffat (1775–1815).
Courtesy of the British Library.

CONTENTS

Preface vii

Introduction: Modernity's Corruption and the Art of Separation 1

1 Corruption and Moral Orders in Eighteenth-Century Britain and India 45
2 Shifting Grounds: The Transformation of the East India Company 82
3 Consequential Reforms and Changing Corruption 119
4 Modern Selves 145
5 Modern Moral Spaces 176

Conclusion 217

Notes 233
References 261
Index 281

PREFACE

To write effective historical sociology—to pull it off, as Dylan Riley might say—is always to dance on a razor's edge. Fall to one side, and you land in a mass of superficial, or even incorrect, historical interpretations, bending them beyond recognition to fit a mold shaped by present-day concerns. Fall to the other side, and you hit a map as detailed as the terrain itself, interesting to historians, perhaps, but rarely useful to guide social scientists. Worst of all, fall awkwardly and your work could end up a messy split that disappoints historians and social scientists alike. But to get the steps right and pull off the dance is to use history to help understand not just the influence of the past on the present but also to show how the categories, concepts, and causes that social scientists sometimes take for granted and treat as though they are universal are, in fact, historical accomplishments that shape, but do not determine, how we think and what we do today.

I cannot tell you if I have pulled it off, of course. That judgment depends on the readers for *Modernity's Corruption*, whoever they turn out to be, and how they receive my argument. But I can tell you what my aims are. This book tries to make sense of *how* "we"—Western, liberal, well-to-do academics, policymakers, and hopefully the general reading public—think about corruption today. It also suggests some reasons for *why* we think about corruption this way and not some other. This kind of argument is inherently historical—it asks how something came to be—and has two main explanatory threads.

The first is raw demonstration: I will try to persuade you that in addition to the contemporary, commonsense view of corruption as a quid pro quo in which some official violates their public duty for private gain, there is another way of thinking about corruption that was at least as important historically. In this alternative view, corruption was deeply "situational," in the sense that cues about what was and was not corruption came from an endless variety of social situations that spelled out not only conduct but also the standards of judgment people should use and even how their senses of themselves as moral individuals were structured.

The second thread is suggestive: I will also lay out one historical path that shifted the dominant understanding of corruption from the situational order to a more familiar framework. The goal here is not to say definitively that this is *the only* way the shift happened but rather to probe one time that it did happen to try and find general conditions that make a shift possible. Here, my goal is to persuade you that a keyword is "empire" and that familiar understandings of corruption came to dominant at least in part because of the characteristic problems of organizing imperial administration.

This is a big argument, and I have developed it in dialog with an epochal historical event: the transition of the English East India Company (EIC) from an organization mostly geared toward commerce (although it did have territorial aspects) to the largest territorial sovereign in South Asia (although it continued some aspects of its commerce). This study of the EIC plays two critical roles in this book. First, it substantiates my argument by giving a detailed look at the perspectives, actions, ambitions, judgments, arguments, lives, and (sometimes) deaths of colonial officials as they interacted with indigenous societies and one another. Second, it also supplies a world-historical, influential case of imperial administration and thus hopefully lays a foundation for comparison and generalization to other cases, both similar and different, to extend the argument I make here.

In pursuing this complicated set of goals, there are many flaws in the pages that follow. Social theorists may find my conceptualization of corruption wanting; scholars of states and empires may reject my characterizations and periodization; historians may wish me bodily harm. In particular, I regret that limitations of language and time prevented me from giving more systematic attention to the dynamics of post-Mughal Indian elites. But even if some do not prefer the tune, I hope there is value in trying to dance.

A book like this is a journey, as anyone who has known me for the last decade-plus will know all too well. And along the way, a variety of venues and people have supported me more than I could have imagined.

This book started its life at the University of Maryland, when I first became interested in, and wrote my undergraduate honors thesis on, the moral dynamics of colonialism. The thesis was produced jointly in the sociology and history departments, and I cannot thank the faculty there enough for launching me on this journey: Meyer Kestnbaum, Patricio Korzeniewicz, and George Ritzer all endured my taking their graduate seminars; and Jeanne Rutenburg and Arthur Eckstein were superlative historians and mentors. Linda Moghadam and Barbara Meeker guided me through the honors thesis process generously and with good humor.

The next step I took in the project that would become this book took place at the University of California, Berkeley. There could hardly be a more idyllic place to find one's intellectual feet, and I turned to the EIC's activities in India thanks to a line from Eric Stokes's *The English Utilitarians in India*, which I read as part of James Vernon's "Making of Modern Britain" graduate seminar. It was also there that I encountered historians whose friendship and intellectual influence has meant more than I can say and who helped shaped this project: Desmond Fitzgibbon, Jo Guldi, Penny Ismay, Radhika Natarajan, and Caroline Shaw. My institutional home in the sociology department also had no shortage of graduate student colleagues from whom I learned: Rachel Best, Jonah Brundage, Ryan Calder, Peter Dixon, Dawn Dow, Barry Eidlin, Sarah Garrett, Kristen Gray, Jennifer Jones, Brian Lande, Laura Mangels, Stephanie Mudge, Freeden Oeur, Jennifer Randles, and Erendira Rueda. And, of course, the faculty was warm, generous, and engaging. The debts I have to the Berkeley sociology faculty are too numerous to mention, but let me single out several faculty members whose efforts crossed from "informal conversation" to "what one would expect of a supervisor anywhere else": Vicky Bonnell, who taught me about historical sociology and everyday life; Claude Fischer, who sharpened my writing and listened to me complain about the Orioles; Marion Fourcade, from whom I learned economic sociology's intersection with morality; Heather Haveman, who sharpened my analytic gaze; Margaret Weir, who put up with my odd questions about political sociology; and Robb Willer, who educated me on the meaning of the phrase "eight hats in a box."

Of course, a project like this, coming as it does from my dissertation, owes its fundamental shape to my committee, above all, to Ann Swidler, who, as my chair, supported my flights of fancy while resolutely tethering me back down to empirical reality, to questions of meaning and organization, and to concrete actions undertaken by real people. Neil Fligstein helped shape this project through his sheer enthusiasm and urged me to think of the EIC as an organizational field while also unflaggingly helping to sustain my spirits and lending me office space at the Institute for Relations in Labor and Employment at Berkeley. James Vernon provided the substantive spine of my dissertation and this book by suggesting the idea—during my defense—of focusing on the intersection of moral images of social order and conflict within the EIC over policy choices. He also arranged for me to undertake the Pembroke College Anglo-California Exchange Fellowship, through which I was able to spend a year at the archives in Britain and to have productive conversations with Professor Sir Christopher Bayly while I enjoyed the hospitality of Pembroke College in Cambridge. And Dylan Riley's relentless, razor-sharp analytic mind invited me to think through the causal claims I was making and to clarify my argument much more than I would have done otherwise.

After graduating, I undertook a three-year postdoctoral fellowship at Yale University, at the MacMillan Center for International and Area Studies, and in affiliation with the sociology department. Steven Pincus was my generous benefactor in this, and from him, I learned how important 1688 was for British history and the value of continued contact between history and the social sciences; meanwhile, Julia Adams was not only a huge intellectual influence (as the following pages show) but also such an enthusiastic supporter that I sometimes worried that she mistook me for a more talented scholar! And if that pair weren't enough, Yale also led me to sustained friendly and intellectual encounters with Emily Erikson, Bruce Gordon, Phil Gorski,

Ayesha Ramachandaran, and Jonathan Wyrtzen. During the crucial period where this project went from dissertation to book, they provided guidance and intellectual companionship. In addition, I was part of a great cohort of postdoctoral fellows, including Sadia Saeed and Matthew Mahler, and encountered another sterling set of history and sociology graduate students, particularly Catherine Arnold, Amanda Behm, Christian Burset, Justin Durivage, Jeff Guhin, Sarah Kinkel, Elizabeth Roberto, and Jensen Sass (again, among many others).

Here at Stony Brook University, I once again benefited from an amazing set of colleagues in both history and sociology. Katy Fallon, Paul Gootenburg, Daniel Levy, and Ian Roxborough were crucial senior colleagues who did much to polish this project, and Eric Beverly, Rebekah Burroway, Jennifer Heerwig, Tiffany Joseph, and Kristen Shorette were amazing colleagues who have heard me agonize over this project one too many times. I am also grateful to S. N. Sridhar for providing me an affiliation to Stony Brook's Center for India Studies.

Beyond those who at least had to listen to me because of some kind of institutional affiliation, a circle of people has also come together around this project who are distinguished simply by their sheer intellectual generosity. Historians like Mark Knights, Phil Stern, James Vaughn, Jon Wilson, and Kathleen Wilson have all generously helped me think through parts of what follows, and sociologists like Gabi Abend, Álvaro Santana Acuña, Stefan Bargheer, Jonah Stuart Brundage, Bruce Carruthers, Rebecca Emigh, Julian Go, Carly Knight, Richard Lachmann, Chris Muller, Ann Orloff, Josh Pacewicz, Monica Prasad, Anna Skarpelis, George Steinmetz, and Iddo Tavory have variously read pieces of this work or improved it through conversation. I also write this in the midst of an ongoing but already enormously stimulating collaboration on the sociology of corruption with Marco Garrido and Marina Zaloznaya.

All of these thanks so far have had a personal dimension, but there are two more that deserve special mention. The first is Anurag Sinha. Since I met him in Phil Gorski's philosophy of social science course at Yale, he has been something of a fellow-traveler for this project. He has shared his superior knowledge of the practices of the EIC with me, his superlative grasp of the history of political thought, and a warm generosity and enthusiasm for the project. He has done all of this while working out a critical, and soon forthcoming, intervention into EIC scholarship (and the history of political thought) that will help to reshape the field.

Second is Damon Mayrl. While the substance of our collaboration is far afield from what you will read, Damon's friendship, relentless work ethic, kindness, fearsome intelligence, and insight have turned me into the scholar I am today, and thus his influence is here, too.

You cannot eat moral support, so I also should acknowledge various sources of funding that have sustained this project. In graduate school, I got a National Science Foundation Graduate Research Fellowship and also enjoyed the Pembroke-Berkeley Anglo-California Exchange Fellowship. At Stony Brook, I was lucky enough to receive a Humanities Institute Faculty Fellowship, which extended my junior leave, and a Trustees Faculty Award. Parts of this work also draws from work I have published as articles; in particular, chapter 5 uses and extends elements of my articles "The Fixation of (Moral) Belief: Making Imperial Administration Modern," which was published in 2018 in the *European Journal of Sociology* and "Moral Accounting as Field Foundation in an Early Modern Empire" from the *Sociological Review*; and chapters 2 and 3 adapt " 'A State In Disguise of a

Merchant?'The East India Company as a Strategic Action Field, ca. 1763–1834," published in *Political Power and Social Theory* in 2015. I am grateful to Cambridge University Press, SAGE Publications, and the Emerald Publishing Group, respectively, for permission to use the material here.

Finally, the *really* personal thank-yous. My mother, Modena, taught me about how ethics and knowledge can come together in the hopes of making the world better; my father, Gary, taught me how to write and to find the sharp details in the world; my brother, Christopher, supported this project and me from as early as I can remember. And, above all, Julie Huang, who, aside from making the ill-considered choice to marry me, is the best person I have met.

Nicholas Hoover Wilson
November 2022

MODERNITY'S CORRUPTION

INTRODUCTION

Modernity's Corruption and the Art of Separation

Am I not rather deserving of praise for the moderation which marked my proceedings? Consider the situation in which the victory at Plassey had placed me. A great prince was dependent on my pleasure; an opulent city lay at my mercy; its richest bankers bid against each other for my smiles; I walked through vaults which were thrown open to me alone, piled on either hand with gold and jewels! Mr. Chairman, at this moment I stand astonished at my own moderation!

—Robert Clive, 1772

THE PUZZLE OF MODERNITY'S CORRUPTION

Robert Clive may or may not have said the exact words shown in this introduction's epigraph, but this passage has become an iconic representation of a corrupt era in the English East India Company's (EIC) transition from a (mostly) commercial concern to something more closely resembling a modern imperial state.[1] By 1772, Clive had been to India in the service of the EIC three times; had distinguished himself through military service when the company increasingly intervened in political affairs on the subcontinent; and had amassed a stupendously large fortune from a variety of sources, both formally sanctioned and, to some eyes, illicit.[2] It was a threat to this fortune that elicited Clive's statement above: by the late 1760s, his organizational enemies had gathered enough strength both in the EIC's Court of Directors on Leadenhall Street in London and in the British Parliament to accuse Clive of having acquired one of the crowning jewels of his Indian fortune—the *jagir*, an annuity drawn from the land taxes of a district near Calcutta and granted to him (and not the company) by the nawab of Bengal and ratified by the Mughal emperor—through corrupt means. They convened a parliamentary select committee to investigate the "Nature, State and Condition of the East India Company" on which Clive sat and by which he was being interrogated when he is said to have uttered his defense.[3]

Normally, a book about the history and social science of corruption would seek to untangle whether Clive really was "corrupt." It might puzzle, for example, over whether accepting "presents" (usually valuables or, in Clive's case, also the *jagir*) counts as a "gift" or a "bribe." Or it might seek to account for why Clive's superiors in the EIC, after he had accepted one such large "present" and was being attacked as a "nabob"[4] on the British political and social scene, thought that he was the perfect anticorruption crusader to be sent back to cleanse the "Augean Stables" of company administration in Bengal.[5] Or, as both amateur and professional historians have done, it could plumb Clive's psychology, ideology, and motivations, seeking to reconcile the various twists and turns of his career. Was he a "heaven-sent general" who saved the company's prospects and with them the British Empire in Asia? Or was he the worst "nabob" of them all, corrupted, like the soon-to-be notorious

Governor-General of India Warren Hastings, by the larger moral decay of his era?[6]

These are all admirable aims, but the goal of *Modernity's Corruption* is different. Rather than attempting to untangle the reality of Clive's corruption, the book instead takes as its puzzle the murky, chaotic world in which Clive's tangled career, the choices he made, and the justifications he offered for what he did made good sense to some observers and were bitterly rejected as moral transgressions by others. This tension resonates in his purported statement that opens this introduction: on the one hand, the difficult temptation of private enrichment while serving others is familiar to us today, but on the other hand, Clive seems to be inhabiting a moral world very different from ours, in which "moderate" indulgence was meant to be virtuous. The puzzle at the center of *Modernity's Corruption* is thus less how to reconcile Clive's behavior and life—and those of the many other EIC servants of whom Clive is an extreme example—with our modern assumptions about virtue and corruption but rather to untangle and explain the chaotic intersection of two moral orders and to uncover a larger story of what corruption is and does.

With this puzzle in mind, *Modernity's Corruption* explores several themes. Most directly, it is about the category of corruption; how and why our understanding of corruption has mutated and transformed over time; and how one view of it has become a familiar, widespread, and "modern" way to judge the conduct of public officials. At the heart of the book's historical account stands the English EIC,[7] a loose subsidiary of the British Empire (at least at the beginning of our account), and the EIC's emergence of the predominant territorial power in much of modern South Asia. My central substantive argument is that when the EIC's affairs became subject to a "distant" metropolitan gaze—that is, when the conduct of its officials was scrutinized by relative "outsiders" with little knowledge of India or the details of company affairs—more modern understandings of corruption (which emphasize deviation of public duty away from private interests) predominated.[8]

This substantive account in turn touches on several issues of recent social-scientific interest. First, recent interdisciplinary scholarly work on corruption has diminished the concept in various ways. Some have reduced "corruption" and its rejection to a matter of badly designed or evolved institutions.[9] Others have argued that humans simply see corruption as unfair because they possess a kind of universal moral sense.[10] Others still tell such particular histories of the category of corruption that it is unclear if the concept holds any general utility.[11] By contrast, along with those who have insisted that corruption is fundamentally a plural concept representing a variety of different forms of social organization and moral transgression,[12] this book stresses the peculiarity of corruption as a social category—how it stands between the particularity of any given moment of social life yet also invokes broad understandings of right and wrong. In other words, analyzing corruption drives us to ask, in turn, How and why do the "moral backgrounds" and "moral orders" of societies shift, mutate, and transform?[13]

Second, in contrast to scholarship, which tends to view corruption as an output or "error" of other social processes,[14] *Modernity's Corruption* emphasizes how corruption is a source of dynamism and change. This is because corruption accusations are always embedded in moments of social struggle and because they inherently draw moral boundaries between good and bad behaviors.[15] In so doing, corruption destroys and constructs political coalitions, enables certain forms of organization and governance while judging that others are out of bounds, and mobilizes resources into political and organizational struggles

INTRODUCTION ᴄʀ 5

while cutting others off. In short, this book views corruption not as an ephemeral indicator of some kind of social dysfunction but rather as a potent *style of moral accusation* made during moments of organizational struggle.

To emphasize how accusations of corruption represent forms of "moral entrepreneurship"[16] raises the question of what was "modern" and new about the category; here, *Modernity's Corruption* emphasizes a particular kind of abstraction. When administrators argued using a language of modern corruption, this required that the logic of the colonial state be disembedded—that it leave behind particularistic local circumstances or concerns about managing concrete networks of interaction as its central governing imperatives and instead shape itself by the moral abstractions of political economy.[17] For individual administrators, this way of thinking about modern corruption in turn relied on a unitary moral biography—a coherent account to link justifications they made to these purportedly universal, ethically disembedded moral spaces. Such a unitary moral biography meant that moments of biographical fragmentation that had hitherto not been problematic suddenly had to be reconciled by narratives of moral conversion or explained away lest they become damning evidence against one's credibility.

In sum, this book recognizes that the moral worlds that anchor claims about corruption form "social imaginaries" of much broader significance for ethical life.[18] By focusing on these accusations and their sources and transformations, in other words, we are provided a unique window into how the moral outlooks of imperial state administrators "became modern." Put differently, *Modernity's Corruption* demonstrates how imperial administrators' corruption arguments were a crucial part of how the state self-constituted as a domain of duty and activity, on the one hand, and how the boundaries among it, the economy, and civil society were delimited, on the other.[19]

"Corruption," in both its modern and nonmodern forms, thus weaves together multiple analytic levels and parts of social, political, and moral life. To unravel these connections, the remainder of this introduction first spells out the book's central contrast between two different modes of corruption in greater detail. Then I discuss the different domains of scholarship informing the book. I then draw from that literature to construct a specific account of corruption that emphasizes its "relational" aspect—the fact that whatever else corruption may be, it is a style of accusation intended to mobilize an audience to one's side during an organizational struggle. Fourth, I discuss why the British Empire in the eighteenth century, and particularly the EIC, is an appropriate case both on explanatory and epistemological grounds. I close with some methodological reflections and provide a roadmap for the remainder of the book.

MODERN CORRUPTION AND ITS COMPETITOR

To call someone or something "corrupt" is one of the biggest but also most beguiling accusations we can make. The concept at once invokes a moralized judgment of the system and person we are accusing and communicates the urgency of our accusation—coworkers do not call each other corrupt for stealing pencils. Partly because it is such an intense accusation, corruption also draws strong contrasts between ourselves and others; *we* are virtuous and being wronged, *they* have morally degenerated to the point that they can no longer competently execute their duty. We sometimes ascribe the causes of this condition to the characters of individuals; more often, scholars instead point to the effects of whole cultures or, more the fashion today, to the specific institutions setting the rules and defining the incentives for people's behavior. Finally, the urgency and passion that the moral accusation of corruption implies is always made to an audience. Except in dramatic moments of a police procedural or in the memoir of a reformed scoundrel,[20] it is rare indeed to accuse someone else of corruption while alone with them; rather, we accuse in order to ask others to join us in condemning a system or person, at a minimum, and hopefully also assist us in struggling for reform against those who have been corrupted.

So far, this account of corruption is only an understanding of *how* we accuse one another and in what tone but not *what* we accuse them of. This is because naming what "counts" as corruption moves beyond the universal form distinguishing the accusation to the particular circumstances in which they are being made. This book's central focus is therefore that while there may be a general *form* to corruption accusations, the *substances* incorporated into that form have seen dramatic historical shifts. For the sake of analytic simplicity, and in spite of significant variations (many of which I will describe, especially in chapter 1), the shift at the heart of *Modernity's Corruption* can be characterized as a movement from corruption understood as a loss of balance among unstable "passions" to the deviation away from institutionalized "interests."[21]

Passions and Public Corruption

The idea that corruption involved "passions" stretches to antiquity. In Greek writing on the nature of the *polis*, for instance, corruption was a key marker for a simultaneous loss of moral balance within individual people and also within a body politic. In Aristotle, to be "corrupt" was to have lost a sense of balance among the various competing "passions"—sexual and culinary appetites; greed; and emotions like pride, anger, and envy—that made up people's sense of themselves and others. The goal of virtue was to hold these various passions in balance against one another, for instance, by appealing to someone's pride to counterbalance their greed or anger, and thus "corruption" meant what ancient philosophers called *akrasia*, or a lack of control over competing impulses.[22] While the understanding of *akrasia* was modified in important ways, especially as it was incorporated into the Christian worldview (above all, by Augustine and later Thomas Aquinas), Niccolò Machiavelli renovated a secular version of this perspective in the sixteenth century.

If this view of the self as a competing heap of different passions is unfamiliar to us today, so too is the way individual corruption intersects with more general social decay. Also beginning in the Greek *polis*, the view was not that specific institutions by design incentivized people to behave in given ways but rather that an individual and their moral outlook was interwoven with society *as a whole*, thus blending together economic, social, and political activity. Because of this deep connection, "corruption" was a condition of *both* the whole social fabric *and* individual people. Therefore, Aristotle could think of both people and polities as having "constitutions" subject to corruption, Aquinas could link public action to the fate of the soul, Machiavelli could argue the relationship between the corruption of a leader and their regime, Michel de Montaigne could view a call to public service by the kind as a threat to unbalance his passions and corrupt him,[23] and Bernard de Mandeville could explicitly connect a sovereign's government as a whole with their ability to manage people's passions.[24]

Interests and Institutional Corruption

By contrast, today, an understanding that is at once narrower and more expansive has taken over several domains of life, most importantly in the works of a broad swath of legal and public policy scholars, economists, political scientists, and international and state administrators.[25] This newer but also more familiar sense of corruption is narrower in that it confines its focus to one thing: the deviation of one's behavior away from a sense of public duty and toward one's private interest. But it is also more expansive insofar as it introduces a world of public and private and of well-understood moral duties to social domains like "the economy," "the state," and "society"—otherwise, what does "duty to one's office" comprise?

By narrowing its focus to specific behaviors and widening its reach to universal, separate moral domains, this way of thinking about what corruption is generates two crucial paradoxes. First, if corruption is a label for a specific act—something someone *does* (and not something they *are*)—this is only sensible relative to some external yardstick of judgment. Indeed, as Alan Ryan has put the point, "any discussion of corruption requires a firm grip on what we think an uncorrupt political system looks like and what a 'clean' economy looks like."[26] Second, this modern understanding also confronts the problem of empirical variation: while corruption is generated by particular institutional arrangements that are different in different times and places, the accusations made of modern corruption act *as though* they reflect universal moral understandings and a shared consensus about how institutions should be arranged. These two paradoxes have been at the heart of much of the contemporary social-scientific scholarship on what corruption is and how to eradicate it.

CORRUPTION AND SOCIAL CHANGE

The social-scientific literature on corruption is an interdisciplinary project that broadly seeks to understand how postcolonial states have transitioned to democracy.[27] The study of corruption accelerated sharply amid the so-called end of history in the 1990s and remains one of the key targets of the international developmental regime today.[28] Originally, corruption was viewed by some scholars as a "good" that made the transition to a universal form of modern societies—with plural democratic governments, capitalist economies, and free civil societies—more efficient, but that view has been abandoned by modern scholarship. Corruption today is seen as a universal harm to government, a drag on economic development, and a distortion of civil society.[29]

The canonical definition of corruption in this literature was provided by Joseph Nye, who wrote in 1967 that corruption was "behavior which deviates from the formal duties of a public role because of private-regarding (personal, close family, private clique) pecuniary or status gains; or violates rules against the exercise of certain types of private-regarding influence."[30] If you are a scholar of corruption, you are already familiar with this formulation, or one like it; such definitions grace many recent works on the subject.[31] One of the features that makes it so ubiquitous is that while it *seems* to provide a specific working definition of the concept of corruption, it does so by pushing nearly all of the *substance* of what makes something corruption outside its boundaries. "Private-regarding . . . gains" are reasonably specific, although one might ask just what makes something "personal" rather than "public," and anyone who has visited an unfamiliar family gathering might marvel at the different boundaries of "close family" to different people.

Yet if we puzzle this phrase out, we encounter two other ambiguities: "public role" and "rules against" certain behavior. What exactly *is* this role? And who sets the rules? What do they say? Is there a universal set of public roles and concomitant rules?[32]

For Nye, the formalism of this definition was intentional; it was meant to overcome the problem of empirical variation. In the same 1967 article, he justified his definition in a remarkable passage:

> In less developed countries, there are two standards regarding [appropriate behavior for a public official], one indigenous and one more or less Western, and the formal duties and rules concerning most public roles tend to be expressed in terms of the latter. In short, while this definition of corruption is not entirely satisfactory in terms of inclusiveness of behavior and the handling of relativity of standards, it has the merit of denoting specific behavior generally called corrupt by Western standards . . . and thus allowing us to ask what effects this specific behavior has under different conditions.[33]

This passage is breathtaking not only because of its substance—blithely dismissing empirical variation and imposing Western standards of judging corruption as (capital U) Universal because it is too hard to accommodate "relativity of standards." It is also pivotal because of the conceptual tension it introduces—one that has been well recognized by postcolonial scholars.[34] On the one hand, the standards of judgment are abstracted outside the definition and stipulated at the outset (an imagined picture of Western practices). On the other, they are to be used to provide causal explanations for specific behaviors in specific contexts *even though* that behavior is or isn't corrupt with reference to tense local collisions of Western and non-Western norms. Thus, in Nye's hands, "corruption" becomes something simultaneously universal and specific, analytically everywhere and nowhere in particular.[35]

Ever since Nye formulated the concept of corruption in this way, social scientists have had to grapple with its tensions. This struggle has produced a heap of fascinating work, from which three main threads of response are distinguishable. The first thread tries to understand corruption by comparing whole regimes and societies rather than simply specific behaviors. Thus James Scott, in his standard-setting *Comparative Political Corruption* (1972), refuses Nye's focus on individual behaviors and instead treats corruption as "a special case of political influence" requiring a mode of analyzing corruption that "embeds it contextually in a broader analysis of a regime's political dynamics."[36] This goal leads Scott to describe corruption in a way that attempts to preserve both its historical variability and its universal sense:

> Much corruption is in a real sense a product of the late eighteenth and nineteenth centuries. Only the rise of the modern nation-state, with its mass participation, broadly representative bodies, and elaborate civil service codes, signaled the transformation of the view of government office, and even kingship, from a private right into a public responsibility.
>
> How, then, can we handle historical comparisons? If, for example, we wanted to compare the practice of bribing to gain appointment to the bureaucracy in transitional England with the same practice in modern England, we could classify such an act as corrupt in the modern period but not in the traditional period, where it often occurred openly and legally. We will want, nonetheless, to compare *practices* that are corrupt only by modern

standards and ask what their causes are in different periods, how they affect the composition of the elite, and so forth. If nepotism or bribery have similar causes and consequences in early France as in contemporary India, that is an important subject for analysis, notwithstanding the fact that legal codes and public standards have changed so much that what was tolerated (not corrupt) in early France is now forbidden by law (corrupt) in India. For our comparative purposes, then, we will refer to pre-nineteenth-century practices which only became "corrupt" in the nineteenth century as "*proto-corruption*." This convention will allow us to analyze the comparative causes and effects of similar behavior while recognizing that such earlier practices did not contravene the existing norms of official conduct and thus cannot be considered corruption as we have chosen to use the term.[37]

Here, Scott starts from the same place as Nye—separating behaviors from standards of judgment—but takes his analysis in a very different direction. Like Nye, he can recognize how the same practice may be considered corrupt at different times and places, yet he insists that such behaviors can be explained only when they are embedded in much wider sets of circumstances of a regime. Above all, this enables the comparison of a wide variety of cases and supports the insight that corruption is a species of political influence like any other, whose propriety is defined fundamentally by whether political institutions supply formal channels of influence to wealthy elites.[38]

But then, why didn't Scott simply title the book *Comparative Political Influence*? After all, Scott is trying to explain not only why practices occur but also why they are sometimes judged appropriate and sometimes not. Because he has so carefully severed behaviors from judgments and because he explicitly deploys cases from times when broad "Western standards" could not be assumed, Scott supplies moral judgment from elsewhere:

> *Our feeling* about corruption often depends on whether this "uninstitutionalized" influence of wealth [exhibited by corrupt activity on political distribution] is undermining a formal system *of which we approve or disapprove.* Thus, corruption in eighteenth- and early nineteenth-century England *seems less contemptible to us* than modern corruption since it involves the subversion of an aristocratic or status-based monopoly of government. Corruption in modern liberal democratic or socialist regimes, on the other hand, seems especially damaging since it undermines both *the egalitarian assumptions of majority rule* and the principles of even distribution of civil and social rights *of which we normally approve.*[39]

There are two ways we could read this passage. The most direct is that the "we" is literally us as readers, supplying our own moral reaction in the place where contemporaries might have. More subtly, Scott may be asking us to understand that, like behaviors such as bribery, our moral reactions are also embedded in much wider worldviews from which our judgments of corruption draw. In either event, we sit squarely back at the tension Nye originally introduced: if we sever a behavior from its judgment to understand "corruption," we are left with the problem of what standards, exactly, should provide the yardstick of judgment.

Another major family of scholarship responsive to Nye's tension focuses not on an entire regime and its relationship to corruption but on its relationship to specific institutions and their structure. And, like institutionalist scholarship more broadly, it comes in many flavors, two of which are of special importance to our focus. One such flavor is derived from rational-choice economics and has perhaps been *the* mainstream of scholarship in corruption in recent generations. This perspective is championed above all by Susan Rose-Ackerman, who inaugurated it with her seminal *Corruption: A Study of Political Economy* in 1978.

The first move in this line of scholarship is to specify corruption even further. From a set of practices, it is usually reduced to only bribery.[40] And, as with Nye, this further narrowing has an admirable payoff: institutions cause more or less corruption to the extent that they are arranged such that the benefits of taking a bribe outweigh the costs of doing so.[41] As with Nye, however, to achieve this insight, a great deal must be swept from view. Consider how Rose-Ackerman handles the problem of cultural variation that so bedeviled Nye: "Obviously, subtle differences in culture and basic values exist across the world. But there is one human motivator that is both universal and central to explaining the divergent experiences of different countries. That motivator is self-interest, including an interest in the well-being of one's family and peer group. Critics call it greed. Economists call it utility maximization. Whatever the label, societies differ in the way they channel self-interest. Endemic corruption suggests a pervasive failure to tap self-interest for productive purposes."[42] At a stroke, Nye's problem of the manifest variation in standards of judgment has become "subtle differences," and the core driver of variation is instead to be found in the "universal" utility maximization. Yet if we look at Rose-Ackerman's work more closely, we can see that cultural variation cannot be dismissed so easily. In 1999's *Corruption and Government*, for instance, culture is given structural prominence.[43] There, Rose-Ackerman describes her scholarly role like this:

> My aim is crucially not to set a universal standard for where to draw the legal line between praiseworthy gifts and illegal and unethical bribes. It will be enough to isolate the factors that

should go into the choice. Culture and history are explanations, not excuses. As an economist, I cannot provide an in-depth analysis of the role of culture and history, but I can point out where the legacy of the past no longer fits modern conditions.[44]

This is a welcome caveat, and I read it as an effort to avoid the cultural condescension that too often follows the analysis of corruption. But Nye's tension again peeks in: just what does it mean for "the legacy of the past" to "no longer fit modern conditions"? Rose-Ackerman spells this out later, at the end of a chapter where she distinguishes among prices, gifts, bribes, and tips:

> The definition of bribes and gifts is a cultural matter, but "culture" is dynamic and constantly changing. If behavior labeled 'corrupt' by some observers is, nevertheless, viewed as acceptable gift giving or tipping within a country, it should simply be legalized and reported. If, however, these practices are imposing hidden or indirect costs on the populace, analysts can clarify and document these costs. Definitions of acceptable behavior may change once people are informed of the costs of tolerating payoffs to politicians and civil servants.[45]

If Scott injects the moral significance back into "corruption" via an invitation to the reader's sympathies, Rose-Ackerman anchors her return in the universalism of the economistic perspective. The persistence of corruption (at least its cultural toleration) is simply a matter of people's ignorance of its costs. Thus, "clarification" is in order, as supplied by economistic assessments of cost and benefits. Moreover, this resolution also simply wishes away what Nye centralized: normative standards are *rarely* held by societies as a whole, and the story of the developing world is not simply that, as a whole, behaviors should be legalized or forbidden but rather that their administrative and political realities reflect the collision of two very different systems of understanding.[46]

Perhaps because of the waning fortunes of rational choice analysis and its supplanting by various strands of behavioral economics, another variety of institutional analysis has grown in popularity in recent years. This approach is best represented by Bo Rothstein's *Quality of Government* (usually abbreviated QoG) approach.[47] From one point of view, Rothstein's departure from Nye is strikingly different from Rose-Ackerman's. Whereas Rose-Ackerman stipulates that human beings are fundamentally self-interested, "impartiality" lies at the heart of Rothstein's "procedural" approach. Impartiality means, simply, that "when implementing laws and policies, government officials shall not take into consideration anything about the citizen/case that is not stipulated beforehand in the policy or the law."[48] Rothstein forcefully argues that this basic norm of impartiality in the execution of government policy can be derived from a careful reading of normative political philosophy, that the approach holds advantages over other attempts to give such a procedural foundation (replacing "impartiality" with "democracy," for example), and that it is amendable to criticism of its austere, hyper-Weberian appearance.[49] But most important for our purposes, impartiality supplies a universal foundation for judgment among societies, and hence comparison. As Rothstein writes,

> [The dominant definition of corruption, à la Nye] makes no reference to what kind of acts constitute the "misuse" or "abuse" of public office, which makes the definition of corruption relativistic. Without a basic norm (such as impartiality), these definitions simply avoid the question of what should count as corruption or, to be more precise, what is the norm or practice that is being "abused" . . . [a definition of corruption based on violating impartiality] has the advantage that what counts

as a breach of impartiality is fairly universally understood and thus not related to how things like "abuse" or "misuse" of public power are defined in different cultures.[50]

Rothstein goes on to use this definition to undertake a rich comparative program, ultimately arguing that poor QoG and concomitant corruption is the result of a collective action problem, in which people cannot trust one another to act impartially and hence will not do so regardless of their judgment of corruption. Put differently, the problem is institutional design, not the possession of different social norms about specific, corrupt behaviors.

Yet for all its empirical productivity, the original tension in Nye's definition of corruption lingers even in Rothstein's analysis. This can be seen most clearly in Rothstein's discussion of where impartiality should apply. Using Walzer's (1983) notion of "Spheres of Justice," Rothstein argues that *every* decision made by a bureaucrat or in a society need not be impartial because "norms should be different in different societal spheres, [and] we should recognize that the same individuals often operate simultaneously in different spheres and are carriers of different norms about what is appropriate in these different spheres." Thus, impartiality is fine, even admirable, during market activity or parenting, but that "those who exercise public power need to know and acknowledge the boundaries between what norms apply in different moral spheres."[51] Yet at the same time, Rothstein argues that Walzer's theory of spheres is itself too particularistic because, for Walzer, the boundaries among spheres are "defined by reference only to historical particularities." In place of this, Rothstein provides a two-by-two table of (presumably universal) moral spheres, along the axes of the "scope of interest" for actors and their "type of interest."[52]

This is an extraordinarily attractive way of providing a foundation for analysis because it both recognizes the historical and internal heterogeneity of societies *and* allows their direct comparison to one another against the "objective" standard of how well they achieve impartiality. As with the other approaches, however, this comes at a high cost. On the one hand, while the norm of impartiality is hard to argue against *in principle*, its role in the analysis is simply to supply another universal sensibility for people in place of self-interest: all people, Rothstein seems to argue, believe that the best governments execute policies impartially. On the other hand, this style of analysis simply transposes the particularity inherent in the definition of corruption from people's foundational motivations and beliefs to where the (still particularistic and historical) boundaries among particular spheres are to be drawn. This seems to recapitulate the original problem of relativism, as in Rothstein and Davide Torsello's analysis of anthropologist's notes about bribery in preindustrial societies:

> Differences in what is understood as corruption lie in the variation of what counts as (and is the extension of) public goods in cultures, and to variation in whether it is morally wrong to turn a public good into a private good. Hence, our hypothesis is that in a culture in which private and public goods are neatly separated both conceptually and customarily . . . there will be fewer problems in distinguishing what is corruption and what is not . . . corruption will be a relevant issue whenever private and public goods overlap or are easily converted by those who have access to them.[53]

Both of these positions on the social science of corruption seek to gain analytic purchase on the concept by stipulating what it *is* at the outset of the analysis. This certainly facilitates broad comparisons, as we have seen, but it also not so subtly assumes an analytic model of Western, bureaucratized states as the yardstick for virtuous government, strongly implying that it represents the models that corrupt states should emulate in their reforms. Understandably, a third line of scholarship, mostly derived from the anthropology of the developmental state, has arisen to criticize these assumptions.[54] This work aims not to understand corruption in the abstract but rather, as the authors of a recent stock-taking special issue put it, at coming to grips with "the practical and social life of these North Atlantic universals."[55] Thus "corruption" is usually thought of as the center of a "corruption complex"[56] touching not only concrete behaviors but also how the meanings of those behaviors reflect *both* on indigenous societies and politics and the broader "developmental community."

This more particularistic approach has a great deal to recommend it, and indeed reading it has inspired parts of the approach I develop here.[57] And yet, perhaps because of its goal to criticize how the concept affects particular societies today, the analysis derived from this approach can sometimes be *so* specific and fine-grained that it is difficult to see what general lessons are to be taken from them. Thus, for instance, while Akhil Gupta has produced a sterling analysis of the biopolitics of corruption, discipline, regulation, and poverty in India, it remains resolutely a study *of India* and develops its theories of concepts specifically for that cause without explaining how they may or may not hold elsewhere.[58] And Steven Pierce, closing his excellent study of the "corruption complex" of Nigeria, discusses the matter of generalization with admirable clarity:

> What does this tell us about corruption as a comparative phenomenon? The argument of [Pierce's] book is that corruption discourse has a long history as a global occurrence, and that history is well known. There is also a long history of articulations between that global discourse and its political use in particular

locales. Understanding corruption requires understanding this history of intellectual and political interaction around the world, all taking place as if corruption were applied to a discrete and coherent object. The history of corruption around the world is a history of global politics, and it is a history bringing together myriad local histories. This relatively grand claim about historical processes can coexist with a number of more modest practical implications. For reformers, ameliorating corruption will require dealing with issues fundamental to the logic of local political culture, and these will vary tremendously from context to context. In Nigeria, the issues involve the intersection of patronage and political life and the distributive issues of revenue across a culturally diverse country. Instead of attempting to prevent officials from diverting public revenue to self-interested ends, Nigerians must face a constitutional challenge: How can public ends be served by accommodating patronage as a fundamental political principle? Exhortation is ineffective, as are investigations and judicial interventions. Instead, the constitutional order must be brought into alignment with political culture. Webs of patronage must be able to constrain official behavior and demand more from it, and the needs of regions must be brought into harmony. That is easier said than done.[59]

The debates about these three positions are ongoing, and if the goal is to attempt to sharpen our analysis of corruption to the point of better understanding its causes and consequences, they have been productive. But if the goal is to resolve the inherent tension present in corruption by definition—that it is behavior deviating *from some standard of conduct*, which meaningfully varies across space and time—the debate has been less productive. Instead of trying to flee from the duality inherent in the phenomenon by either universalizing or particularizing corruption,

I propose instead centralizing it. This transforms the question of corruption from why certain behaviors occur or not (which assumes the point of reference to licit or illicit actions) to why and how certain selves, actions, and understandings are embedded in organizational fields, and in turn how, under certain conditions, actors in those fields come to find an "interest in disinterest."[60]

A RELATIONAL THEORY OF CORRUPTION

Sociology attempts to understand the nature of concepts, for both the people who live with them and those for whom they are unfamiliar. And so, for a sociological understanding of corruption to be adequate, it should squarely focus on the fact that "corruption" at once depends on concrete behaviors undertaken by specific people in particular times and places *and also* invokes general judgments of right and wrong. As we have seen, the mainstream of modern scholarship on corruption either wishes this away by stipulating what "should be" corrupt or takes it as a warrant to refuse generalization altogether.

Sociology, however, provides a promising direction through the "relational" style of analysis. While this approach has existed since sociology's organization into a self-conscious discipline—and, depending on one's philosophical interpretations, well before too—it is today enjoying a renaissance.[61] The core of this approach is to reject the idea that social things have essences or characteristics "in themselves" but rather that any such aspects are instead defined by the relationships such entities have with others we define as relevant and the contrasts we draw among them.[62]

Thinking of corruption as something inevitably suspended in and defined by a web of other relations—that form economic, political, social, and cultural orders—risks simply transposing the concept into a description of those very relations, hence falling back into relativism and losing the ability to say anything broadly about the concept.[63] I seek to address this risk in two ways. The first is to recognize that the very charge of relativism is itself grounded in the assumption that there is a universal, timeless definition of corruption that can be stipulated, uncovered, or derived.[64] As I will suggest, this assumption *is* a major aspect of one configuration of corruption, but to convert this empirical fact into an analytic assumption is to bracket major historical aspects of what corruption is and has been. Instead, along with others,[65] I emphasize what corruption as a concept or category *does*—what judgments it enables or forecloses, what coalitions it builds or breaks, what kinds of careers and organizations it makes and destroys, and what "ways of being" it opens up or closes off.[66] The second reason to focus on a relational approach to the concept of corruption is epistemological. If we think of corruption as always embedded in a set of relations instead of one that can be treated as discrete from those relations for the purpose of analysis, then to examine what "corruption" is to different groups and at different times is to examine that web as best we can; in Clifford Geertz's words, the point of approaching corruption in this way is that it "light[s] up a whole way of going at the world."[67]

With these risks of a relational approach in mind, we can turn to its profits for conceptualizing corruption. Rather than the label for some essence or behavior, I see corruption as, first and foremost, *a form of moral accusation made by one party against another in appeal to an audience.* If we are to understand this view of corruption, we need to see what such accusations are made of.[68] To do this, I will first propose a set of mechanisms that seem important to how corruption as a moral accusation works, then discuss how they may come together in different configurations to produce different styles of corruption. In my view, corruption is at least composed of: morality, abstraction, biography, and escalation. I therefore call this the model of corruption.

Morality

While there has been a laudable effort to avoid stigmatizing corruption, particularly in the developing world by drawing attention away from the motives of people to give and accept bribes, for instance, it remains that to sensibly call an act, person, or organization "corrupt" is to say something fundamentally *moral*.[69] By this I mean that there is a special significance to a corruption accusation as opposed to one of, say, incompetence or impropriety. By using "corruption" and its cognates specifically, we invoke the profane,[70] touching on judgments of "what is right, good, permissible, obligatory, admirable, etc." in a society by making claims about what *isn't*.[71]

But just how do we know which judgments we should make, given the flux of particular situations we find ourselves in? To ground our judgments, Gabriel Abend argues that we rely on and draw from *moral backgrounds*, or understandings of what the world has to be like for any individual judgment to make sense. Thus, these moral backgrounds, which Abend calls "second-order," facilitate and give force to "first-order" evaluations of things, people, institutions, and behaviors.[72]

Judgments that are anchored in moral backgrounds are different from everyday choices; instead of the trivial choice of what route to take home from work, for instance, or what to order at a restaurant, a moral judgment says something about who we *are*. In the words of Charles Taylor, it is a "strong evaluation": "To know who I am is a species of knowing where I stand. My identity is defined by the commitments and identifications which provide the frame and horizon within which I can try to determine from case to case what is good, or valuable, or what ought to be done, or what I endorse or oppose. In other words, it is the horizon within which I am capable of taking a stand."[73] To call an act, institution, or person "corrupt" is thus much more forceful than to say that we have found an inefficiency, incompetence, or even suspicious behavior or characteristic. Instead, it is to touch on some of our deepest assumptions about the structure of the social order we inhabit and, by extension, who we see ourselves as being.

Abstraction

As Taylor notes, because making an accusation of corruption is to invoke a moral judgment, and because that judgment involves balancing the interface of particular events "from case to case" with more general principles of judgment, corruption accusations therefore inevitably involve *abstraction*. In one way, this is not at all surprising because as bare cognitive and social matters, categories are the bedrock of social organization. They provide us with means to organize our perception[74] and our social relations (the basics of role structure). And when categories grow increasingly abstract and incorporated into systems of understanding, they provide the grounds for complex social organization.[75] When we turn from thinking about abstraction as part of categories and concepts themselves to an act undertaken in interactions—that is, as a labeling process[76]—we can see the special significance it has for corruption accusations.

This is because a given person, act, or organization we wish to label corrupt inevitably has a variety of *potential* significance, and to call something "corrupt" is to invite its subsumption into a specific *set* of those meanings.[77] Moreover, when discussing *social* things, and not merely the "brute facts" of material life, these processes of abstraction and categorization can be essential parts of what makes that thing what it is. Thus, certain labels and pronouncements actually *make* a husband and wife,[78] or, in the case of corruption, a gift represents corruption when it takes place in some social domains (governmental contracting relations, for example), and not others (a family gathering for the holidays).

Biography

So far, I have been using the language of "behaviors" or "acts," "persons," and "organizations" in my discussion of corruption accusations. But just what *are* these things? This question turns out to be harder than it seems to answer because to call a *person* corrupt, for instance, is to aim at the social category of their "character," proposing that they have not only acted in a corrupt way in the past but that there is also something *about them* that suggests they *also* are suspect of doing so in the future. Similarly, when we call an *organization* corrupt, we are presented with the question of whether there are thoroughgoing-enough reforms that it might no longer require the label. Even an *act* is hardly self-evident; the famous U.S. Supreme Court ruling in *Citizens United* revolved, in part, around just what defined a "corrupt act." Was it the *appearance* of corruption to a reasonable observer or a "bright line" statute, or was it a tightly bounded quid pro quo exchange?[79]

Put simply, accusations of corruption stick to acts, people, and organizations because the people making those accusations seem credible in their moral judgments.[80] But what makes them credible? One crucial resource is the *biographies* on which the accusers rely.[81] At base, this is simply a claim to a related series of events whose unity is a resource to corroborate that claim. In the case of an organization, this may be shared history or collective values; for people, it is often socialization or disposition; and for acts, it is often that acts of that type have in the past led to an outcome or that they will have predictable effects. But whatever the style of the claims and their variations,[82] it remains that an accusation must stand on *some sort of* biographical claim.

Escalation

The foregoing discussion of how corruption is a form of moral accusation presumes that such accusations are made before an audience. This is because it is the rare corruption accusation indeed that is made without any expectation that others will join in one's outrage, and that the label will produce some sort of meaningful change. In other words, a corruption accusation is meant to *escalate* a local conflict.

The escalation of a conflict happens in a predictable way.[83] First, escalation happens during conflict that has been contained within boundaries, whether they are organizational, legal, national, or any other form. Escalation is an effort to expand the conflict beyond its current boundaries and to mobilize the audience beyond those boundaries into the conflict. Second, it is rare indeed for people who are *winning* a local conflict to seek to escalate it. Whistleblowers, in other words, are almost never the incumbents who benefit from corruption but instead are those who *lost* a local conflict and thus are appealing for help outside it. Finally, the *outcome* of an escalation depends a great deal on the position of the conflict among a set of interlinked conflicts.[84] In some cases, a given conflict may be embedded within another, larger conflict (as a human resources department, for instance, is part of a larger organization), or in a relationship closer to a "horizontal" one among coequals (as when legal compliance and acquisitions departments come into conflict within an organization). In either case, the audience to the conflict who may be mobilized into it depends on the structure of these links.

STYLES OF CORRUPTION: MORALITY, ABSTRACTION, BIOGRAPHY, AND ESCALATION IN COMBINATION

As I argue throughout this book, the model of corruption has historically come together into at least two very different configurations. By that, I mean that while corruption is everywhere a form of moral accusation before an audience, such accusations can be made in very different ways. To get a sense of this, consider how abstraction works in corruption accusations. A corruption accusation asks us to categorize something by abstracting its particulars into a category, but this begs the question: abstract them *into what*? Or, to phrase it in terms of the morality aspect of the model, what moral backgrounds make corruption accusations sensible, and (to shift to escalation) to what kinds of audiences? And (biography) what sort of claims make those accusations credible?

TABLE 0.1 TWO CONFIGURATIONS OF THE MODEL OF CORRUPTION

	Situational	Universal
Morality	Contextual	Transcendental
Abstraction	To similar contexts	To disembedded spheres
Biography	Localized	Unitary
Escalation	Familiar	Unfamiliar

In the remainder of this book, I will argue that there have been at least two such systems, summarized in table 0.1. One, which I call *Situational*, is and has been fundamentally oriented around abstraction into a set of similar contexts, which the accuser can reasonably claim are directly relevant to making their judgments. Of course, to say that such judgments were contextual does not mean that they were purely relative; instead, it is to say that the moral background was an interlocking set of connections, blending together one's own position with political, economic, familial, cultural, and historical concerns into a more or less "harmonious" order.[85] And, as we shall see, because EIC administration could involve shifting among radically different contexts and seemingly discordant histories, the claims to biographical credibility were consequently localized, and there was much less emphasis on consistent behavior or justification across varying contexts. Finally, these facets of this configuration of corruption were in turn shaped by dependence on an audience's familiarity with the context of one's claims; those making accusations relied on the audience to their appeal "knowing how it was on the ground." By contrast, the second and more familiar system of corruption, which I call *Universal*, abstracts into principles of action that purportedly transcend any given circumstance, derived from a disembedded or universal moral background where entities like "the state," "society," "the public," and "the economy" are all distinct from one another.[86] Moreover, because this moral background was supposedly universal, escalating appeals could be made to those *un*familiar with the details of the struggle taking place, and claims made in this register would be especially persuasive if the accuser could demonstrate their own moral consistency and their target's hypocrisy.

A key point that I develop throughout the book is that the Situational and Universal configurations of corruption are each associated with very different arrangements of how administrations operate and how conflict occurs within them. Speaking broadly (I will discuss relevant nuances throughout the book), the Situational configuration of corruption lends itself to cosmopolitan and patrimonial forms of administration.[87] Officials can still be "corrupt" in this configuration, but this means the loss of decorum *given the local context* in which a behavior occurred. And so too does moral regulation depend on the concrete examples of superiors for those officials, and a relatively tighter binding of administrators to claims of ethnographic knowledge or "capital" with respect to the populations they govern.[88]

The Universal configuration, meanwhile, is associated with a very different style of administration. Because its sense of "corruption" is meant to transcend any particular circumstance, it became convenient, even necessary, to sever the connection between officials, especially but not only colonial ones, and the actual populations and processes they oversaw. Thus, *distance* became a crucial vector shaping modern corruption, and just as it was shaped by the distance of the audience to the concrete circumstances of corruption accusations, so too did it in turn open a gulf between officials themselves and their administrative objects. And in this gulf, we will find critical foundations for our peculiar, modern capacity to take ourselves as objects of analysis and also to puzzle over the universality of the principles of the social orders we inhabit. This autocritique is at the heart of postcolonial theory[89] and is also the essence of calls to probe the "historicity of reason" itself.[90] Put differently, one central argument of *Modernity's Corruption* is that, in these corruption arguments, we find the germ of such paradoxical modern phenomena as "the liberal art of separation,"[91] the "rule of colonial difference,"[92] and "liberal strategies of exclusion."[93]

CORRUPTION IN THE EIGHTEENTH-CENTURY BRITISH EMPIRE

As much of the foregoing discussion has suggested, *Modernity's Corruption* is a book of historical *social science*, and while I hope that it will be informative to historians, it is not a "vanilla" history of corruption or of Britain and the EIC in the eighteenth century. So why sacrifice the ability to interview officials, observe their activities, conduct surveys, or even run experiments?

There are biographical, substantive, and methodological reasons to pursue the "case" of the EIC. Biographically, I came to my interest in corruption laterally—originally, I studied land tenure administration systems,[94] but I noticed that EIC administrators bitterly accused one another of corruption more often than not. From there, I found the vast heaps of archival and published material on corruption and began reading secondary sources emphasizing its centrality to eighteenth-century discourse.

These materials emphasized strong substantive reasons for pursuing an analysis of corruption and the EIC. For one thing, the EIC and its history, spanning 258 years from the end of the Elizabethan age in 1600 to the height of "modern" imperialism in the middle of the nineteenth century, is the very time that most analysts agree "modernity"—whatever *that* term refers to[95]—emerged. More specifically, the EIC was a pivotal player in the transition between Britain's "first" settler-based and Atlantic empire and its "second" empire, rooted in the "indirect" imperial domination of Asian and African subjects.[96]

With my eye toward corruption and its dynamics, moreover, the EIC is a good case "to think with." This is because analyses of corruption today have to reckon with the fact that there is a dominant view of what corruption *is* within the scholarly, policy, and development community. This view in turn exerts a subtle but powerful constraint both on any observations a scholar might conduct because people know "in the back of their heads" what the basic consensus on the nature of corruption is, and it has been a fundamental aspect of postcolonial development, and this consensus also inevitably sets the boundaries of analysis. By contrast, even though part of the project of historical social science is to maintain a dialogue with that contemporary scholarly knowledge of corruption and its dynamics, and some historical social scientists attempt to study the past explicitly as though it is an extension of the present, to study corruption in the eighteenth-century EIC is to study it in an environment where empirically no such consensus on the nature of corruption exists. To put it bluntly, rather than hashing matters out under-the-table or in smoke-filled rooms to conceal it from disapproving authorities, EIC officials literally fought duels with one another because they had different understandings of corruption. To study corruption in such a setting inevitably reframes scholarly understanding of its dynamics.

Finally, there is also a methodological reason for studying corruption over two hundred years ago. In part *because* there were such different views of what corruption was, and because this caused such misunderstanding, there was a great deal of explicit, even public argument about the topic, and officials felt compelled to justify their conduct explicitly. This fact, of course, gives us a unique window into how corruption connects with deeper moral frameworks and allows us to see a critical transition in the emergence of modern life taking place.

All these advantages do not come without trouble, however. Most important, the field of British studies is one of the historiographically "densest" that exists, and I therefore am, at least implicitly, taking a stand in a debate about the timing of changes in the eighteenth-century British Empire. Some scholars have pushed the seeds of a modern state bureaucracy further and further backward into the late seventeenth century, so that by the period I discuss, modern anticorruption views were already dominant.[97] By contrast, another group maintains that, aside from a few radical voices, the system of "old corruption" persisted until at least the turn of the nineteenth century.[98] My argument falls somewhere in the middle of this debate: I think that, on the one hand, it is true that you can find arguments that seem surprisingly quite modern early on; on the other hand, you can also find ones that seem shockingly anachronistic being taken seriously quite late. In other words, along with several scholars of corruption, the EIC, and Britain, I think the period under study is one that was deeply ambiguous (even "enigmatic," as you will see in chapter 1), where government institutions, civil society, economic interests, corporate organization, and political power blended together.[99] Further, to demonstrate the moral frameworks that this ambiguity contained and sometimes even obscured, I have (especially in the first chapter) worked with broadly "cultural" sources—that is, intellectual, economic, and political discourse and debates to the relative neglect of the nitty-gritty organizational politics that they animated.

In thinking about my choice to study the EIC, I have been drawn to an analogy with paleontology. William Sewell once compared the work of historical social science to that of natural history,[100] and to my mind this implies two different techniques for examining the historical record. One might drill for core samples, collecting many from all over the world and comparing them to one another to formulate generalizations. Or, as in this book, one might search for particularly informative outcroppings, where the bedrock of moral and political life has sedimented and been exposed to view by natural processes. From this view, the EIC is a *very* large outcropping. But at the same time, thinking about it in this way also takes us far afield from traditional social-scientific methods, so it seems worth spelling out my approach more formally.

FROM VARIABLES AND VALUES TO POWERS AND PROPERTIES

The focus of *Modernity's Corruption* is on a difficult-to-study social-scientific topic—corruption—and the book examines it through a case with few obvious comparisons—the British EIC's transition to a territorial power. An obvious question is, How I can be sure, even relatively sure, that my argument is basically correct for my case, to say nothing of generalizable beyond it? To answer this question means wading into the nettles of historical social-scientific methodology. The generations of scholarship since the explicit organization of the field into subdisciplines has produced a multitude of options: I could compare the company and its experience to other cases, both similar and different, to search for key causes of the emergence of the category of modern corruption; I could search for patterns of evidence that support my argument against imagined "counterfactual" alternatives; or I could trace the "biography" of a particular causal process using a variety of evidence to spell out my best (scholarly) guesses about its causes and consequences.

Each of these alternatives has its merits, but none is, on its own, adequate to explain the complicated emergence and institutionalization of a complex social phenomenon. Macro-comparative analysis has long been criticized for too readily disembedding cases from the time and place they occur, falsely treating them as interchangeable units, like animals ripped from their environment to be judged in sterile laboratory conditions.[101] Counterfactual analysis, meanwhile, typically depends on the stability of the entities being analyzed, which is precisely what *cannot* be taken for granted in this book. And the strategy of process tracing can often yield rich and adequate analytic descriptions that turn out to be difficult to generalize elsewhere.[102]

With the criticism of these approaches in mind, this book blends them. It takes as its fundamental aim to explain how the category of corruption, as employed and understood by EIC administrators, came loose from one moral background and became anchored to another, and what were the consequences of this transition. In pursuit of this goal, I attempt to balance thinking of "The East India Company" as simultaneously a single organizational entity—because, like any other organization, it was set up to coordinate the activities of its agents in the service of a single enterprise—and as an organizational "field" in which individual administrators and internal interest groups struggled with one another.[103] This kind of analytic image transforms the question, Why did one category of corruption predominate? into a set of others: Why did particular administrators begin to argue with one another using the language of modern corruption? How persuasive did people inside and outside the company find these arguments? And how did these arguments begin to supply a logic for organizing the company's activities?

In different ways, each of these questions is also accessible to the methods I described above. Comparison, for example, plays two roles. Asking what conditions made modern corruption arguments more persuasive to the audience for intra-administrative conflicts means analyzing changes in the company's relationship to the British state and its political publics—that is, comparing the company's relationship at an earlier time with that of a later time. Meanwhile, to understand the variety of different appeals being made, comparison also works *within* the EIC, showing how different groups of administrators with different backgrounds and working in different parts of the company made different sorts of arguments about what corruption was.

So too it is with process tracing. The technique operates in this book to show the role of corruption categories in the overall trajectory of the EIC—as it shifted from a largely commercial enterprise semi-independent from the (then) English state in the seventeenth century to a wholly owned subsidiary of the British Empire in the middle of the nineteenth century. But it *also* works on the level of individual administrators, showing, for instance, how the career of Robert Clive came to be subject to increasing scrutiny and pressure, not as his behavior changed but rather as the category of corruption itself changed *around* him. Finally, the book also traces the process of change in the categories of corruption themselves—here, I suggest that the interrelationship among the elements of the model were reconfigured, in part, by moral entrepreneurs in the middle of the eighteenth century.

Counterfactual reasoning also plays a crucial role in my argument. Most centrally, my argument is that, if EIC affairs had not been subject to "distant," "disinterested"[104] metropolitan gazes, the more disembedded category of corruption would not have enjoyed nearly the ascendancy that it did. But this larger, more macro-sociological causal claim is built on a host of other, smaller counterfactual arguments—that, for instance, if Sir John MacPherson had been appointed the first governor general of India rather than Lord Cornwallis in 1785, the historical sociology of the category of corruption in the EIC would have been very different.

Thus, in contrast to the standard ways each of these methods is used in historical social science, my goal in *Modernity's Corruption* is to use each as needed to illuminate the rise to dominance of one category of corruption at the expense of another. This goal is as methodologically ambitious as it is analytically difficult and empirically demanding, and I cannot promise success. But in the service of these goals, I have sought to marshal as much evidence as I can, and I have used sources ranging from archival materials to published historical documents, fictionalized accounts, demographic data, commercial returns, and secondary historical monographs and publications by experts on the company and Indian history. And with each type of evidence, I have worked to make clear how I see it fitting into my account—obviously, I will judge the fictionalized work of G. M. Trevelyan in *The Competition Wallah* or the verse of *Tom Raw* quite differently than an administrative minute, a commercial filing by the company, or a parliamentary debate. Likewise, I have tried to maintain careful sensitivity to different historiographical schools when invoking secondary literature.

This kind of empirical strategy is deliberately eclectic, and it invites charges of bias. After all, aren't I risking simply looking for material that confirms my preconceived account, to the neglect of that which might challenge it? To this question, I have two responses. The first relies on the evidence of my own intellectual biography. I didn't set out to study corruption in the EIC; indeed, my first intention was to follow up on research I conducted on variations in land tenure arrangements codified by the company.[105] But I repeatedly encountered charges of corruption in primary documents and accounts of its role in the secondary literature—both of which seemed to me to take the category far too much at face value. Put differently, I didn't go looking for the category of corruption; it found me.

My second response to the risk of bias in my empirical approach is that there are benefits that outweigh this risk. While the EIC's archival record is unusually strong—mostly because many documents were copied in triplicate, and one copy was sent to the company archives in London, which has been unusually well cared for and combined with a variety of relevant private papers over the years—it is *still* an eighteenth-century archive, meaning that, at times, the type of evidence available for a given aspect of my argument may vary tremendously. Thus, on the one hand, I didn't want to undertake an archival empiricism, simply transcribing what was there and providing what Bernard S. Cohn called "simply a list of documents and regulations."[106] On the other hand, however, I didn't want to so constrict my empirical approach in the service of standardizing my evidence that I left our crucial aspects of my account. I tried to find a middle way—in particular, I followed Philip S. Gorski's realist exhortation to use methods as a guide, as "a diagnostic tool to strip a model down to its barest assumptions."[107]

INTRODUCTION ⚬δ 39

Taken as a whole, this methodological approach inevitably implies a view of what the social world is like. It seems worthwhile to state this directly because the social sciences have recently been engulfed by a war of method, which has generally been as vituperative as it has been disappointing and unproductive. Its terms are broadly set by a defense of (a version of) positivism, with its emphasis on causal inference, empirical observation, and the (now tempered) search for lawlike generalities, on the one hand, and varieties of post-positivism that emphasize that the social world is made up of very different kinds of structures and entities and is not easily reducible to a single substance, cause, or force.[108]

To my eyes, every practicing historical social scientist mixes both sides of this debate, and its intensity is best interpreted as an effort to maintain the boundaries and coherence of scientific and/or intellectual movements.[109] Thus the approach I have taken here maintains empirical care, analysis, and a search for more general conclusions than the particularity of the EIC's history, but it also shifts the emphasis of my account away from a view founded in "general linear reality," where more or less self-contained entities act on one another through various forces, and toward one in which entities can be formed, transformed, and decomposed, and are endowed with certain affordances and properties.[110]

To make sense of this shift in emphasis, I have found Nancy Cartwright's notion of "nomological machine" very useful, in spite of its jargonistic label. From the standpoint of corruption, a nomological machine is simply the way that the different elements of the model of corruption are arranged so that they produce regular outcomes. Thus, when moral judgments, abstraction, biography, and escalation are linked together in relation to a disembedded moral background, for instance, corruption accusations shape and facilitate the rule of colonial difference, as we shall see. Of course, it is in principle possible to drill down into moral judgments, abstraction, biography, and escalation, as I have briefly done in developing the model in this introduction. But the nomological machine emphasizes the power of those elements *in combination* and how that combination persists in stable arrays, demonstrates emergent properties, and reacts with its environment. Cartwright uses the example of an engine to demonstrate this point: the gears, steel, and fuel that make up the engine all have discrete properties that are (reasonably) universal and afford a wide variety of outcomes. Yet *in combination*, they form an engine with a completely different set of properties and affordances. It is the same with corruption: while the structure of complex social activity, biographical accounts of official behavior, escalations of intraorganizational conflict, moral conceptions of the self, and the "moral background" and "social imaginaries" of social action all exist semi-independently and at various timescales, they have been brought together more or less intentionally into different combinations to produce nomological machines of corruption that in turn have very different powers and properties.

This ontological view seems to me to carry distinct advantages for historical social science, especially when it is applied to matters such as the changing category of corruption. For one thing, its shift from a radical epistemological skepticism to (tempered) optimism implies that we can indeed actually infer aspects of past events and structures, and it avoids the epistemological reductio ad absurdum that historical sociology is essentially impossible without strict adherence to the bare "artifacts" of the archival record.[111] Instead, the powers and properties approach lends itself to what historical social science does quite well—searches for emergent phenomena through history and explores *both* the typical properties of these phenomena as well as the unique features of them as they are embedded in particular historical environments. Finally, in destressing empiricist bias, the aim is to infer to the "best explanation" *for now*—my claim is not to have uncovered the unwavering truth of corruption but instead to have exposed a variety of powers and properties to the category in different configurations that may stimulate further empirical investigation. In other words, the goal of *Modernity's Corruption* is not to explain the prevalence of corruption or present means to eliminate it. It is rather to trace the unique powers and properties facilitated by the shift to one (now predominant) way of thinking about what corruption *is*.

PLAN OF BOOK

As may be evident by the foregoing discussion, the argument of *Modernity's Corruption* functions at several levels, and this is reflected in the structure of the book. Chapter 1 sets the scene for the narrative that follows, exploring the (sometimes loose) structure of the moral backgrounds in eighteenth-century Britain. It does this by probing intellectual discussions, class and political structures, and everyday practices of moral regulation. The central point of the chapter is that there were at least two moral backgrounds giving corruption accusations their sense, that they were the cause of considerable conflict, and that the more contextual and situational background formed the apparatus of practical moral regulation within the British EIC until at least the middle of the eighteenth century.

Chapter 2 begins the main analysis, describing how the EIC came to be put under dramatic organizational pressure both in Britain and India. In India, this happened fundamentally because the EIC (sometimes because of the freelancing of its agents and officials) was drawn into the expanding economic system and transforming political relations begat by the decay of the Mughal political system. This pressure fractured the EIC's organizational insulation and provoked new attention from a new domestic audience that was unfamiliar with the details of life and moral organization in India.

Chapter 3 turns from a large-scale view of the EIC's circumstances in Britain and India in the middle of the eighteenth century to a more fine-grained analysis of how these circumstances shaped organizational conflict within the EIC. The EIC's organizational structure had always encouraged conflict among its officials, and participants in these conflicts had always tried to escalate the conflict by appealing to audiences, but before the middle of the eighteenth century (with a few exceptions), these conflicts had remained "within" the EIC's organizational structure and visible to audiences who either had themselves been officials in India or were deeply conversant with the contextualist moral backgrounds that made corruption accusations comprehensible. *After* the transformation of the EIC's metropolitan circumstances, however, a new class of "distant" audience was in play, and consequently an initially fragmented but increasingly cohesive set of corruption claims based on more modern understandings began to hold sway. In turn, these new types of corruption claims, when they triumphed over those made in the older key, facilitated concrete organizational changes in how the EIC operated, including the imposition of a government oversight board and the replacement of the most senior ranks of company leadership in India with outsiders.

INTRODUCTION ❦ 43

Chapter 4 addresses the self-presentation of company officials in the aftermath of the reform. Whereas a contextualist understanding of moral regulation (and an understanding of corruption as the loss of balance among competing passions) implied a localized sense of self that could radically change its behavior and moral posture as social settings varied, the universalist understanding of morality and corruption ushered in by company reforms demanded a much more unitary self-presentation and consistent set of self-justifications. I demonstrate accordingly that the EIC at the end of the eighteenth century was populated by both officials who followed the older system of moral regulation and those (primarily outsiders who needed to mobilize external support) who presented themselves in terms of the new one. As a consequence, when officials struggled with one another in this period, the outcome was often misunderstanding, incoherence, and distrust. A key tool in these struggles, I argue, was the emergent moral biographies by which officials began to explain their seemingly aberrant behavior.

Chapter 5 combines the insights of *Modernity's Corruption* to show how company reforms extended beyond merely regulating the moral self-presentation of its officials. Justifying behavior in terms of universalistic moral spaces meant also that those spaces—"the state," "society," and "the economy"—had to be disentangled from one another. Thus, the turn of the nineteenth century found officials defining their behavior no longer in terms of concrete commercial exchanges, the imperatives of particular state treaties, or their concrete peers (whether Indian or British) but instead speaking in terms of abstracted social spaces that could compel their senses of duty. "Corruption" thus came to mean not the loss of balance among these moral spaces but rather their entanglement, and efforts to disentangle them were at the heart of modern empire's "rule of colonial difference," or the requirement to set colonial society decisively apart from colonizing officials.

The conclusion explores the broader lessons we can take from *Modernity's Corruption* and applies some of them to the present via an analysis of the tangled moral politics of corruption under Trumpism.

1

CORRUPTION AND MORAL ORDERS IN EIGHTEENTH-CENTURY BRITAIN AND INDIA

Julia Adams called the eighteenth century "enigmatic"[1] because it is a peculiar mixture of modern and nonmodern forms across the range of sociological analysis: from political economy to the structure of the state to culture, social structures, and family relations, it is hard to know whether to read the century as one in which "traditional" patterns continued to obtain or one in which structures recognizable to us today emerged. Although the question of when, where, and why "modernity" emerged still implicitly undergirds much work,[2] in recent years historians and historical sociologists have forcefully rejected such straightforward dichotomies and instead have shown how different structures and practices emerged over a "long" early modernity that stretches (sometimes) all the way back to the Renaissance in Europe and through the middle of the nineteenth century.

So too it is with corruption. As felicitous as it would be to be able to trace a clear, dichotomous shift in the meaning of the concept, I will argue several points to the contrary in this chapter. First and most broadly, I will argue that "corruption" is, in general, best understood as embedded in systems of moral regulation and order and that this insight is particularly useful to make sense of what it meant in eighteenth-century England. Second, and following the path I outline in the introduction, if we adopt this "embedded" perspective on the nature of corruption, we see that the concept is best understood in its connection to two major moral backgrounds:[3] one emphasized contextual ethics, a fragmented structure of identity, and a blended moral order of society, and another stressed more familiar aspects of clear-cut duty to well-defined organizations, a unitary sense of self, and an ethics stressing universal rules. Third, the eventual eclipse of the first of these two systems was not inevitable; rather, in the eighteenth century, these two moral orders (and, by extension, these two understandings of corruption) were both "live" ethical options in Britain, and tension between them and among their different facets were central features of intellectual, cultural, and political conflicts.

To address these points exhaustively even for a single case is far too large a task for a single chapter or even a book,[4] so here I focus on matters that figure directly into transformation of the concept of corruption within the East India Company (EIC).[5] Building from a variety of sources, both primary and secondary, I take up these three points in turn.

CORRUPTION AS AN EMBEDDED CONCEPT

As I noted in the introduction, as social scientists, we can think of the meaning of "corruption" in two fundamentally different ways. First, we can stabilize the concept by trying to supply a behavioral (or, even better, material) definition that is objective and context-independent. Or we can attend to its meaning as actually used in different contexts and seek the connections that supplied its force. In this section, my goal is to persuade you that the second alternative is the most profitable way to analyze (one aspect of) England's "enigmatic" eighteenth century.[6]

To begin, consider Samuel Johnson's *A Dictionary of the English Language* from 1755 (see figure 1.1). It lists the following definitions for "corrupt" as both a verb and adjective:

> To CORRUPT v. a. 1. To turn from a sound to a putrescent state; to infect. 2. To deprave; to destroy integrity; to vitiate; to bribe. 3. To spoil; to do mischief.
> CORRUPT adj. Vitious; tainted with wickedness; without integrity.
> CORRUPTION. n. f. [*corruptio*, Lat.] 1. The principle by which bodies tend to the separation of their parts. 2. Wickedness; perversion of principles; loss of integrity. 3. Putrescence. 4. Matter of *pus* in a pore. 5. The means by which anything is vitiated; depravation. 6. [In law.] An infection growing to a man attainted of felony or treason, and to his issue: for as he loseth all to the prince, or other lord of the see, so his issue cannot be heir to him, or to any other ancestor, of whom they might have claimed by him; and if he were noble, or a gentleman, he and his children are made ignoble and ungentle, in respect of the father.[7]

While these definitions are still in dictionaries today, their senses seem unfamiliar from the vantage of modern scholarship on corruption.[8] Above all, this is because, of the ten definitions of "corruption" listed, only part of one ("to bribe") resonates with contemporary, universalist definitions of what corruption is. Likewise, only some of these senses of corruption could even theoretically be judged by reference of objective material states—anyone can tell whether there is pus in a pore or some

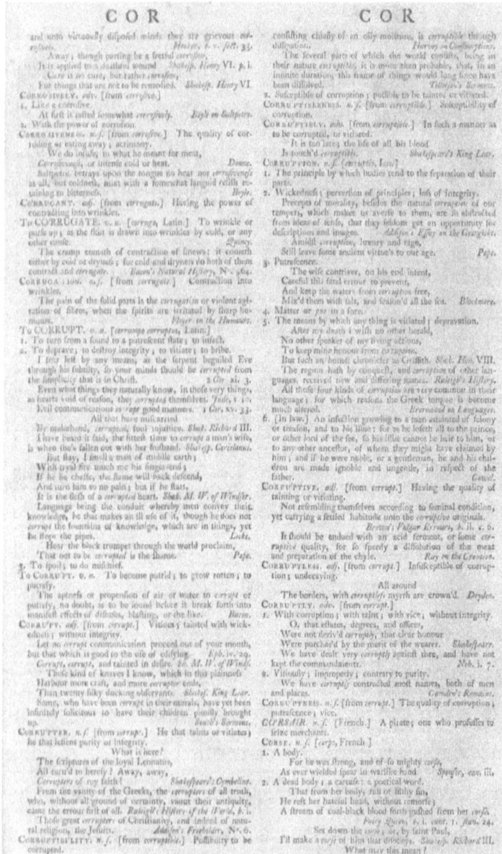

FIGURE 1.1 Samuel Johnson's 1755 *A Dictionary of the English Language*, page listing "corruption."

Source: Samuel Johnson, *A Dictionary of the English Language*, 1755, 1773, edited by Beth Rapp Young, Jack Lynch, William Dorner, Amy Larner Giroux, Carmen Faye Mathes, and Abigail Moreshead. 2021. https://johnsonsdictionaryonline.com.

food is rotting, but people might disagree whether something is "tainted with wickedness."

Instead of referring to physically identifiable states, the definitions of corruption involving human action almost all refer to much broader senses of human enervation ("depravation," "vitiation," or "wickedness"). But how are we to know "wicked" from "not wicked"? To provide grounding for such judgments, the definitions involving human action refer to *other* meanings.[9] Take "Wickedness; perversion of principles; loss of integrity." The central theme, of course, is deviation *away from* some state of virtue or righteousness, but the definition is actually purely formal. In other words, for us to be able to tell what "corruption" meant, we need to know what systems of moral order it was embedded in.[10]

MORAL ORDERS OF CORRUPTION

As hinted by Johnson's definitions of "corruption," the term is only sensible with reference to the moral order in which it is embedded.[11] For many scholars today, that order is supplied by a universal and behavioral set of meanings that carefully strip away variations in the hopes of facilitating predictability and transposability of findings (among other things). But in eighteenth-century England, there were at least two major systems in which the term found meaning.[12]

A Universal Moral Order

The first of these two moral orders is familiar because it reflects our typical modern sensibility. An excellent practical illustration of it comes from Thomas Hobbes's *Leviathan*, when discussing the structure of judicial precedent:

> [A]ll the sentences of precedent judges that have ever been, cannot altogether make a law contrary to natural equity...'tis against the law of nature, *to punish the innocent*; and innocent is he that acquitteth himself judicially, and is acknowledged for innocent by the judge. Put the case now [i.e., consider the example], that a man is accused of a capital crime, and seeing the power and malice of some enemy, and the frequent corruption and partiality of judges, runneth away for fear of the event, and afterwards is taken, and brought to a legal trial, and maketh it sufficiently appear, that he was not guilty of the crime, and being thereof acquitted, is nevertheless condemned to lose his goods; this is a manifest condemnation of the innocent.[13]

In this passage, "corruption's" role is to pervert the course of justice and "to punish the innocent." This is done, moreover, by the familiar trope of a judge displaying "partiality" in the service of "the power and malice of some enemy."[14] And if we invert Hobbes's example, we find that these evaluations rest on a recognizable moral order: judges are meant to be impartial and independent, no matter who appears in their court; there is a constant, unchanging sense of innocence and guilt that is itself independent of the particular judgment rendered and ultimately derives its force from "the law of nature," and the accused person maintains his innocence consistently through both unjust and fair judgments against him. Thus, as early as 1651, we find an instance of corruption gaining its sense via (1) a universal ethics independent of particular circumstances, and (2) the expectation of agents (here, the accused and the judge) to act consistently in service of those ethics.

If we dig beneath the surface of this example, we also find deeper assumptions about the relationship between the self, moral responsibility, and the structure of the moral order. On this count, a clear statement comes from John Locke's *Essay Concerning Human Understanding*, which was broadly congruent with Hobbes's view because both Hobbes and Locke were empiricists and naturalists seeking to banish all trace of inherent "essences" in their theories of human nature.[15] Locke's argument began by asserting that moral order had the same sources as all other ideas, impressions, and categories: direct experience by "consciousness."[16] The experiences by the consciousness provided the basic unit of accountability and judgment for individual people, and also supplied the raw material for Locke's moral order. People were motivated by a variety of goals, and Locke argues in one section that "good" and "bad" obtain their basic sense as labels for anything that causes pleasure and pain, respectively. Thus, for instance, the passion of "joy," usually identified as "good," is simply the label we attach to the state of anticipatory pleasure at satisfying a goal.

This account of the origin of moral judgments may work well enough when we imagine an isolated person confronted with a moral quandary at one single time, but in more realistic circumstances, important tensions arise. The first trouble Locke confronts is one that would go on to occupy much modern moral philosophy: if the "self" can be reduced not to some "soul" or other unobservable essence but rather to a "consciousness" having experiences,[17] and given that experiences can and do change, what supplies our sense of being more or less the same person over the course of our lives, and why can we be treated as such? The answer Locke gives is that our consciousness, combined with the actions we take and our experience of them, constitute a "Person": "That with which the *consciousness* of this present thinking thing [an individual] can join it self, makes the same *Person*, and is one *self* with it, and with nothing else; and so attributes to it *self*, and owns all the Actions of that thing, as its own, as far as that consciousness reaches, and no further; as every one who reflects will perceive."[18] So far, so good; Locke is articulating a familiar, modern sociological model of "the self" as the combination of our experiences and memories. But this, of course, begs the question: What happens when the consciousness is fragmented (as happens with amnesia and madness)? Locke admits that, in these rare circumstances, it is possible for there to practically be "two Persons"[19] because of the divergence of memory and experience. Yet he insists that these circumstances *are* exceedingly rare and that, in the main, people ought to be held to account for their behavior even when a man is "beside himself."[20] To emphasize why, Locke makes the case for why blackout drunks should be held responsible for their behavior:

> But is not a Man Drunk and Sober the same Person, why else is he punish'd for the Fact he commit when Drunk, though he be never afterwards conscious of it? Just as much the same Person, as a Man that walks, and does other things in his sleep, is the same Person, and is answerable for any mischief he shall do in it. Humane Laws punish both with a Justice suitable to their way of Knowledge: Because in these cases, they cannot distinguish certainly what is real, what is counterfeit; and so the ignorance in Drunkenness or Sleep is not admitted as a plea. For though punishment be annexed to personality, and personality to consciousness, and the Drunkard perhaps be not conscious of what he did; yet Humane Judicatures justly punish him; because the Fact is proved against him, but want of consciousness cannot be proved for him. But in the great Day, wherein the Secrets of all Hearts be

laid open, it may be reasonable to think, no one shall be made to answer for what he knows nothing of; but shall receive his Doom, his Conscience accusing or excusing him.[21]

To excuse the potential "injustice" of punishing a riotous drunk, Locke introduces more familiar wrinkles, even if their legal merit is still debated today. For one, the standard of practical judgment remains empirical insofar as we can only know *for sure* what can be established as matters of fact; thus, a drunk cannot *prove* that they in fact were blacked out. In other words, there is a strong sense in which the self is *unitary* even under very different circumstances (even intoxication and sobriety), and coming with that unity is a (somewhat paradoxical) demand that any given person hold their own behavior and action to rational, "disengaged" reflection in light of their own conscience.[22]

This last point—that moral conduct is simultaneously to be judged by concrete experience yet is also connected to God's knowledge of our interior thoughts and feelings, which transcends any particular circumstance—opens the second major tension in Locke's presentation of a familiar, modern moral order. This is because Locke's empiricist account remains fundamentally one of the *origins* of our moral sensibilities and tells us little about how they were supposed to be configured, especially when others are involved; for that, Locke argued that there were composite "Modes" of moral judgment that consisted of behaviors combined with judgment of their significance in terms of some larger standard of propriety. These standards, in turn, came in three different varieties: religious dictates and civil law, as in the example of the accountable drunk above, and customary practices.

The problem with the standards of law, religion, and custom, from the viewpoint of Locke's *Essay*, is that they vary. Locke openly acknowledged that moral modes varied considerably historically and geographically, yet at the same time, he resisted accusations that he was producing a relativist, even atheistic account of moral order. To square this circle, Locke made a breathtaking logical turn:

> [T]hough perhaps by the different Temper, Education, Fashion, Maxims, or Interest of different sorts of Men it fell out, that what was though Praise-worthy in one Place, escaped not censure in another; and so in different Societies, *Vertues* and *Vices* were changed: Yet, as to the Main, they are for the most part kept the same everywhere. For since nothing can be more natural, than to encourage with Esteem and Reputation that, wherein every one finds his Advantage; and to blame and discountenance the contrary; 'tis no Wonder, that Esteem and Discredit, Vertue and Vice, should in a great measure every-where correspond with the unchangeable Rule of Right and Wrong, which the Law of God hath established. . . . And therefore Men, without renouncing all Sense and Reason, and their own Interest, which they are so constantly true to, could not generally mistake, in placing their Commendation and Blame on that side, that really deserved it not. Nay, even those Men, whose Practice was otherwise, failed not to give their Approbation right, few being depraved to that Degree, as not to condemn, at least in others, the Faults they themselves were guilty of: whereby even in the Corruption of Manners, the true Boundaries of the Law of Nature, which out to be the Rule of Vertue and Vice, were pretty well preserved.[23]

This passage is extraordinary for the bluntness with which it expresses its contradictions. Moral order is maintained via the "Law of God" *even though* it is evident that "in different Societies, *Vertues* and *Vices* were changed" (i.e., subject to variation).

And *even though* there are people whose practices have been "corrupted," it is simultaneously true that they themselves recognize a universal moral order, if only honored in the breach of their own judgments of others.[24]

Finally, it is also worth noting that Locke's expression of this tension extended beyond the abstract phrasing he gave it in the *Essay*. In his *Some Thoughts Concerning Education* (1693), Locke summarized advice for child-rearing for well-to-do families in a way that centralized moral education. The process of this education had a strikingly-similar structure—and tension—to that of the variations described above. This emerges because Locke argued that, while young children manifestly expressed competing passions—what Locke calls "that pretty perverseness which [parents] think well enough becomes that innocent age"[25]—it was essential that these be subjugated to the dictates of reason.[26] According to Locke, parents, "by humoring and cockering [their children] when little, corrupt the principles of nature in their children and wonder afterwards to taste the bitter waters, when they themselves have poisoned the fountain."[27] In other words, for Locke, there was indeed a universal "principle of nature" that could be "corrupted" by ill breeding and that explained the variations in moral virtue expressed by adults.

The Universalist moral order thus has aspects that are deeply familiar to us today: it supplies an objective basis for ethical judgment, whether from religion, law, or custom; by extension, it is the duty of any "good" agent to act impartially or disinterestedly in service of those standards; and a firm expectation that actors will be held to account for their behavior over time and in a consistent manner, whether by the judgment of others or through the mirror of their own conscience. Yet while they may be less familiar, the tensions this order engenders are no less striking. While the basis for moral judgment is supposedly observable experience and matters of fact, reactions only *become* moral judgments when combined with standards that can and do vary; while people should be accountable for their moral biographies, this accountability relies on sometimes dubious "matters of fact" and has a tangled relationship with a person's own account of their experience and interior reactions to their own behavior, and finally, while acknowledging that people may have competing impulses, desires, and interests, this perspective subsumes them under a single entity, whether it is called "consciousness," a "person," or "the will."

A Situational Moral Order

If the Universal moral order is familiar to those of us who have lived Westernized, middle-class lives, the Situational moral order is much less so. The reasons for this go beyond the fact that it is the order that was eclipsed; it is also because it was empirically less a *single* intellectual program and instead was made of multiple interweaving threads. The most important of these threads stretched back to Greek antiquity and composed the warp and weft of ancient, Renaissance, and early modern religious and political thought.

Broadly speaking, this multifaceted Situational moral ordered revolved around the idea that humans acted as they did because they were guided not only by reflecting reason but also by *passions*. While these are sometimes anachronistically reduced to the more familiar term "emotions," passions are better defined as "thoughts or states of the soul which represent things as good or evil for us, and are therefore seen as objects of inclination or aversion."[28] It is hard to find a definitive list of such passions or much consensus on their relation to each other: Aristotle is inconsistent between his *Rhetoric* and *Nicomachean Ethics*[29] about whether the passions are to be thought of as components of virtues and vices or something else to be "found in the soul";[30] Augustine found three and labeled them sins—lust for money, power, and sex;[31] Thomas Aquinas found six "concupiscible" (oriented toward pleasure) and five "irascible" (oriented toward usefulness in spite of their difficulty) but admitted yet more "psuedopassions" could be formed by their combination;[32] René Descartes identified six and related them to bodily sensations to be controlled by a "higher soul" representing the will;[33] and Niccolò Machiavelli wrote that there were "in the main" only two—love and fear.[34]

Whatever their inconsistencies and disagreements, from the vantage of understanding them as a moral background, all of these formulations present a striking contrast with Universal moral orders because they are oriented around a different set of problems. The first cluster of problems involved the structure of the passions in action: if there was no "master" rationality or a "will" strong enough to simply do what was right in spite of countervailing passions, then the question of how to dampen, manage, or even harness them became crucially important.[35] The general prescription provided by classical scholars of the passions was that the goal of human existence amounted to the confrontation and restraint of the passions in light of knowledge, repeated practice, and rational examination. But the struggle was not, as in the Universal moral background, about how to reconcile a person's action with their ultimate conscience or matters of fact but rather the struggle against the fragmentation of one's identity into a disorganized heap of impulses that could easily leave one beyond the bounds of moral rescue. Thus Aristotle, for instance, was at great pains to distinguish those who were merely morally incontinent from those who were self-indulgent.[36]

Aristotle thought that the incontinent were so overtaken by their passions as to be "in a similar condition to men asleep, mad or drunk,"[37] but that they were not yet overtaken to the point of "making him ready to believe that he should pursue such pleasures without reserve."[38] The self-indulgent, meanwhile, had allowed themselves to be so corrupted by passions that they made the active *choice* to pursue vices strategically and systematically, leaving them "incurable . . . for wickedness is like a disease such as dropsy or consumption, while incontinence is like epilepsy; the former is a permanent, the latter an intermittent badness."[39]

Crucially for this Situational moral order, this risk of decaying into a capricious heap of passions or a self-indulgent dissolute could only be countered by interrelated micro- and macro-sociological forces in the pursuit of virtue and happiness.[40] The micro-sociological side depended on careful education and moral practice to train habits of virtuous choice and moderation of one's passions, as well as the careful cultivation of a group of friends, because "the friendship of bad men turns out an evil thing (for because of their instability they unite in bad pursuits, and besides they become evil by becoming like each other), while the friendship of good men is good, being augmented by their companionship; and they are thought to become better too by their activities and by improving each other; for from each other they take the mould of the characteristics they approve."[41] But if the micro-sociological structures like friendship and moral education could help to regulate the passions, the situation was more unstable at the macro-sociological scale, as outlined most famously by Machiavelli in *The Prince* and his *Discourses on Livy*. This was because, on the one hand, all regimes had a semi-inevitable tendency to decay from a state of virtue to corruption—Monarchies to Tyranny, etc—and for the states of individual citizens to decay in parallel.[42] On the other hand, however, the imperative of a ruler, the eponymous prince, was also guided by the need to manipulate the passions of his citizens and to do so in a way that was responsible to variable circumstances, which Machiavelli terms "Fortune." Crucially, for Machiavelli, governing was *not* a matter of enacting a deeply held sense of duty to confront shifting circumstances; rather, it was a matter of adapting one's self-presentation in light of those circumstances. Thus, "it is necessary [for a prince] to know how to colour over his nature effectively, and to be a great pretender and dissembler. Men are so simple-minded and so controlled by their immediate needs that he who deceives will always find someone who will let himself be deceived . . . to appear merciful, faithful, humane, trustworthy, religious, and to be so; but . . . his mind [should be] disposed in such a way that, should it become necessary not to be so, he will be able and know how to change to the opposite."[43]

In eighteenth-century Britain, there were few more forceful (if controversial)[44] statements of a Situational moral order than the Anglo-Dutch physician Bernard Mandeville's *Fable of the Bees*, first published in 1714 in London and significantly expanded thereafter.[45] The core purpose of the *Fable of the Bees* was communicated by its subtitle, *Private Vices, Publick Benefits*, and its main target was a group Mandeville called "sagacious Moralists," among them the Earl of Shaftesbury, whose thought is discussed below.[46] To Mandeville, these moralists made two mistakes: in seeking to extinguish vice, they neglected the public good, such as economic growth, that it could produce; and in assuming that people were basically sociable, they mistook both the substance and structure of human nature. The Mandevillian self was "A Compound of Various Passions," each of which could only "be subdued by a passion of greater violence"[47] rather than rational reflection on appropriate virtuous behavior. The core passion was self-love, and it could be put to social ends by the "dextrous management of a skillful politician";[48] thus, governance was a matter of deploying flattery, a "bewitching Engine,"[49] to accomplish the ends of state because "the Moral Virtues are the Political Offspring which Flattery begot upon Pride."[50]

Taken together, this sometimes fragmented tradition of Situational moral order is radically different than Universal orders in two main ways. First, rather than giving a single "consciousness" a unified pride-of-place at the wellspring of social action (as Hobbes and Locke preferred), this moral order instead saw the self as a sort of composite. This composite included rational, self-reflecting elements, of course, but it *also* could be driven by a variety of different "passions" spanning a wide variety of present-day labels, from emotional reactions (anger) to desires (hunger), to more social relational states (pride, envy, greed). But their key feature for our purposes is that they could all impinge upon and bias "pure" ratiocination.

The second major feature of Situational moral order that is important for our purposes derives from this first point: because the passions were no longer subordinated to reason, how to appropriately "govern" them became a major question. There were two major ways that this governance could occur—one could ask or demand that someone *restrain* their passions in the name of virtue, through something like "modesty" or prudence enforced by direct social or religious influence, or one could *counterweigh* the excess of one passion through the invocation of others. Broadly speaking, the Aristotelian avenue of self-governance pursued the first route, and the Mandevillian/Machiavellian influence pursued the second.

CORRUPTION AS A SOURCE OF CONFLICT

These two moral orders, and the modes of thinking about the nature of corruption that went with them, were a major source of conflict in eighteenth-century Britain. While it is again impossible to detail—or even completely summarize—the nature of the conflict with all its nuance and frequent ambiguity, three aspects of it are especially salient for the account of *Modernity's Corruption*. The first relevant axis of conflict was *political* because "corruption" (embedded in either moral order) came to be one of the most salient means of organizing political conflict in eighteenth-century Britain. The second is *cultural* because the tension between these two moral orders implied different meanings to social action, different lifestyles, and different psychologies. Finally, how exactly the tension or transition between the two moral orders was to be managed, its impact on the structure of the self, the most felicitous social order that could be fashioned in congruence with it, and the best way to judge the ethics of conduct were all main features of *intellectual* debate, especially among moral philosophers, during the eighteenth century.[51]

Political Conflict

British elites constructed their moral self-understandings and self-presentations as part of a broader effort to reconstitute a political order that seemed shattered after the religious and political conflict and economic instability in the seventeenth century. Political uncertainty, of course, had exploded into violent conflict in the seventeenth century and was nominally resolved by the Glorious Revolution of 1688, "a coup d'état undertaken by an adventurous foreign prince [the Protestant

William of Orange] and his mercenary army, supported by local aristocracies" to depose the Catholic James II.[52] Against the lingering shadow of the passionate religious sectarianism that had partly motivated the English Civil War[53] and internal military threats from Catholic Jacobites (which culminated in unsuccessful rebellions in 1715, 1719, and 1745), the Whigs (who had supported the Glorious Revolution) and the Tories (who had opposed it) sought to justify their participating in a new political order that centralized parliamentary sovereignty counterbalancing the monarchy. The Tories gravitated toward the orbit of Bolingbroke, who struggled to justify support for Hanoverian regime, while the Whigs thought, according to one of their chief propagandists, Anthony Ashley Cooper, the third earl of Shaftesbury, that the Glorious Revolution had removed "the Credit of a Court" and "the Awfulness of a Church" as sources of legitimate order.[54] While many claimed that the Glorious Revolution had definitively installed liberty and property as the governing principles of British politics, in reality the restoration of monarchy, and particularly the Hanoverian accession in 1714, represented an effort to sidestep not only clarity on the precise nature of parliamentary relationship to the crown (because there was no constitution) and thus avoid the most radical implications of 1688.[55] Indeed, both Whig and Tory used the language of liberty and property to very different purposes over the first half of the eighteenth century, even as concrete differences between the two groups were supplanted by the more vital cleavage of those with and without access to the crown.[56]

These anxieties over the foundations of legitimate social order were compounded by the perceived erosion of the lesser gentry's social and economic position. In the first half of the eighteenth century, land taxes levied for war caused steady consolidation of landed estates into larger and larger units, piquing the anxiety of largely Catholic gentry shut out of the emerging English fiscal-military state.[57] The lesser gentry vented anxiety in two directions: toward the wasteful luxury that beneficiaries of wartime spending exhibited, thus driving up the cost of competitive consumption and, through mercantilist reasoning, deflating the value of land, and the new fiscal relations that moved the locus of capital from land to the Bank of England, public debt, and joint-stock companies.[58]

While these concerns over the influence of vice and luxury were widespread, they found a forceful, if multivocal, formulation in the language of corruption. There *was* political concern over how bribes, kickbacks, and embezzlement threatened the effectiveness of the navy and the state's tax apparatus.[59] Yet at the same time, those accused of corruption in government service sometimes dissembled but also often excused their behavior as legitimate, and concrete accusations also often mixed financial impropriety or bias with sexual and religious innuendo.[60] This link was not accidental; indeed, one of the most important languages of corruption down to the time of the American Revolution used "civic republicanism" to connect concerns over moral judgment and behavior to the larger decay of the body politic.[61]

These anxieties over corruption were so salient because, in the aftermath of the Hanoverian succession, the Whigs installed a political order that endured for nearly fifty years. Based around upholding the ill-defined "principles of 1688" and defending a constitution on whose content no one could agree, this order rested on Whig ministers' ability to convince the king that Jacobitism was a real threat to his rule and to "manage" Parliament through a vast network of state-provided offices and pensions.[62] Although the extent to which this practice of management actually influenced voting on specific policies is dubious,[63] there is little doubt that all members of Parliament sought at least some preferment from their seats. Elections, after all, were expensive, even though they were rarely contested, and a stint in the Commons was an expected vocation for the eldest sons of the British political and social elite.[64] But the patronage network extended well beyond Parliament, linking British elites together both horizontally and vertically. Horizontally, it bound British merchant, church, military, and political elites together because it was common for siblings in the same families to occupy patronage positions in each domain. For example, a wealthy gentleman could send his younger sons into church, army, and East India Company positions, while his eldest inherited the family's estate.[65] And likewise, a sitting member of Parliament was likely to have extended family members occupying military, ecclesiastical, or colonial positions.[66] Vertically, it linked elites to social subordinates via petty positions that the elites controlled, and occupants of powerful positions could expect to be bombarded with supplicating requests from "friends."[67]

After 1760, however, this political apparatus was severely strained and transformed. From one angle, it was ironic that 1760—the date of George III's accession to the throne—would mark such a transformation. A final Jacobite uprising centered in Scotland had been crushed in 1745, and the Seven Year's-War (1756–1763), although extremely expensive,[68] not only increased the universe of available patronage positions within the British state[69] but it also marked the extension of British power in both India and the Americas.[70] Moreover, increasingly robust economic growth seemed to vindicate the Whig focus on commerce at the same time that it threw up a new "middling sort"—a petty, urban commercial class who was an increasingly important cultural, political, and social force and held aspirations to gentility and (as I discuss below) "politeness."[71]

But even given these seemingly favorable circumstances, George III's accession marked the beginning of a significant reorganization of Britain's ruling structure for two key reasons. He was deeply, personally hostile to the Whig oligarchy that had ruled Britain for nearly fifty years, and he consequently attempted (and failed) to rule via his ineffectual favorite the Earl of Bute. George also refused to acknowledge the trumped-up threat of Tory disloyalty that had been used by the Whigs to maintain the favor of George's predecessors and welcomed Tories into the government. Combined, these moves dissolved the old distinction between Whig and Tory (after 1768, no Tories stood for election to the Commons) but drove the "Old Corps" of Whigs, including the duke of Newcastle and marquis of Rockingham and their "new" followers, into the unfamiliar territory of opposition to government.[72]

Thus driven into opposition, this group of Whigs found the spigots of patronage shut off and no natural patron of their own to organize their opposition. Newcastle's departure from the ministry was accompanied by the "massacre of the Pelhamite innocents," a wide-ranging and unprecedented administrative purge of even the low-level officials whom Newcastle had patronized for their support during the administration of Henry Pelham.[73] Not only did this grossly antagonize the outgoing Whigs but it also meant that political instability ramified throughout elite patronage networks for the first time since the Hanoverian succession.[74] Because George III had no mature, politically active heir at the time of the Old Corps' exit, they could not organize around the Prince of Wales and his smaller yet still significant font of patronage at Leicester house. The men who benefited from the patronage system that had underwritten Whig rule in the first half of the eighteenth century were thus placed in the difficult position of following Newcastle out of their secure positions or remaining at the cost of abandoning their patron.[75]

The behavior of these Whigs (soon to be called, after their younger leader, the "Rockingham" Whigs with the breakdown of the earlier Whig/Tory distinction) in opposition had lasting consequences for the structure of politics and elites' moral self-presentations. Drawing from the complex early eighteenth-century political discourse that emphasized the efforts of independent "Country" (as opposed to the power center of the Court) opposition to defend the hard-won liberties of 1688 and was deeply hostile to the acrimonious faction of party politics, the Rockingham Whigs ironically constructed a justification for a permanent parliamentary opposition as necessary for the very defense of liberty itself.[76] This permanent opposition was justified as a reflection of the "honorable connections" among men who were "united in principle, concurring in sentiment, and bound together by affection,"[77] and its requirement of united principles lent it an unprecedented ideological uniformity as a basis for party organization; as Edmund Burke, the Rockinghams' chief ideologue, noted, this form of opposition party structure was needed to put "the great strong-holds of government in well-united hands, in order to secure the predominance of right and uniform principles."[78] To such organized, principled opposition members, the greatest political sin one could commit was to appear to have been bought out by the crown at the cost of one's principles. Thus, the opposition mounted a sustained attack on the corrupting influence of the king's patronage, and William Pitt the elder was hounded for his acceptance of a peerage and lucrative pension. The attacks on Pitt centered around his outward conformity to the rhetoric of oppositional patriotism without authentic commitment. As a sarcastic newspaper advertisement lampooned Pitt:

Lost supposed to be Stolen by a SCOTCHMAN [The Earl of Bute]. A PATRIOTIC MASK, decorated with many fine flowers of Rhetoric, and set round with Tropes, long sounding Words and Similes. Whoever shall find it and bring it undamaged, to a qoundam *Great* Commoner [Pitt], so that he may wear it again, shall receive a Gouty Shoe and an old pair of Crutches for his Pains.[79]

Over the course of the eighteenth century, then, corruption was an important orienting vocabulary, but it remained ambiguous: Was it linked to a Universal moral background of duty and a strict separation of public and private duty and self-interest? Even as the parliamentary and political system of "Old Corruption" came under increasing pressure at the turn of the nineteenth century, both languages remained powerful.[80]

Cultural Conflict

Given that the political scene was riven by tensions over social disorder and the perceived corruption of the structures developed to stymie it, it is no surprise that conflicts over the best mode of moral regulation echoed into broader cultural politics. This echo was amplified by the structure of elite society in eighteenth-century Britain. Put simply, rather than being cleanly demarcated into straightforward social classes, cultural distinctions were made along increasingly fine distinctions that microscopically separated, say, a wealthy member of the gentry from a minor member of the aristocracy.[81] When combined with an economy that was throwing up nouveaux riches and casting down old money without clear class referents, a member of the aspirational or secured social elite in Britain would have confronted murky and treacherous waters.

How could these cultural waters be navigated? Via two main strategies that often interlinked. First, the fortunes of any individual could be indirectly hedged against by treating a *family* as the unit of strategy, accumulation, and political action.[82] And often this strategy reached beyond Britain itself to become a kind of imperial hedge and accumulation net, even as political and cultural events strained its internal fabric. For instance, the Johnstone family originated in provincial lowland Scotland, and the marriage of Barbara and James in 1719 eventually produced eleven children who survived infancy. There were four daughters, one of whom died in political exile in France, but the rest remained in Scotland. Of the seven sons, two joined the army, two the navy, two joined the East India Company, and only one remained in Britain his whole life (William, who also became quite rich after marrying an heiress). Throughout all this, the specter of debt and risk to the family estate and fortunes lingered.[83]

Beyond such family strategies, British elites in the eighteenth century also emphasized the practical management of self-presentation in interactions, calling such management "politeness." As it was to be understood in the eighteenth century, politeness began as an explicitly political attempt to justify Whig participation in government in the aftermath of the Glorious Revolution and to knit together the ideological strands of elite society into some cohesive form. Along with mainstream Whigs such as Joseph Addison and Richard Steele, politeness was most articulately advocated by Shaftesbury. Shaftesbury unified two seemingly opposing sources: the courtly "manners" discourse traditionally associated with French *politesse*, and the ruggedly independent civic humanism characteristic of the "country" opposition (consisting of both Tories and opposition Whigs) to the new Whig regime—as he paradoxically declared, "all politeness is owing to liberty."[84]

This reconciliation between two competing impulses—individual liberty and behavioral conformity to social norms—was justified in Shaftesbury's mind because people were naturally sociable, and by consequence creating the conditions for sociable, pleasant interaction took priority over the pursuit of individual urges and passions. Politeness therefore stressed the "art of pleasing in company" and argued that moderate, urbane discourse would lead to social order, intellectual creativity, and the realization of human virtue. As Shaftesbury put the point, "We polish one another, and rub off our Corners and rough Sides by a sort of amicable Collision. To restrain this, is inevitably to bring a Rust upon Mens Understandings. 'Tis a destroying of Civility, Good Breeding, and even Charity itself, under pretence of maintaining it."[85] Formulated in this way, politeness privileged form over content and contextual sociability over what Shaftesbury criticized as the abstract egoism characteristic of Locke and Hobbes's natural law perspectives.[86] But perhaps because of its protean formalism, politeness became an organizing metaphor for a wide swath of elite cultural behavior in the first half of the eighteenth century in Britain, touching literature, artistic production, philosophy and science, and even architecture.

Although the relational quality of politeness escapes easy substantive definition,[87] the fact that in the eighteenth century it generally came to mean "that *je ne sais quoi* which distinguished the innate gentleman's understanding of what made for civilized conduct"[88] gave it advantages. For one thing, it left the definition of precisely who was and was not a gentleman to a matter of performance and behavior, meaning that anyone who could behave politely could gain admittance to Britain's eighteenth-century elite social structure, constructed around a nearly infinite gradation of hierarchical ranks in which the members of one rank attempted to emulate those above them (in the hopes of joining them) and exclude those below them.[89] In this kind of organization, marks of status that could be learned and enacted were of an immense advantage. As a consequence of this advantage, the education of "politeness" became a key component of any education that pretended to prepare children to be members of the elite.[90]

While politeness had its advantages, it also presented key tensions. While Shaftesbury himself strongly argued that politeness expressed man's "natural" virtue (although he himself struggled with this formulation and diluted it over the course of his life), what polite behavior represented was deeply ambiguous, especially in its vulgar forms. Was it an authentic expression of virtue or simply a callous manipulation of social convention to gain status in a group? One of the better-known contemporary definitions of politeness, after all, channeled a Situational moral order, calling politeness "a dextrous management of our Words and Actions, whereby we make other people have better Opinion of us and themselves."[91] The risk that politeness would deteriorate into superficial "dextrous management" was especially high when gentlemen supplicated themselves before patrons,[92] and this strategy was explicitly advised, for example, by Lord Chesterfield to his illegitimate son in 1748: "I need not (I believe) advise you to adapt your conversation to the people you are conversing with: for I suppose you would not, without this caution, have talked upon the same subject, and in the same manner, to a minister of state, a bishop, a philosopher, a captain, and a woman. A man of the world must, like the Cameleon [sic], be able to take every different hue; which is by no means a criminal or abject, but a necessary complaisance; for it relates only to manners, and not to morals."[93] Chesterfield may have weakly gestured to the fact that the social manipulation he

CORRUPTION AND MORAL ORDERS ᛞ 71

advised was no matter of morals, yet he so strongly emphasized the importance of social context that the expression of authentic, individual motives and desires—core concerns of the expression of virtue—was erased. Most strikingly of all, nothing in the structure of politeness demanded a unity of one's behavior or judgment as contexts varied; in other words, it was an expression of a much more fragmentary structure to identity and moral life than is familiar today. Indeed, it is part of what has been called the "*ancien regime* of the self."⁹⁴

The ongoing cultural tension between Universal and Situational moral orders can be seen in the satirical poem *The Passions, Humorously Delineated*, published in 1810. Figure 1.2 shows the fourth plate in the work, which is accompanied

FIGURE 1.2 "Avarice & Dissipation."

Source: *The Passions, Humorously Delineated; Plate on Avarice and Dissipation*, by John Collier under the pseudonym Tim Bobbin (1810).

by the story of a nameless lord who, having fallen into gambling debts, defrauds the banker Screwby by providing false security for a mortgage. Screwby discovers the fraud and sets out to find the lord, but his compatriots lie on his behalf, and Screwby commits suicide in despair, despite still maintaining a large fortune.

Some aspects of the poem and the illustration strongly suggest a Situational moral order based on the interaction of the passions. For instance, the visual arrangement of figure 1.2 suggests that Screwby is meant, as the figure on the left, to represent the passion of avarice or greed, and the lord (on the right) that of dissipation. Represented this way, they are direct symbols of passions rather than reasoning characters. The plot, likewise, is driven not by reasoned choice but by the passions: the lord "heard old Screwby oft supply'd the needs/Of broken rakes, who had good title deeds" and seeks only to make the fraudulent gains "fly 'mongst courtiers, girls, and plays" and "wheels off to gambling, rakes, and whores"; Screwby's good sense not to take unsigned deeds is overcome when "old Screwby sore did fret/That he cou'd not this precious morsel get." Screwby's mood, moreover, vacillates from skepticism of the Lord's offer to greed, to joy, to regret, and finally to despair over the course of just twenty stanzas.

Yet there is also a note of a Universal moral order presenting itself. After all, the lord himself is never actually named, focusing our imaginations on Screwby and his behavior, and the poem's narrative certainly draws us to judge his behavior *as* a parable of the folly of avarice, and makes the lord's dissipation incidental. Yet the poem closes with an ambiguous couplet that seems to pull back toward a more Situational perspective: "Calm reason judge; give sentence if thou can, Which murder'd most the character of man!"

Intellectual Conflict

Along with political and cultural struggles, tension between Universalist and Contextualist moral orders also set the groundwork for a great deal of intellectual ferment over the course of the eighteenth century. Much of this ferment swirled around finding an answer to Mandeville's central challenge: Just what were the practical ethical foundations of social order supposed to be in a rapidly transforming commercial society, especially when the options offered by the likes of Hobbes and Locke were themselves highly controversial?[95]

To be sure, this was a shift that had a multitude of sources, and because the shift to secular and self-consciously sociological bases of social order is usually one of the hallmarks of "The Enlightenment" and modernity more broadly, its general character is well-covered terrain by intellectual historians.[96] Rather than rehash that ground, my goal here is to make a more focused point: that whatever the larger shift was that may have been taking place, at least until the second half of the eighteenth century, British intellectuals were still struggling to resolve the question, and no definitively Universalist resource was popular.[97] But one of the most important manifestations of intellectual conflict in Britain occurred in the aftermath of the political turmoil surveyed above after 1760: institutionalized, oppositional party conflict emerged as a feature of political life, elite patronage networks consequently fractured, and opposition ideologues began to criticize the practice of patronage itself as "corrupting." Combined with the radical voices of politics out-of-doors,[98] strained colonial relations,[99] and rising provincial and commercial centers in the British Isles,[100] politeness as a means of judging moral propriety—and supplying a language of elite sociability that could underwrite social order and grease the wheels of patronage—suffered enormous strain. In search of a new answer to how to judge the propriety of action in the face of this combined instability, British elites reformulated strands of moral philosophy that emphasized different elements of the Whig inheritance of 1688.

The core of this reformulation took place as part of the "Scottish enlightenment," which was rooted in 1707's act of union that merged the Scottish and British parliaments and opened the English economy to Scotland, actions that accelerated after the final defeat of Jacobitism in 1745. A prominent figure of the Scottish enlightenment (and indeed of the European Enlightenment as a whole), David Hume adopted the discourse of politeness' view of humans as basically sociable and cultivated a deep hostility to Robert Walpole's oligarchical patronage politics.[101] Hume, however, worried that advocates of politeness had little way to guarantee that discourse did not decay into factional disputes driven by irrational "enthusiasm."[102] To rectify this flaw, Hume grounded his claim that man was naturally sociable even more strongly than Shaftesbury had, discarding any latent claim to the expression of quasi-Christian virtuous essences and instead rooting the drive for sociability in epistemological skepticism. For Hume, the foundations of moral philosophy had to be grounded in an empirical account of how people actually related to one another, and this account in turn had to be founded on an analysis of people's direct experience of the world around them.[103] This direct experience, noted Hume, included people's feelings of empathy and sympathy for others, and it was those natural, innate structures of approbation and disapprobation of others that constituted the judgment of action's propriety. In other words, considering "willful murder,"

[T]he vice entirely escapes you, as long as you consider the object. You never can find it, till you turn your reflexion into your own breast, and find a sentiment of disapprobation, which arises in you, towards this action. Here is a matter of fact; but 'tis the object of feeling, not of reason. It lies in yourself, not in the object. . . . Vice and virtue, therefore, may be compared to sounds, colours, heat and cold. . . . Nothing can be more real, or concern us more, than our own sentiments of pleasure and uneasiness.[104]

Thus, although he shared some concerns with the earlier debates on politeness and vice, he took elements of both to refashion the foundations of his moral philosophy in a way that would prove profoundly influential. From advocates of politeness, he took a concern for how moderation and restraint could supply the interpersonal fabric of social order.[105] But to explain how this moderation took place, Hume drew from the Mandevillian tradition that viewed actors as composed of competing passions. Hume demoted the role of reason and promoted sensibility, but for our purposes, a crucial aspect of his work is that at the center of his thought lies an individual relying on his or her own perceptions to judge right and wrong. In other words, he attempted a reconciliation of Universal and Situational moral orders.

Although picked up by many Scottish enlightenment moral philosophers, the question of how best to adapt politeness to the needs of a dynamic commercial society was most forcefully and systematically taken up by Hume's famous friend and correspondent Adam Smith in his *Theory of Moral Sentiments*. First published in 1754 and revised repeatedly until 1790, *Theory of Moral Sentiments* was typical of the Scottish enlightenment in that it was meant both as a theoretical model of human behavior and "a . . . casuistical armoury to instruct young men of middling rank in their duties as men and as citizens of a modern commercial society."[106] Indeed, like *The Wealth of Nations*, the *Theory of Moral Sentiments* was an elaboration of Smith's lectures in moral philosophy at the University of Glasgow.[107]

The central question of *Theory of Moral Sentiments* asks how people decide whether actions are good or bad. Smith built his answer to this question from Hume's foundation, namely, that people arrive at these judgments through the experience of feelings of approval or disapproval of other's actions, which Smith called sympathy. Smith thought that this sympathy was rooted in people's literal identification with those around them, as "when we see a stroke aimed and just ready to fall upon the leg or arm of another person, we naturally shrink and draw back our own leg or our own arm."[108] Although rooted in these physical sensations and sentimental passions, sympathy for others was actually an act of imagination in which identification with others is achieved "by conceiving what we ourselves should feel in the like situation."[109] The next step in this imagination, and the core of Smith's theory, was the impartial spectator. This spectator was made when people "endeavour to examine [their] own conduct as [they] imagine any other fair and impartial spectator would examine it."[110] This spectator was at once "real" in the sense that he represented the sum of the experience of actual spectators and real judgments a person had had over the course of their lives but was also an "abstract man" located "within the breast"[111] representing how the person would judge themselves if they observed their own action as an unbiased spectator. As Smith summarized it,

> I divide myself, as it were, into two persons; and that I, the examiner and judge, represent a different character from that other I, the person whose conduct is examined into a judge of. The first is

the spectator, whose sentiments with regard to my own conduct I endeavour to enter into, by placing myself in his situation, and by considering how it would appear to me, when seen from that particular point of view. The second is the agent, the person whom I properly call myself, and of whose conduct, under the character of a spectator, I was endeavouring to form some opinion. The first is the judge; the second the person judged of.[112]

Smith wove the impartial spectator and a sympathetic concern for others together into a forceful prescriptive model of how people judged the propriety of action in uncertain times:

The man of real constancy and firmness, the wise and just man who has been thoroughly bred in the great school of self-command, in the bustle and business of the world, exposed, perhaps, to the violence and injustice of faction, and to the hardships and hazards of war, maintains this control of his passive feelings upon all occasions; and whether in solitude or in society, wears nearly the same countenance, and is affected in very nearly in the same manner. . . . He has never dared to forget for one moment the judgment which the impartial spectator would pass upon his sentiments and conduct. He has never dared to suffer the man within the breast to be absent one moment from his attention. . . . He does not merely affect the sentiments of the impartial spectator. He really adopts them. He almost identifies himself with, he almost becomes himself that impartial spectator, and scarce even feels but as that great arbiter of his conduct directs him to feel.[113]

Thus, Smith both summarized and proposed a subtle yet profound transformation of the judgment of the propriety of action. The "bustle and business of the world" experienced by the gentry was one riven by "the violence and injustice of faction" and "the hardships and hazards of war." In the face of this, and like earlier advocates of politeness, Smith recommended above all moderation and control of passions. This control was to be learned in "the great school of self-command" and actuated through constant attention to the impartial spectator's judgment. But this constant attention meant a new depth to the self that underlay behavior; this control of emotions was meant to extend across social domains, "whether in solitude or in society," and the impartial spectator's voice was meant to be so strong that it could shape the structure of people's emotions and passions such that one listening to him "scarce even feels as that great arbiter of his conduct directs him to feel."

The voice of the impartial spectator, as proposed by Smith, was extremely strong and so too was the "great school of self-command" that trained it. This school was made up of socialization by a community of like-minded people, and it began in early childhood:

> A very young child has no self-command; but, whatever are its emotions, whether fear, or grief, or anger, it endeavours always, by the violence of its outcries, to alarm, as much as it can, the attention of its nurse, or its parents. . . . When it is old enough to go to school, or mix with its equals, it soon finds that they have no such indulgent partiality. It naturally wishes to gain their favour, and to avoid their hatred or contempt. Regard even to its own safety teaches it to do so; and it soon finds that it can do so in no other way than by moderating, not only its anger, but all its other passions, to the degree which its play-fellows and companions are likely to be pleased with. It thus enters into the great school of self-command, it studies to be more and more master of itself, and begins to exercise over its own feelings a discipline which the practice of the longest life is very seldom sufficient to bring to complete perfection.[114]

Smith's articulation of progressive self-mastery through socialization—indeed, through the natural process of sociability playing out in the structure of the self—is remarkable for two reasons. First, it deftly combines the various strands of debate over moral propriety together. Following Shaftesbury, it views people as naturally sociable—after all, each lesson of self-command above is learned through a "natural" discourse with others from whom one seeks approbation. Yet it draws the mechanism that makes such lessons salient for people from Mandeville (and more proximately Hume); it is self-regard, the desire "to gain favor and avoid hatred and contempt of others" that teaches people to subordinate their passions. Thus combined, the impartial spectator was simultaneously the residue of other people's judgment left in a person's conscience and a universal figure of "reason, principle, and conscience" with "a voice capable of astonishing the most presumptuous of our passions" and reminding us "that we are but one of the multitude."[115]

Smith's discussion is also remarkable, however, for the silence it continues. For while characterizing the impartial spectator's voice as simultaneously one of quasi-universal reason and accrued social experience with others, any significant discussion of the substance of the impartial spectator's injunctions is curiously absent. In other words, Smith gives the impartial spectator a strong voice, but one struggles to find any reference in *Theory of Moral Sentiments* to what the impartial spectator says about the propriety of action. While this omission is shocking to our eyes for a prescriptive text like this one—and has led to misconceptions of Smith as a protomodern virtue theorist—it makes a little more sense when placed in Smith's intellectual and social context. Intellectually, Smith was still responding to Hume's turn in moral philosophy, shifting his emphasis from the ends people pursue to an empirical account of how people make moral judgments.[116] Second, considering his target audience and his own experience, the reference group forming the impartial spectator must have seemed obvious to Smith. His lowland Scotland was the upright, sober, and rapidly commercializing and urbanizing world populated by friendly, urbane associational clubs.[117] Thus, for Smith, the impartial spectator represented a mechanism through which people adopted and internalized the directives of an audience whose views could be safely assumed.

Smith's moral philosophy may have depended on its embeddedness in the world of Scottish enlightenment "polite" society, and its core mechanism of judging moral propriety may have been a systematization and extension of Hume's skeptical turn. But when considered as practical advice to university students—those of the "middling sort" who composed an important part of British elite society—and placed in contrast with previous formulations of politeness, Smith's impartial spectator takes on a new significance. The spectator was meant to stabilize and reinforce the experience of approval and disapproval people collected over the course of their lives, but in order for the spectator to speak with a coherent voice, it also assumed a fundamental unity to the self. Rather than the "cameleon"-like conformity suggested by some advocates of politeness or the fractured, multiplicitous self that Mandeville saw, the impartial spectator was supposed to speak in the same way across social domains and circumstances. Hence, while the two models look similar when both were embedded in eighteenth-century elite British society, they carried with them strikingly different underlying assumptions about the role of the self in the judgment of moral propriety. The focus of politeness was on the conformity of behavior to shared social norms, but the impartial spectator carried the potential for the foundation of at least locally autonomous moral judgments.

CONCLUSION

As this chapter has demonstrated, there were at least two different moral backgrounds to which accusations of corruption could be attached in eighteenth-century Britain. One is quite familiar to us today, and I call it *Universal*: it emphasized moral judgments that transcended particular situations, abstraction to disembedded value spheres, and a unitary structure to moral identity. Another background, which I term *Situational*, stressed judgment in light of particular circumstances and situations; abstraction to an identifiable, embedded context; and a comparatively fragmentary structure of moral identity. These two moral backgrounds fueled tension and struggle in eighteenth-century Britain, which cut across political organization, cultural meaning, and intellectual discourse.

As the next chapter will explore, this was the scaffolding on which the East India Company's system of moral regulation was built and the setting for its extraordinary and dramatic transformation.

2

SHIFTING GROUNDS

The Transformation of the East India Company

Chapter 1 highlighted the various and ambiguous meanings that "corruption" could take in eighteenth-century British politics, culture, and intellectual discussion, and stressed how these meanings were driven by attachment to Situational or Universal moral orders. This chapter advances the story of *Modernity's Corruption* to the East India Company (EIC) itself. I first describe the company's organizational structure and its presence in India, emphasizing how, until the middle of the eighteenth century, its affairs were generally insulated from prying eyes in Britain (especially those without direct experience in India themselves) and how its system of regulating its officials and settlements in India strongly suggested that a Situational moral order predominated within it. I then go on to show how this system, because of its embedding in political, economic, and social relations in both England and India as well as an international terrain of globalizing military conflict, profoundly strained this system in the second half of the eighteenth century.

CORRUPTION AND MORAL REGULATION IN THE EIC

In one form or another, the English EIC existed for 271 years—from 1600, when its original charter was granted by Queen Elizabeth just before her death, until 1871, when its final shareholders were compensated by act of Parliament after the company's territorial possessions had formally been folded into the British Empire. The remainder of *Modernity's Corruption* traces the variation in the nature of the company's activities, as well as its relationship with its own servants, Indian politics and society, and domestic English (and then British) affairs. For the moment, however, our discussion is aimed at demonstrating two points about its history until the middle of the eighteenth century: first, that even with a few major exceptions that nevertheless prove the rule, its affairs were insulated from the prying eyes of domestic groups who lacked direct experience in India, and second, that the discipline and ethical regulation of the EIC's settlements in India, and the modes of struggle among its officials over accusations of corruption, expressed a Situational moral order.

The EIC's Organizational Insulation

The English EIC was founded in 1600 as a joint-stock "adventure" and began its operations on the Indian subcontinent within a decade.[1] Until the middle of the eighteenth century, it oversaw small but politically and economically significant outposts, called "factories," dotting the coastlines on both the east and west coasts of India.

The English EIC had to balance the demands of two large-scale political entities even as it carved out significant state-like political functions—administering law, raising an army and a navy, and minting currency—for itself. On the one hand stood the English (and, after the Act of Union with Scotland in 1707, "British") state, which itself transformed radically over the course of company history. On the other hand was the political mosaic of South Asia, dominated in the seventeenth century by the Mughal Empire and competing political entities, which themselves went through radical transformations that accelerated after the death of Aurangzeb in 1707. The mechanism connecting the company to both political domains was the sovereign charter: from the English/British monarch, and, after the Glorious Revolution in 1688, Parliament, the EIC received exclusive trading privileges between Asia and England; from the Mughal emperor or his (increasingly independent) regional subordinates, the company negotiated *firmans* ("imperial decrees") authorizing its commercial activities at favorable customs terms.

By the close of the seventeenth century, the key company settlements in India were Bombay, on the West coast and given as a dowry gift to Charles II by the Portuguese before being transferred to company control in exchange for a loan to the English crown; Fort St. George on the southeast coast of the subcontinent, sited since 1640 where the city of Chennai (long called Madras) now stands; and a new settlement in the Bay of Bengal, Calcutta. Each of these settlements served as a semi-independent home base for EIC operations[2] and oversaw satellite trading posts staffed by officials charged with exchanging bullion that the company shipped to India and minted into coins called "pagodas" for the various trade goods—primarily high-value cloths like silk—that were shipped back to Europe and resold. The company did not manufacture these goods in India itself; rather, its factories were really warehouses meant to store goods bought through Indian middlemen from local producers and stored until they could be periodically shipped. From the point of view of London and the English crown and Parliament, the terms of the EIC's charter, although subject to contentious negotiations over its renewal throughout its history, granted the company extensive authority over its employees, possessions, and economic activities "beyond the Cape of Good Hope."[3] Indeed, the company minted its own coinage in its factories, dispensed civil and military justice, maintained a standing army, undertook displays of state-like authority (such as prominently displaying flags and surrounding its officials with ornate retinues), and regulated the commercial activities of its own officials and other Europeans via a system of "passes" granted to trade under its own (customs-favorable) authority.[4] In each case, the company clearly derived part of its authority from its royal charter but also sought to adapt English law, customs, and commerce to the Situational circumstances in India.

Of course, such an intensive and extensive set of powers was repeatedly threatened in Britain—above all, because the company's charter granted it a *monopoly* over trade between India and England, which established an oligarchy at the expense of entrepreneurial "free merchants."[5] Especially after the Glorious Revolution of 1688, in which James II was overthrown and exiled, and William of Orange was enthroned along with an enduring shift toward parliamentary sovereignty within England's "mixed constitution," the company's cozy relationship with the crown via its royal charters became a liability.[6] Partly because of the company's own aggressive activity toward European interlopers, a coalition rallied in Parliament under the banner of "free trade,"[7] and the EIC found itself at the center of a struggle between the crown and Parliament over its prerogative to grant charters. Interlopers who had been ejected from Asian waters or had their goods seized protested the EIC's "arbitrary" actions, the company's activities were briefly scrutinized by parliamentary and Privy Council committees, and in 1697 a competing "New" East India Company was even chartered on behalf of the interlopers.[8] And amid these events, accusations of corruption, bribery, and "despotical" behavior flew in all directions. Yet the fact of competing companies was widely seen as untenable, and after negotiations (and the equivalent of a hostile takeover of the "new" company by the committees of the "old" one) a compromise was reached in 1709 by which the two companies would be combined into a "United" successor. On the one hand, this compromise resulted from unprecedented royal and parliamentary scrutiny into EIC affairs and allowed new kinds of intervention into company activities. On the other hand, the compromise placed the newly united company firmly at the center of the newly constituted British political order,[9] and while the practical outcome of the companies' unification was temporarily chaotic in India, "there was no fundamental ideological rift in the Old and New Companies' approach to authority and governance in India."[10]

The EIC's Moral Order

Just what was the EIC's "approach to authority and governance in India"? To answer this question, let us begin by recognizing that the actual company presence in India at the beginning of the eighteenth century was tiny. The largest settlement, Madras, had twenty-seven company servants and twenty-nine "Free

Merchants," as well as something like four hundred European soldiers; Bengal had a similar size and proportion to its population (especially when subtracting the sometimes large, transient population waiting to sail for Europe); and Bombay, which was recovering from the disastrous "Child's War" against the Mughal emperor, was home to only about seventy-five company servants.[11]

These tiny company factories were organized around a president, who oversaw a council responsible for commercial and civil matters in the factory, and aided by various subordinate official grades, down to the lowly "Writers," who were so titled because they literally copied official documents in triplicate. The traveler John Fryer neatly captures the social structure of the company factory in Bombay in 1672, as well as its isolation from Indian society except for intermediary *banians*[12] and the typical ambitions motivating officials:

> The whole Mass of Company's Servants may be comprehended in these Classes, *viz.* Merchants, Factors, and Writers.... The Writers are obliged to serve Five Years for 10 L. *per Ann.* giving in Bond of 500 L. for good Behaviour, all which time they serve under some of the forementioned Officers: After which they commence Factors, and rise to Preferment and Trust, according to Seniority and Favour, and therefore have 1000 L. bond exacted from them, and have their Salary augmented to 20 L. *per Ann.* for Three Years, then entring into new Indentures, are made Senior Factors; and lastly, Merchants after Three Years more; out of whom are Chose Chiefs of Factories, as Places fall, and are allowed 40 L. *per Ann.* during their stay in the Company's service, besides Lodgings and Victuals at the Company's Charges.
>
> There in their several Seigniories behave themselves after the Fundamentals of *Surat*, and in their respective Factories live in

the like Grandeur; from whence they rise successively to be of the Council in *Surat*, which is the great Council; and if the President do not contradict, are Sworn, and take their place accordingly, which consists of about Five in Number, besides the President, to be constantly Resident.

Out of the Council are elected the Deputy-Governor of *Bombaim* [i.e. Bombay] and Agent of *Persia*; the first a Place of great Trust, the other Profit; though, by the appointment from the Company, the second of *India* claims *Bombaim*, and the Secretary of *Surat* the Agency of *Persia*, which is connived at, and made subject to the Will of the President, by the Interest of those whose Lot they are; chusing rather to reside here, where Consignments compensate those Emoluments; so that none of the Council, if noted in *England*, but makes considerably by his Place, after the rate of Five in the Hundreds, Commission; and this is the *Jacob's* Ladder by which they ascend.

It would be too mean to descend to indirect ways, which are chiefly managed by the *Banyans*, the fittest Tools for any deceitful Undertaking; out of whom are made Broakers for the Company, and private Persons, who are allowed Two *per Cent.* on all Bargains, besides what they squeeze secretly out of the price of things bought; which cannot be well understood for want of knowledge in their Language; which Ignorance is safer, than to hazard being poysoned for prying too nearly into their Actions: Though the Company, to encourage Young men in their Service, maintain a Master to learn them to Write and Read the Language, and an Annuity to annexed when they gain a perfection therein, which few attempt, and fewer attain.[13]

Beyond its dramatic reference to poisoning, several aspects of this account stand out. The first is that company officials were extremely poorly remunerated for their work; £10 in 1682 was only £2,216 in 2020.¹⁴ In place of those paltry wages, the real goal was to rise enough in seniority that an official could "make Considerably by his Place" via the country trade—or the allowance of company servants to trade within Asia and remit home for their own profit (see figure 2.1 for an example of the explicit recognition of the country trade).¹⁵ And because the favorable positions for an officials' country trade depended first on where they were stationed and their position within the company and second on their access to a murky network of Indian intermediaries, EIC factories in India risked becoming warrens of infighting where every advantage was "connived at."

The chaotic potential in this image of company factories in India seems to have been realized. For instance, in 1682, what was then the Court of Committees¹⁶ wrote in exasperation to the factory at Fort St. George:

> Long experience with [a] variety of Persons and humours hath convinced us of these following Truths:
>
> 1st. That long, tedious, and cross examinations in INDIA, with bundells of attestations, accusations, defences, apologies, certificates, and such other like Trumpery¹⁷ (of which We have had Loads in our Time) do signify just nothing, but chime as many changes as the best Ringers in LONDON can do with seaven Bells, and that the worst of men will contrive their business so as to furnish themselves with the Largest Fardle¹⁸ of such sophisticated Ware.
>
> 2dly. That without such a Bustle, a wise Agent and Councill may easily, after a few admonitions, descern which Factory doth well, and which not, and may shrewdly guess whether it be depraved by the malignant influence of the Chief, or whether the Chief be good and those under him idle or obstinate, which seldom happens.

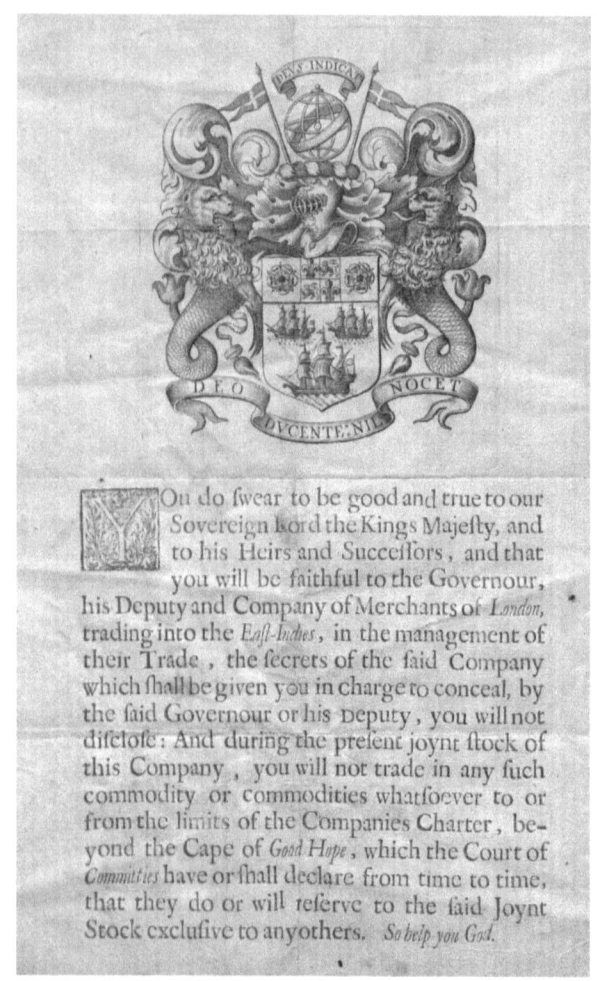

FIGURE 2.1 Late eighteenth-century oath of allegiance to the East India Company, sworn by officials.

Source: Elihu Yale Papers, General Collection, Beinecke Rare Book and Manuscript Library, Yale University, https://collections.library.yale.edu/catalog/16495091.

SHIFTING GROUNDS ⊗ 91

3dly. That great abuses, unfaithfulness, or neglect can hardly hold long in any Factory where the Chief is tollerable, nor be ever possibly cured till at Least the Chief be changed.

4thly. That in a Factory totally corrupt and depraved, as METCHLAPATAM was many Years, the charge of the Chief may make a partial, but can never make a thorough Cure, without displacing the Chief and every person of the Councill.

5thly. That a Person once habituated to and contaminated with Infidelity, sloth, or Luxury, will never mend to that degree as is fit for us to trust him again.[19]

This admonition by the Court of Directors forcefully demonstrates a Situational moral order. First, it acknowledges the difficulty of judging conduct in India because any audit from London will lead every actor to try to "furnish the Largest Fardle" of positive references. Second, because of ambiguity, the center of moral order and fidelity in EIC settlements in India was the senior merchant at a given station; it is only through their "wisdom" and "shrewdness" that the tangle of competing claims can be pierced. Third, that such senior officials held a pivotal position in the moral order because, if *they* became corrupted, then "great abuses, unfaithfulness, or neglect" would run rampant. And finally, this corruption was *not* the product of systemic factors shaping people's actions because of distorted incentives but rather the "habituation and contamination" of passions like "Infidelity, sloth, or Luxury."[20]

Faced with such chaotic factories, the Court of Directors sent plenipotentiaries to restore order. One of the most important was Streynsham Master, who was charged by the court in 1675 "to take an inspection into all Our Affairs and to regulate and sett in Order what you shall find amiss" such that they "may not be prejudiced by their Divisions."[21] And indeed, Master seems to have found a great deal to be amiss. For instance, the company's organization in the Bay of Bengal appeared to be dangerously ambiguous. It was nominally run out of Fort St. George itself, yet factors in different outposts repeatedly refused to recognize this authority, instead arguing for a more democratic "Council of the Bay" to make decisions. In 1679, Master thus presided over the trial of Joseph Hall, a company factor who had apparently clashed with nearly everyone he met.[22] The reason for the trial was that Hall was charged by Walter Clavell, then chief of the Bay of Bengal, with (among other things) beating one of his colleagues:

> [Hall is charged by Clavell] That he, after a most barbarous manner, cause Mr. Nurse, then appointed to keep a diary a Ballasore, when he was on his Cott quietly reading, to be seized on by Peons who bound him and tore almost all his clothes off, and afterward, as Mr. Nurse affirmed, beat him with a Caine himselfe, and being bloody, and without a hat or other Clothes, thrust him into the street out of the Honourable Companyes Factory, not permitting him to returne again to his Lodgeing. And afterward, feareing what the issue of this might be, insinuated into Mr. Nruse maliciously, telling him that [Hall] had order from Mr. Clavell for soe doeing as he did to him, when it is well knowne the Quarrell betwixt them was for words of difference uttered on to another some time before.[23]

Remarkably, Hall's defense to this charge was less that he was not guilty but rather that Clavell had in fact ordered him to beat Nurse, and, moreover, that Clavell had previously beaten Nurse himself: "By for Mr. [Clavell's] abuseing [Mr. Nurse], throwing him downe stairs as is said, and for Mr. Vincents [one of Clavell's witnesses against Hall] abuseing him at Cassambazar in like nature without cause, [know] noe reason any of them can give for it."[24] In other words, the moral order of this dispute is deeply Situational: Hall asks to be excused because his immediate superior, Clavell, behaved in the same way he did; at the same time, Clavell's complaint against Hall was less that he had behaved violently against a colleague and instead that he had falsely done so under Clavell's authority and hence violated his contextual role. Given his charge to root out disorder, it is not surprising that Master dismissed Hall.[25]

In the face of such conflicts, Master implemented a new form of moral discipline for company servants with the explicit endorsement of the Court of Committees. He did this in order to combat, as William Langhorne complained, "emoulation envy & backbiting so much in use . . . that we tax poore Machivelly."[26] The committees wrote:

> We have againe Seriously considered what you write about keeping a Publick Table, and do adjudge It Both most honourable and Convenient to have it mayntayned; and the Sitting of the youths at the same Table with you can no way abridge you of any freedome; and [in] Suratt and Bombay our President practices the Same; and We are Sure it must be of great advantage to the Youthes by enjoying So good an example and preventing them from keeping ill Company.[27]

As hinted at in this description, the "Publick Table" was literally collective dining, meant to be required of all the company officials resident in the factory. The chaplain John Ovington provides more detail about the structure of the table and its purpose:

> Each Day there is prepar'd a Publick Table for the Use of the President and the rest of the Factory, who sit all down in a publick place according to their Seniority in the Companies Service. The Table is spread with the choicest Meat *Suratt* affords, or the Country thereabouts; and equal plenty of generous *Sherash* Wine,

and *Arak* Punch, is serv'd round the Table. Several hundreds a Year are expended upon their daily Provisions which are sumptuous enough for the Entertainment of any Person of Eminence in the Kingdom: and which require two or three Cooks, and as many Butchers to dress and prepare them. . . .

The President and Council only meet at Supper, for the maintenance of a Friendly Correspondence, and to discourse of the Companies Business, and prevent all Jealousies and Animosities which might obstruct the publick Affairs from that Progress, which a joint Unanimous Affection might carry them on with. For the Current of the common Interest has been sometimes very much lessen'd and diverted by the unhappy Intervention of private misunderstandings and Quarrels. And tho' it has been a repeated Contrivance of some leading Men, to play their Servants in *Indica* on against another, and to set them as Spies of each others Actions, yet I'm sure the publick Affairs have suffer'd when the Design has been unmask'd, and the Jealous Eye has been awaked. For nothing vexes a Man of Honour, and who is conscious of his own Integrity more, than to find himself suspected of Dishonesty, and Designs laid by those to intrap him in his Actions, who have the least Reason in the World to distrust his Fidelity.[28]

Thus, the goal of the public table, in a direct echo of Anthony Ashley Cooper's, the third earl of Shaftesbury, theory of moral regulation through politeness, seems to have been based on direct proximity and conversation, which would in turn facilitate the company's commercial success. In other words, it assumes a highly Situational moral order, and it generated exaggerated accounts of the harmony in some factories. For instance, Master described the operation of the system in the Surat factory in 1672, first by praising the "Company's Commandments" of moral regulation (prohibiting profanity and requiring church attendance), and then describing how their enforcement was redoubled in the factors:

> These Rules and orders of the Companys not requiring any Penalty for the breach of them, the President and Councell thought fitt to continue their owne orders which have been many yeares in the Factory, wherein Severe Penalties are required for omission of Prayer and Divine Service and Commission of any Debauchery, and these orders are much more sutable to the place and custome of the Country for the well Government of our People, then the others are . . . and these Penaltys are some of them, allmost as often inflicted, as the offences are Committed, Soe that by the Smart thereof and the good example of the President and Councell here is a most excelled govern'd Factory, indeed more like into a Colledge, Monasterie, or a house under Religious order then any other, for We have much more Discourse of Religion, Philosophie, the government of the Passions and affections, and sometimes of history, then of trade and getting Mony for ourselves.[29]

Of course, this "rose-colour"[30] account is belied by the voluminous records of struggle and tumult that dot the EIC's records. After all, Master himself, as well as the two other plenipotentiaries the company dispatched in the same era, each clashed bitterly with each other, their subordinates, and even the court itself. These struggles often followed a characteristic pattern of escalation: beginning between two or a few officials in a settlement over matters intertwining friendship or enmity with activities in the country trade or preferment for promotion, and would turn into appeals to both parties' allies in the relevant factory council. At times, the struggle would stop there, but often appeals would be carried further to the EIC Court of Directors. And at times, officials' actions in India were so dramatic that they became matters of general concern in England. Yet even in these cases, the company successfully maintained (or reestablished) an organizational insulation of its affairs in India.

One of the clearest such examples was the affair between Edward Winter and George Foxcroft, which occurred just before Master's perambulation and indeed was a significant cause of his being dispatched to restore order in the first place. Frustrated by Madras's chaotic commercial administration in the 1650s, the directors empowered Winter[31] as the new governor in 1661 and granted him "despotic powers to examine the whole question" of the country trade, and he "was at liberty to dismiss and even imprison, and to confiscate the goods of any persons whom he detected in unlicenced trading, whether they were free men or the servants of the Company."[32] Winter initially antagonized his subordinates, who complained to allies on the court that Winter himself was embezzling money.[33] In disgust and exhaustion, Winter resigned and the directors appointed Foxcroft[34] to succeed him. Foxcroft sailed for Madras with his son Nathaniel, arriving in 1665. In the meantime, however, Winter had "made good friends with his colleagues" and no longer wished to resign.[35] Consequently, while he handed over power to Foxcroft and was offered the second in council, Winter

> awaited his opportunity and watched his enemy. [Foxcroft] was an uncompromising old Puritan; and it was not long before he expressed opinions about the King and his debauched court in words which were nothing less than treasonable in those days. Sir Edward was ready; he denounced the astounded President and his son, who had come out with him, as traitors. The Garrison and the majority of the merchants were on Winter's side, and an attempt was made to arrest the Foxcrofts. They resisted, aided by

a few friends, and there was a fight between the two parties, in which one man was killed. The Foxcrofts were overpowered and imprisoned, and Sir Edward Winter once more resumed the reins of government.[36]

Both sides sent justifications back to London, and Winter went so far as to write both the king and archbishop of Canterbury with his explanation.[37] The directors, however, became convinced that sedition was widespread in Madras and dispatched commissioners in force, prepared to blockade the port; they were able, however, to negotiate the peaceful handoff of the fort back to Foxcroft and allowed Winter to wrap up his commercial affairs before returning to London.[38]

Viewed from the perspective of the EIC's moral order in India, Winter's overthrow of Foxcroft is significant for three reasons. First, it revealed the extent of malfeasance in India in commercial as well as political matters. As part of their investigation of the overthrow, for example, the court discovered corruption by the chief at Masulipatnam. They dismissed him in writing in 1669:

> And for as much as we are informed, that Mr. William Jearsey hath contemned our Orders, and permitted grosse prophanes, and scandalous vices to be practiced in our Factories at Mesulapatam, to the dishonour of GOD, and discredit of the Protestant religion, and hath carried on a private trade not in INDIA only, but promoted the same, out and home, overating our Goods, and making use of our Stock, for his own private advantage, and finding that he hath made verie short returns of what is come to his hands, and hath neglected to send us his accompts, or any Advices of his proceedings, We have and doe hereby discharge him from his Chiefship.[39]

Second, the conflict between Foxcroft and Winter also revealed how closely the moral orders used in administrative conflicts in India were linked to England. Foxcroft could be criticized for sedition, and Winter could defend his actions directly as an effort to defend sovereign prerogatives. Indeed, the depositions sworn by Winter's faction in the conflict repeatedly referenced Nathaniel Foxcroft's sedition in terms that would be directly comprehensible in England. For example, Joseph Farley's deposition swore that "the said GEORGE FFOXCROFT Agent, did assert after that his son NATHANIELL FFOXCROFT had maintained that the present Kind of ENGLAND had no other title to his Crone then that of Conquest."⁴⁰ But equally important, the Court of Directors, likely to prevent the conflict from spilling beyond its borders, refused to acknowledge these terms of the conflict, writing coldly in their recall orders that "ffor what concerns personall controversies, wee forbeare to writ anything, for that [the commissioners] will find out the truth thereof by examination upon the place."⁴¹

Finally, the substance of the accusations in the conflict reveals a striking deployment of the language of passions and Situational moral order. For instance, during the height of the Foxcroft/Winter struggle, Henry Gary, then deputy governor of Bombay, issued a proclamation in support of Winter. Foxcroft wrote to Gary admonishing him for intervening and issuing him "a friendly Caution to you not to intangle nor intytle your selfe to the damage of the Honourable Company or their unlawfully Imprisoned servants."⁴² To this, Gary responded,

> If you know no what spirit you are yourself, how blinded and thick and noysome foggs of your passion, yet I and others doe, and so being acquainted with the principalls and sentiments of your heart, out of the abundance whereof your fowle mouth speaks I wonder not at that [*sic*] your sordid language, and dirty dyalect, that is the true Sibboleth of a person of your party.⁴³

THE COMPANY'S TRANSITION IN INDIA

With this highly Situational moral order in mind, we can now turn to the course of events that transformed the EIC's position in India. By the first half of the eighteenth century, there were three main "presidencies" in India, all operating semi-independently of one another at the same time that they were bound together by the company's organizational apparatus and trading imperative: Bombay, which, in the aftermath of the disastrous defeat in the Child's War and until the start of the nineteenth century militarily contained by the Maratha Empire, was a comparative administrative backwater;[44] Madras on the southeast coast near the French settlement of Pondicherry; and the newest presidency in Bengal, contending with the powerful Nawab of Bengal. All three settlements relied on a Situational moral order and understanding of corruption to discipline their own officials and troublesome European interlopers at the periphery of company service and, as political competition on the subcontinent militarized, both Madras and Bengal became embroiled.

Madras

The regional political field the EIC faced in South India was shaped by the decline of the Mughal Empire. The empire had reached its apotheosis under Aurangzeb at the turn of the eighteenth century, but after he died in 1707, subsequent emperors rapidly lost control over their satraps throughout the subcontinent. This process of imperial contraction was especially pronounced south of the Deccan Plateau, where Mughal power had only recently—and fleetingly—been exerted. (The rulers of the area immediately surrounding Madras had only sworn fealty to the Mughals in 1693.) However brief its presence, the

Mughal Empire's withdrawal left an arena of small, competitive, and militarized Hindu and Muslim states in its wake. The midsized states with Muslim rulers—the Nizamat of Hyderabad in the Deccan Plateau, the Nawabi of Arcot (after 1749), and the Sultanate of Mysore (after 1763)—each sought to subordinate semifeudal Hindu vassals, each of whom occasionally claimed independence and had to be forcibly subdued. Most significantly for regional politics, these rulers included the rajahs of Travancore and Tanjore, as well as smaller agrarian elites called poligars living in the southern reaches of the Nizamat of Hyderabad (which was an area that would be called the "Ceded Districts" when it came under the control of the British in 1801).

This pattern of fiscal-military competition increasing as a hegemonic empire loses control of a region is typical in world history, but in southern India this process was amplified by the presence of European merchant empires. The French had important settlements at Pondicherry and Mahe; the Dutch at Negapatam; and the English at Masulipatam, Fort St. David, and Madras. Each of these settlements was chartered by the local Indian ruler (whether Muslim or Hindu, and whether a petty magnate or larger ruler), and each was thus at least nominally subservient to the ruler's will.

As relations among the European powers represented in India grew more contentious, however, the relative quiescence enjoyed by the companies deteriorated. Starting with the War of Austrian Succession (1740–1744), relations between the French and English East India Companies became increasingly contentious. The English issued letters of marque against French shipping in the Indian Ocean, and the French trained an army of Indian sepoys ("soldiers") and marched on Madras itself, capturing it in 1746 over the objections of the Nawab of the Carnatic. Most important, the French defeated the Nawab's army, commanded by his son and charged with forcing an end to hostilities among the European powers, at the battle of St. Thome in 1746.

The battle of St. Thome was significant for two reasons. First, it inaugurated an era of both direct and indirect conflict between the French and English in southern India that would end only with the death of the French proxy Tipu Sultan in 1799. But more immediately, St. Thome also signaled a further escalation of military conflict south of the Deccan—and for the first time, a European-style army armed with muskets and modern artillery had defeated a vastly larger Indian force armed with flintlocks and ineffective cannon. Indian rulers predictably rushed to equip their armies with modern weapons and recruit European mercenaries to train them in Western tactics, and both the French and English companies, eager to compete with one another by proxy, aided them in this effort.

The consequences of this further escalation of the cost of military competition in South India were complicated, both for the European companies and Indian rulers. Indian rulers faced a common fiscal dilemma: European-style armies were professional armies that could no longer be raised or equipped through a feudal ban, and thus the question became how best to raise the money to pay for them. Some rulers, like the sultan of Mysore, sought increased revenues from his subjects by radically centralizing and bureaucratizing his tax administration,[45] while others, like the Nawab of Arcot, greedily eyed rich territories around them.[46] These fiscal concerns were redoubled, moreover, by promises the ruler made to European companies for military and financial support during succession disputes.

These fiscal questions were no less pressing for the Europeans. The companies themselves, after all, served both "mars and mammon"[47] in the sense that, after the middle of the eighteenth century, they were required to raise and maintain armies while returning profits to shareholders at home. On the one hand, aiding Indian rulers and successfully defeating competing European companies was good for business because the supported rulers were likely to grant favorable terms of trade and prices would be better in the absence of competing buyers. On the other hand, however, war meant the disruption of production, trade routes, capital flows, and shipping. In this sense, it damaged commerce.

Beyond concerns of commercial profitability, Indian fiscal-military competition also had important consequences for European company servants in their private capacities. Some, like Claude Martin in Awadh and George Paterson in Madras, abandoned their companies altogether and found employment at the courts of Indian rulers, serving as political liaisons with the European powers and even training troops. Others, such as Paul Benfield (of whom much will be said later in this chapter), began speculating in Indian rulers' bond debt from the relative safety of Madras and a position as a company contractor. But even those who remained in official positions in the companies had stakes in the outcomes of Indian fiscal matters. Successfully supporting a claimant to the throne of Arcot or Hyderabad meant "presents" (in the form of cash and jewels), and almost all officials in Madras held at least some Indian debt bonds. But above all, if the company army were loaned out to an Indian ruler (which happened increasingly as the eighteenth century wore on), its operating costs must be paid for by that ruler.

Thus, the question of land revenues lay at the heart of many competing interests. Indigenous rulers were in a bind: to pay down debts accrued as they fought for their thrones, they had to extract more money from the land they had or conquer new territories, but to conquer new territories took even more money. Desperate to survive and maintain independence from European powers even as they fought against recalcitrant vassals, some rulers (especially Arcot and Hyderabad) chose to begin directly mortgaging territories to the English. According to deals signed in the early 1760s by Arcot and Hyderabad, the English were promised the whole revenues of Indian territories and, in some cases, were drawn into direct administration and collection of revenues (at least down to the district level where they dealt with local tax officials, or *amildars*).

Thus, by the middle of the eighteenth century, South India was a cauldron of fiscal-military competition. In this way, it represented a common pattern of protostate formation (resembling, for example, Western Europe and the Chinese "warring states" period),[48] yet the conflicts among Indian rulers was overshadowed by the presence of European merchant trading companies that, because of conflicts with each other, had militarized. As discussed in the last section, this combination of fiscal pressure and readily available military might for hire led to a cycle of increasing indebtedness.

One of the analytically clearest examples of this dynamic was also one of the most empirically fateful for the institutional logic of Madras administration. This was the Nawab of Arcot (and nominal ruler of the whole Carnatic region), Muhammad Ali Khan al-Walajah, who ascended to the throne over a French-backed rival in 1749 with the assistance of the British (see figure 2.2).[49] Khan succeeded his father's five-year reign, and while he technically was connected by a chain of vassalage that stretched through the Nizam of Hyderabad back to the Mughal emperor, in reality he ruled over an independent state.[50]

When he rose to the throne, Khan had firm control over only Arcot itself via a network of fortified towns. He faced vassal rajas in Kalahastri, Turaiyur, Ariyalur, Warriarpollam, Venkatgiri, and Pudukkotai who were reluctant to pay revenues; rival claimants

FIGURE 2.2 Muhammad Ali Khan al-Walajah, Nawab of the Carnatic, 1772–1776.

Source: © Victoria and Albert Museum, London.

from the Muslim Navaits whom his father had replaced;[51] and restless poligars in Trichinopoly, Tinnevelly, and Madura could only be violently subdued and only with British assistance beginning in the 1750s.[52] Moreover, the Nawab endured rebellions by his own military commanders and succession intrigues by his two sons.

If these challenges vexed the Nawab from below, his relationship with the British company proved even more difficult. Beginning with his succession in 1749, but especially with the Peace of Paris in 1763, the Nawab came to be seen as a direct feudal lord to the poligars and his subsidiary rajas. At the same time that it inflated his own ambitions for rule over the whole Carnatic, the terms of the peace also exaggerated British estimations of his suzerainty and expectations that he would be able to collect the full three million pagodas (approximately £300,000) thought to be the potential tax revenues of the region.[53]

But these revenues were never realized, mainly because of the extraordinary pressure placed on the Nawab's revenue administration by the demands of repaying the company for the army used in his ascension struggle.[54] The size of the initial debts was large, estimated at 1.2 million pagodas or £120,000 in 1756–1757,[55] and to finance them, the Nawab was forced to rely on Gujarati moneylenders (called *sarkars*) and eventually (in 1763) on mortgaging the lands immediate around Madras—called the company's *jagir*—until the loans were repaid.[56]

Rather than diminishing, however, the Nawab's debts spiraled. To the company alone in 1761–1762, they totaled 2.6 million pagodas, or £260,000,[57] forcing the Nawab to rely increasingly on sarkars, from whom he borrowed 1.1 million pagodas (£110,000) between 1758–1759 and 1766.[58] When he exhausted these creditors, the Nawab turned, fatefully, to European creditors and began issuing interest-bearing bonds on his debt in the early

1760s.[59] Guaranteeing a 3 to 4 percent compounding monthly interest rate,[60] the bonds proved a popular way for Europeans to invest their salaries, through their dubashes, because the country trade had been depressed by incessant warfare in the Carnatic.[61] As more and more Europeans clamored to purchase bonds, they also began lending to the Nawab's amildars, who in turn used the advances to pay the Nawab but who promised interest out of future revenue returns.[62] These debts were compounded, finally, in the mid-1760s when expensive military campaigns against Ramnad and Tanjore led the Nawab to grant his customary "presents" to company officers in the form of bonds carrying 20 percent monthly compounding interest. Between 1763 and 1766, for example, the Nawab is estimated to have granted 929,355 pagodas, or about £92,000, in these bonds.[63]

The Court of Directors had gotten wind of the Nawab's escalating debts by 1766 and dispatched a letter ordering a reduction of all outstanding loans to 10 percent annual interest,[64] but by this time the genie was out of the bottle. Nearly everyone in Madras owned at least some of the debt, and "the inner group of leading creditors were in effect the Board" of Madras.[65] Over the rest of the 1760s and into the early 1770s, junior company servants who arrived in Madras demanded even higher interest for their loans to the Nawabs, and an active bond market developed containing complicated financial instruments issued on the Nawab's debt and managed primarily by Paul Benfield, a sometime architect and victualler for the company's army who soon abandoned EIC employment for a fiscal and political career.[66]

Given the extensive debts the Nawab had to the company as an official body and to its servants in their private capacities, the risk that the Nawab would be unable to repay his loans began influencing the company's policy in South India. Since the Nawab's prime source of revenues was from land taxes, he turned to the province of Tanjore, one of the richest in all of the Carnatic (it was composed of rich riverine farmland) and ruled over by the Nawab's nominal Hindu vassal (according to the Treaty of Paris in 1763). The Nawab sought to subdue the rajah of Tanjore by force, even though the rajah was himself a treaty ally of the company; in this ambition, the Nawab was supported by many of his creditors (who made up a majority on the Madras council) and saw Tanjore as the means to have their private debts repaid. Thus, the company's army marched on Tanjore on the Nawab's behalf in 1772 and 1773, and its revenues were subsequently assigned to the Nawab.

Bengal

While the Mughal Empire's grip on Southern India had never been strong, Bengal (along with Bihar and Orissa) had been one of its key possessions since they were first conquered in 1575. But after Aurangzeb's death in 1707, Bengal too began to slip from Delhi's grasp. When Murshid Kuli Khan ascended to the seat of Nawab of Bengal in 1716, he combined the two most important imperial administrative posts—that of Diwan, responsible for collecting and remitting revenues to the emperor, and Nizam, responsible for maintaining the military and law and order—for the first time. In addition, Kuli Khan and his successors renegotiated the prebendal *jagirs* through which administrative officials were remunerated and began directly managing revenue collection, thus more forcefully stepping between the flow of money between Bengal and Delhi. Thus, "Murshid Kuli Khan had in effect founded a dynasty,"[67] although, as was common in imperial states, one with uncertain succession. Thus, upon Kuli Khan's death in 1727, his chosen successor was overthrown by his own father, and when that Nawab (Shuja Khan) died in 1740, the son was again overthrown, this time by the governor of Bihar, Alivardi Khan.

When he became Nawab of Bengal, Alivardi Khan faced daunting challenges. From one side, he had to placate numerous constituents: powerful Begali elites, including the residual Mughal aristocracy; administrative officials; large Hindu landholders, called *Zamindars*; merchants and bankers, including the powerful India-wide house of Jagat Seth; and European trading companies, including the English at Calcutta, the French at Chandernagore, and the Dutch at Dhaka. From the other side, Kuli Khan faced external pressure from the Hindu Maratha confederacy; the rulers of Avadh (another semi-independent Mughal successor state); and even from the Mughal Empire itself, which had grown restive at declining tribute from Bengal.[68] Thus, the decade from 1742 to 1752 saw Alivardi Khan nearly constantly campaigning in western Bengal and Orissa, and culminated in him being forced to ransom all of Orissa to the Marathas.[69]

As it had for the Nawab of Arcot in southern India, these extended military campaigns both increased Alivardi Khan's debts and also damaged the ability of his subsidiary zemindars to pay. Fears of the Marathas' stark brutality seem to have kept the zemindars and Mughal elites from defecting from Alivardi Khan, but the system as a whole could not survive another death and succession struggle. Indeed, when Alivardi Khan died in 1756, he named his grandson Siraj-ud-Daula to succeed him, and at least initially Daula was able to overcome challenges from the Mughal aristocracy (in the form of a rebellion by the *faujdar* of Purnea, Shaukat Jang). But Daula also acted imperiously, not only cutting Alivardi Khan's administrators out of the new regime but also extorting money from the

Jagat Seths and even personally beating the head of the banking house when he refused.[70]

But most fatefully, Daula also turned against the Europeans along Bengal's shores. He demanded nearly three quarters of a million rupees combined from the French and Dutch factories, but in order to reduce the symbolically disgusting military fortifications around Calcutta, the Nawab sacked the city in June 1756.[71] After British people smothered to death while imprisoned in Daula's famous "Black Hole of Calcutta," the company sailed an army under Robert Clive from Madras in December 1756 with the help of a crown fleet and artillery. Clive's force was "an entirely new element [in] the politics of Bengal, a highly professional European army,"[72] and although Daula at first tried to negotiate with the British, he could not stand British demands that he destroy French settlements in Bengal and took up arms. But Daula had alienated too many of his own bases of support, and the Jagat Seths negotiated with the British to attack Daula while Daula's own top aides—Mir Jafar and Rai Durlabh—stood aside. The British accepted the deal, defeated the small fraction of Daula's army that was loyal at Plassey in June 1757 with trivial losses, and installed Mir Jafar as the new Nawab.[73] As part of the deal for support, Jafar signed a treaty promising a crore of rupees (one million, or about £100,000) for indemnity to the company.[74] This led the Bengal Council to write the Court of Directors, excitedly reporting that bullion exports from London could be suspended and a dividend could be promised to company investors.[75]

Plassey thus ratified the British position as regional military players and involved them deeply in the political economy of Bengal. Company servants tried to draw the EIC's interests closer to Britain's national ambitions because Plassey took place in the context of the Seven Years' War and the consequent militarization of the French and English East India Companies.⁷⁶ As William Watts, a key player in the intrigues leading up to Plassey and author of a self-aggrandizing memoir he published in London in 1760, wrote: "This stupendious [sic] Revolution may be also considered as equally glorious and advantageous to the *British* Nation. We may be allowed to say, because the Fact cannot be disputed, that it is a signal Proof of the Utility of Maritime Empire."⁷⁷ Although it initially seemed to be a boon for the company and its servants, Plassey proved to be profoundly destabilizing. At first, company influence over the new Nawab promised not only reimbursement for its military expenditures but also favorable trading concessions and protection from European rivals in Bengal.⁷⁸ But instead of stabilizing, company relations with the Nawab's deteriorated, and the Bengal Council overthrew Mir Jafar in 1759 in favor of his son-in-law, Mir Qasim, only to overthrow Qasim and reinstall Jafar in 1763. Rai Durlabh crossed into open rebellion against Jafar (followed by some key zemindars), and Alivardi Khan's wayward son Siraj-ud-Namjh was an active pretender to the throne. Finally, the Wazir of Avadh and the Mughal emperor had recognized the threat that company control posed and hence rallied behind Namjh. Collectively, these events were so disruptive that by 1765, the Nawab's original indemnity promised to the company had yet to be repaid.

One reason the Nawab (whoever it was at the time) was so slow to repay—and indeed, a key source of the disorder overall—was that, with each succession struggle, company servants who supported the successful claimant stood to make huge fortunes from *inams* ("presents"). Indeed, between 1757 and 1772, when the Nawabs' sovereignty in Bengal was much more directly folded into the company's, a 1772 parliamentary committee estimated that £2,000,000 was distributed as "presents" among company servants at various levels.[79] Before Plassey, the company's select committee negotiated a set of private "presents" for themselves and the army and navy for supporting Mir Jafar's claim to the throne, totaling forty lakhs of rupees (about £440,000) for military officers and troops and twelve lakhs (about £144,000) for the councilors.[80] Soon after Mir Jafar was installed as the new Nawab in Murshidabad, company servants were dispatched to the treasury to settle the debts, which was done before Mir Jafar began paying the huge indemnity owed to the company and residents of Calcutta in a "public" capacity.[81] But above and beyond these payments to company and crown servants generally, Mir Jafar showered particular rewards on Clive. Clive was given sixteen more lakhs of rupees (about £175,000) outright and was created a *Mansabdar* ("imperial official") within the Mughal empire. Along with his title of Zubdat ul Mulk ("Select of State"), Mir Jafar also invested Clive with a prebendal annuity, called a jagir, from the twenty-four Pergannahs immediately surrounding Calcutta. Mir Jafar had already ceded these lands to the company but reassigned their revenues—amounting to £27,000 yearly—to Clive personally.[82] In sum, the House of Commons Select Committee estimated that the 1757 payments to company servants alone amounted to £1,250,000,[83] and P. J. Marshall estimates that, in total, £15,000,000 of private profit were remitted home by company servants between 1757 and 1784.[84]

The promise of fortunes like these (as well as favorable trading concessions granted to interloping European allies) also destabilized the Bengal Council. In fact, because the governor could be overruled by his own council on matters of foreign policy and even war and peace, local company attitudes toward the Nawab oscillated according to who controlled quorum in Calcutta. Most important, when a dissenting faction obtained quorum to overrule Clive's successor, Henry Vansittart, in 1763 and unseat Mir Qasim, Qasim retreated into Bihar after a military defeat and was joined by Emperor Shah Alam and the Wazir of Avadh in united opposition to the company. These forces were defeated, however, at the hands of the company's army in 1764, and in 1765 the company was granted the *diwani*, or right to collect territorial revenues from Bengal.[85] This was to be done in the name of the Mughal emperor, such that the company de jure stood as a vassal to him, and de facto controlled Bengal outright. (Indeed, it was they who appointed the next Nawab and who named his administrative *naib* responsible for collecting revenues.)

The grant of the *diwani* shortly predated Clive's return to India as governor. In his time in England, Clive had dabbled in both company and parliamentary politics, but especially because he felt his jagir might be under threat from the Bengal Council,[86] Clive accepted the charge to "clean the Augean stables" of corruption on the council and returned to Calcutta in 1765. He reported a bleak picture to the directors just after landing:

> Upon my arrival, I am sorry to say, I found your affairs in a condition so nearly desperate as would have alarmed any set of men, whose sense of honor and duty to their employers had not been estranged by the too eager pursuit of their own immediate advantage. The sudden, and among many, the unwarrantable acquisition of riches, had introduced luxury in every shape, and in it's [*sic*] most pernicious excess. These two enormous evils went hand in hand together through the whole Presidency, infecting almost every member of each department. Every inferiour [*sic*] seemed to have grasped at wealth, that he might be enabled to assume the spirit of profusion which was now the only distinction between him and his superior [*sic*]. Thus all distinction ceased, and every rank became in a manner upon an equality. Nor was

this the end of the mischief, for a contest of such a nature among your servants, neccessarily [sic] destroyed all proportion between their wants and the honest means of satisfying them. In a country where money is plenty, where fear is the principle of government, and where your arms are ever victorious; in such a country, I say, it is no wonder that corruption should find its way to a spot so well prepared to receive it. It is no wonder that the lust of riches should readily embrace the proffered means of its gratification, or that the instruments of your power should avail themselves of their authority, and proceed even to extortion in those cases where simple corruption could not keep pace with their rapacity. Examples of this sort, set by superiors, could not fail of being followed in a proportionate degree by inferiours [sic]. The evil was contagious, and spread among the civil and military, down to the writer, the ensign, and the free merchant.[87]

How could Clive possibly justify such a diagnosis, when he himself had sailed to India in part to protect his own "acquisition of riches"? An answer to this question starts with Clive's emphasis on "unwarrantable" acquisition and on how "all distinction ceased, and every rank became in a manner upon an equality." Under the older, patrimonial, proximate mode of judging moral propriety that Clive championed, "[i]t was the practice of the eighteenth century to accept advantages which were consecrated by custom, or which did not threaten the interests of the State,"[88] so Clive openly wrote to the Court of Directors about the presents distributed in Murshidabad in 1757 and was congratulated in return.[89] Likewise, William Watts also wrote openly (if with some circumspection, couching personal emoluments as "Satisfaction for the Losses private Persons had sustained") in his *Memoirs of the Revolution in Bengal* (published in London in 1760) of how "the unliquidated Demands in the Sketch [of a treaty between Mir Jafar and the English] should be reduced to a Certainty."[90] Clive provided a good summary of administrators' attitudes at the time when he casually wrote to a friend to justify accepting £175,000 from Mir Jafar:

> Exclusive of which Treaty or any Agreement whatever, the Nabob of his own Free will from the Services rendered him made me a present much beyond my Expectations, part of which I bestowd on those immediately about me & one or two of the principal Officers: I never made the least Secret of this Affair—but always thought the World ought to be acquainted with the Nabob's Gratitude.
>
> As to what was given to the Committee, perhaps you will say very undeservedly, I may venture to assure you, what is no Secret, that without some such provision I should have found it a difficult Task to have executed the late Glorious Expedition.
>
> Thus Sir you have matters of Fact as to Private Money Concerns; if I had been disposed to grow rich by receiving presents from any other Hands but those of the Nabob, surely no one had ever the like Opportunity; but there is not that main living among the daily Temptations which Offerd who can accuse me of receiving anything of Value but from the Nabob himself. I have troubled you with these particulars because among some it may be computed as a Crime my being rich: if it be a crime, you Sir are truly acquainted with the Nature of it.[91]

From the vantage of the kind of moral justifications of concern, Clive's justification is striking. He openly declared taking a present from the Nawab in his private capacity for a duty nominally performed in his public capacity, yet he stressed how he distributed some of this present among his subordinates. Clive also stressed how the gift was given "of [the Nawab's] own Free will," implying that a coerced gift would have been inappropriate, yet he spoke of the presents to the Bengal Council and Clive's own personal intervention as though they were tools of statecraft, implying they would have had to be at least suggested beforehand. And most important, the shadow of even greater "Temptations" from "any other Hands but those of the Nabobs" loomed as the alternative to the gifts Clive actually took—clearly implying that the Nawab's present counterbalanced Clive's passionate desire for even more. In other words, the Nawab's gift was justified because of Clive's service and position of seniority in the company, and more generally because generous gifts that demanded reciprocal gratitude and loyalty (if the receiver wished for another gift) were a way to control officials' greed. But above all, Clive's present was appropriate because it was being given to him as the most senior company servant and because his proper example of moral restraint would be reflected in the behavior of his subordinates. Indeed, in the view of historian Lucy Sutherland, the view of many like Clive was the following:

> A man should, if he survived (as many of course did not) make a considerable fortune in the Company's service, but only if he had worked his twelve or fifteen years through the ranks and given the Company the benefit of his industry and acquired experience. While making this fortune through the recognized channels of perquisite, private trade, and money-lending, he need not reject presents from wealthy and important Indians, but he ought to do so if in return he had to sacrifice his employers' pecuniary interests, and he must not permit his private concerns to monopolize his attention to the detriment of his public duties.[92]

Thus, among old-school company servants, the "corruption" endemic in the aftermath of Plassey stood not for the acquisition of a fortune per se but for that acquisition to be out of step with the EIC's patrimonial hierarchy in Bengal. As Harry Verelst, Clive's immediate successor, well summarized the perspective of old India hands:

> The dissolution of government in Calcutta kept pace with that of the country. A general contempt of superiors, a habit of equality among all orders of men had obliterated every idea of subjection. To reclaim men from dissipation, to revive a general spirit of industry, to lead the minds of all from gaudy dreams of sudden-acquired wealth to a patient expectation of growing fortunes, were no less difficult in execution than necessary to the existence of the company. Large sums of money, obtained by various means, had enabled many gentlemen to return to Europe. This cause . . . occasioned a very quick succession in the service, which encouraged a forward spirit of independency, and produced a total contempt of public orders, whenever obedience was found incompatible with private interest.[93]

When this overall view of the sources of corruption in Bengal are combined with Clive's own narrative of how his temptation of riches could be balanced by accepting them from honorable sources (if still as a personal "present"), Clive's suggestion for how best to reform the conduct of administrators makes more sense. In fact, the core of his proposal to the Court of Directors rested on the *diwani* itself. As he wrote:

> I have at last, however, the happiness to see the completion of an event, which in this respect [of rampant corruption and insubordination among company servants], as well as in many others, must be productive of advantages hitherto unknown, and at the same time prevent abuses that have hitherto had no remedy. I mean the dewanee which is the superintendancy of all the lands, and the collection of all the revenues of the provinces of Bengal,

Bahar and Orissa. The assistance which the Great Mogul had received from our arms and treasury, made him readily bestow this grant upon the Company, and it is done in the most effect manner you can desire. . . . Revolutions are now no longer to be apprehended; the means of effecting them, will in future be wanting to ambitious Mussulmen, nor will your servants—civil or military—be tempted to foment disturbances, from whence can arise no benefit to themselves. Restitution, donation mony [sic] &c. &c. Will be perfectly abolished, as the revenues from whence they used to issue will be possessed by ourselves. The power of supervising the provinces though lodged in us should not, however, in my opinion be exerted . . . though we may suffer in the collection yet we shall always be able to detect and punish any great offenders, and shall have some satisfaction in knowing that the corruption is not among ourselves. By this means also, the abuses inevitably springing from the exercise of territorial authority, will be effectually obviated.[94]

In other words, Clive presented the *diwani* to the directors at home (shortly after Clive returned to India to reign in the administrative chaos in Bengal) as a panacea: (1) it would definitively stabilize EIC finances in Bengal and London (because it would mean that the company could pay for its commodities without exporting bullion); (2) it would rein in corruption by reducing the temptation presented to company officials because it could and would be administered indirectly by Mughal officials with company oversight; and (3) it would stabilize Bengali politics by placing the company in a supervisory role and removing the motivation to overthrow the Nawab.

Even after the company's position in Bengal had been transformed, administrators still clung to a conception of the moral propriety of their action that was at once deeply patrimonial and which relied on the moral example of immediate peers and superiors for its force.

CONCLUSION

This chapter explored two main features of the EIC's organizational apparatus as it spanned London and India. First, it argued that the EIC's moral order was, in the main, situational and that, until the middle of the eighteenth century, the company's management generally successfully suppressed attempts to escalate struggles originating in India beyond the bounds of the company and its structures themselves. Second, it also argued that, beginning in the middle of the eighteenth century, the company became embroiled in geopolitical competition with other European (especially French) companies and the successor states of the Mughal Empire. Together, these forces (further) militarized the company's activities and further transformed the significance of the "country trade"; after all, "private" economic activity had a very different valence when backed by an army than when undertaken otherwise. And because the "private" activities of company interlopers and hangers-on could suddenly upend state relations between the company and Indigenous Indian political forces, the EIC's operations in India were thrown into chaos, which radiated back to Britain after news of Plassey and its aftermath arrived nearly at the same time as George III took the throne.

The next chapter analyzes how the EIC's affairs subsequently became the subject of public scrutiny in Britain; how this changed the company's relationship to the British state; and how, in turn, the organizational consequences of this shifted relationship opened the door for a transformation in the moral order of EIC officials and consequently how they viewed corruption.

3

CONSEQUENTIAL REFORMS AND CHANGING CORRUPTION

The radical transformation of the East India Company's (EIC) position in India, as it militarized and was drawn increasingly into the succession politics of the fragments of the Mughal Empire and other political entities on the subcontinent, reverberated back to London beginning in the eighteenth century. At first, this was an intense struggle within the "Theatre of Disputes"[1] that was the company's General Court and Court of Directors. But as the struggles threatened the fiscal health of the British state itself and domestic financial markets, and as rumors of officials' misconduct and the extravagance of returning "Nabobs" grew louder, unfamiliar eyes turned toward company affairs. As I show in this chapter, the sense in which the company was called "corrupt" in these struggles was by no means clear, mixing Situational and Universal moral backgrounds, but the organizational compromise between the EIC and Parliament that was eventually struck in Pitt's India Act of 1784 *did* decisively transform the senior ranks of the company's administration.

THE COMPANY'S TRANSITION IN BRITAIN TO 1773

In London, the news of the *diwani* exacerbated an already delicate political situation, with the EIC's Court of Directors at its center. At first, the directors' goal was to use the revenues from the *diwani* as a means finally to hush bullionist (and ironically, mercantilist) criticisms that the company exported silver by directly providing money in India to remit company goods home.[2] This policy demonetarized the Indian economy, however, and damaged trade; by January 1767, the Bengal Council was already complaining to the Court of Directors of "a stop to all important of Treasure from Europe" that "no kingdom can support long."[3] Thus, George Dudley, chair of the Court of Directors, instructed Robert Clive in 1766:

> [I] also induce . . . you to take every measure in your power to put them [the revenues] into a flow of cash, by sending home large quantities of goods, supplying the China supercargoes with great sums of money and providing Bombay with what ever treasure they may want, and lastly by drawing upon the Court of Directors for as little money as possible. These are the two grand points to be now attended to, for if we do not find ways and means to bring our great acquisitions to centre in England neither the Company nor the nation will reap the expected benefit from them.[4]

But this anticipated boon was soon attacked from two main directions: from below, as company shareholders and returning servants eager to guarantee their fortunes began interfering in the directorate; and from above, as Parliament became increasingly interested in company affairs.

From below, a shareholder uprising demanded an immediate dividend from the *diwani*'s unrealized revenues, and director's elections became hotly contested events notorious for "stock-splitting" among factions of investors with political and financial aims (see figures 3.1 and 3.2).[5] These collisions became particularly heated between Laurence Sulivan, who aimed to preserve the company's largely merchant character, and Clive, who, besides being interested in protecting his *jagir* and newly minted position as a member of Parliament (MP), also believed that territorial revenues held the key to the company's long-term political and financial prosperity. Contention between the two figures got heated enough, particularly surrounding the directors' elections of 1758 and 1763, that Parliament was forced to intervene (in the form of two investigatory committees).[6] These committees largely stayed out of the details of the company's organization in India itself but did depose Clive at length and forced him to justify his acceptance of the *jagir* and other

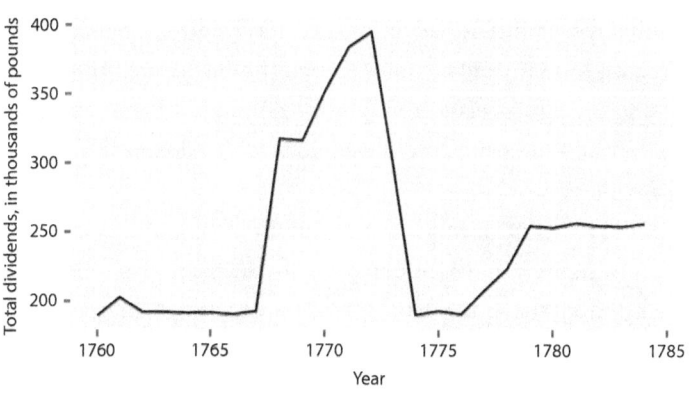

FIGURE 3.1 East India Company dividends, 1760–1784.

Sources: Bowen (2020); East India Company: Trade and Domestic Financial Statistics, 1755–1838 (data collection); UK Data Service. SN: 5690, doi:10.5255/UKDA-SN-5690-1.

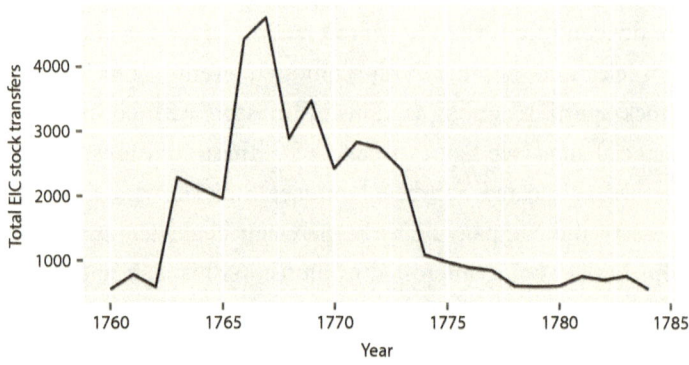

FIGURE 3.2 East India Company stock transfers, including individual and by attorney, 1760–1784.

Sources: Bowen (2020); East India Company: Trade and Domestic Financial Statistics, 1755–1838 (data collection); UK Data Service. SN: 5690, doi:10.5255/UKDA-SN-5690-1.

emoluments from Mir Jafar, which he did (as discussed in the introduction) in heavily Situational terms that relied on local Mughal custom and the behavior of his immediate peers among company servants in Bengal. Clive survived the skirmish, but because so many outsiders to company affairs were now attentive to the EIC's finances and internal politics,[7] the court began to feel new pressure to respond to a wider domestic political constituency.

One index of this wider attention to company affairs can be seen in figure 3.3, which compiles the number of publications in London about the EIC from 1600 to 1784.[8] There is little attention paid to company affairs for most of the seventeenth century by the general English public, and there are no more than a handful of publications about it every year. There is a relatively large output at the turn of the eighteenth century, when

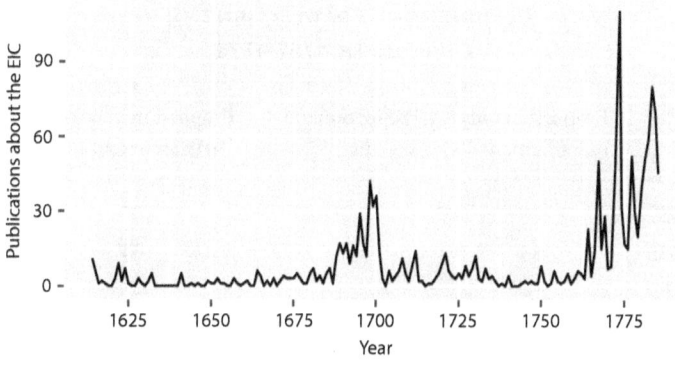

FIGURE 3.3 Publications discussing the East India Company in Britain, 1600–1784.

Source: Catherine Pickett, Bibliography of the East India Company: Books, Pamphlets and Other Materials Printed Between 1600 and 1785, United Kingdom: British Library, 2011.

(as recounted in chapter 2) there were actually *two* companies competing for a parliamentary charter after the Glorious Revolution. Attention to company affairs again falls after the two companies were "united" early in the eighteenth century, and its patronage and profits were integrated into the new parliamentary regime.

Another important sign of this pressure can also be seen in the volatile composition of the Court of Directors in the key period between 1757 and 1773, which is displayed in table 3.1. The table displays the proportion of the directorate who had *only* served in India during their lives (who we can broadly interpret as the Court of Directors' "incumbents"), those who likewise had *only* service in Parliament (broadly, "insurgents" from outside the company seeking to influence its affairs), and those who had done both (a composite of loyalists to the company and

TABLE 3.1 PROPORTIONS OF COURT OF DIRECTORS WITH EXPERIENCE IN PARLIAMENT, IN INDIA, OR IN BOTH, 1757-1773

Year	Proportion only in Parliament	Proportion only in India	Proportion in both Parliament and India
1757	.09	.23	.05
1758	.13	.17	.04
1759	.04	.26	—
1760	.08	.21	.04
1761	.9	.26	.04
1762	—	.43	—
1763	.14	.14	.05
1764	.13	.22	.04
1765	.2	.36	—
1766	.19	.35	—
1767	.33	.33	—
1768	.39	.17	.04
1769	.30	.09	.22
1770	.29	.25	.08
1771	.23	.23	.15
1772	.27	.23	.15
1773	.14	.21	.14

internally insurgent "nabobs" like Clive, who wished to protect their fortunes or influence politics).[9]

Several features of these data stand out. First, in 1757, the court's largest constituency was "India hands" who became directors after service in India, such as the dominant director at the time, Laurence Sulivan. By 1767, however, this group—which then was a third of the directors—was evenly matched by insurgents from Parliament.[10] By 1769, only a tenth of the directors constituted this "old guard"; instead, about a quarter of the directors had *both* Indian *and* parliamentary experience. Taken together, in other words, the Court of Directors after about 1765 was decisively penetrated by outside political interest in Britain, and there was a countermovement of EIC officials to Parliament as the center of political gravity over the company's affairs drifted in that direction.

From above, the company also faced increasing pressure from Parliament. This came from a desire to get a piece of the promised revenues from Bengal (because the crown's fleet had been instrumental at Plassey) and took the form of the Chatham ministry's efforts to formalize the legal relationship between the company and crown over the *diwani*. The struggle over the *diwani* took the form of complicated legal disputes in the gray area of the company's chartered monopoly, as backroom negotiations between the ministry and directors. But in brief, the company used its formal vassalage to the Mughal emperor Shah Alam as a means to shield the *diwani* legally as a "grant" rather than as a "conquest" to prevent the revenues from legally defaulting directly to the British state.[11] For its part, the ministry saw the *diwani* as a way to alleviate a spiraling domestic debt, which by 1767 had reached £131 million,[12] and to ministers hungry for revenue, a share of the £2 million annually that Clive privately estimated to Rockingham and Chatham was a great prize, especially given the rising crisis in the Atlantic empire over colonial taxation.[13] (Clive publicly declared in 1765 to the Court of Directors that the *diwani* would mean "a clear gain to the Company of 122 lack of sicca rupees, or £1,650,900, which will defray all the expence of the investment, furnish the whole of the China treasure, answer all the demands of all your other settlements in India, and leave a considerable balance in your treasury besides.")[14] While the ministry was unable to gain control over the revenues outright (in part because it wanted no part in their actual administration and collection), in 1767, the directors agreed to a yearly payment of £400,000 to Parliament.[15]

These two pressures on the company—from its shareholders to distribute revenues on earnings that had not materialized in London and from the ministry to contribute what amounted to a tax share of its new revenues—combined with a more general economic downturn in England in the early 1770s to produce a general fiscal crisis. In 1772, the company declared that it could not make its annual payment to the crown, and, in the face of a shareholder sell-off of its stock and sudden absence of purchasers for its bonds, would instead need a loan from the state and might suspend its dividends altogether.[16] This financial crisis was compounded by a new controversy relating to the company's administration in Bengal. William Bolts, a sometime employee of the company, had repeatedly abused the company's trading privileges in Bengal's interior (much to the aggravation of the Nawab, Mir Qasim) and was deported by the governor (and Clive's post-Plassey successor), Harry Verelst, in 1768.[17] Upon his return to England, Bolts sued Verelst (who also returned shortly thereafter), and although the company indemnified Verelst against the trivial damages awarded Bolts, Bolts also engaged in a public broadside against Verelst by publishing *Considerations on Indian Affairs* in 1772.[18]

The book proved extremely popular (going through three editions), and Verelst felt compelled to respond to it, which he did in his *A View of the Rise, Progress, and Present State of the English Government in Bengal* of the same year. This public debate was remarkable not only because it was one of the first times that debate about the company's Indian administrative policy took place publicly (and so polemically) before British eyes but also because of the contrasting views of corruption, its sources, and the appropriate foundations of administrative order the two works represented. For "thwarted" servants like Bolts, the source of corruption was the disordering of the company's old patrimonial organization, and the answer was to ratify solutions to the problem of moral order that rested on radically new, autonomous moral foundations; for Bolts, "free trade," if practiced, would draw together Britain and India in harmony. For Verelst (responding publicly to Bolts), the answer was to empower the governor such that his local, patrimonial authority to deport nettlesome characters like Bolts could not be questioned.

In addition to proliferating these abstract moral frames, the outcome of this domestic period of disorder was the passage of the compromise Regulating Act of 1773. The key provisions of the act were, first, to limit the payout of company profits in dividends until it repaid its loans to the Bank of England and, second, to empower a governor-general to oversee a Supreme Council in Calcutta. The governor-general-in-council was to stand superordinate over Madras and Bombay, and the council itself was to be a composite of both company and parliamentary interests.[19] The governor-generalship was a matter of consensus: it was to be Warren Hastings, who was "the one Company servant with a reputation which made him at that time widely acceptable within the Company and to a wider public without."[20]

But the composition of the council stood much more debate and yielded dubious results: Richard Barwell, "a typical 'Nabob' of the kind that had grown rich since Clive's conquests"; General John Clavering, "who possessed, though he hardly deserved, the confidence of the king as a soldier and man of good sense and integrity"; Colonel George Monson, "no more than a mediocre soldier of good political connections"; and Philip Francis, "both desperately ambitious and so virulent of in tongue and per as to wreck the success of any team of which he formed a part," and who was a last-minute replacement for a man who refused the personal hazard of Indian adventures.[21] Of the newly constituted council, only Hastings and Barwell had ever been to India.

Thus, by the early 1770s, the company's position had been transformed in Bengal, as had its relationship to Parliament and the crown in London. But the transformation was incomplete. The EIC collected revenues from the whole province of Bengal, but it did so indirectly and technically as a vassal to the Mughal emperor. The British state's attention had been drawn to the structure of its administration, yet Parliament had avoided direct intervention, assigning politicos to serve under an old India hand, Hastings, whose position the court and the company had only tepidly empowered. State interventions and new promises from the directors seemed to guarantee that official abuse and corruption in India would be reformed, but the character and progress of that reform rested on an uneven terrain of competing visions of what the company's moral order was to be. As the next section will show, those competing visions were to clash repeatedly over the next decade and a half in Bengal.

CONTINUING DISORDER IN INDIA

In the aftermath of the Regulating Act of 1773, conflict in India continued in Madras (as discussed in chapter 5) but in Bengal, it coalesced around the figure of Warren Hastings. Hastings' administration in India is often seen (and indeed, was excoriated by Burke) as an era in which "Asiatic Despotism" crept into and corrupted British administration.[36] And if such were the case, Hastings's career would mark the crucial point at which an abstracted "state"—even of an "Asiatic" variety—became a key organizing logic of company administration.[37] Yet the practical organization of Hastings's administration, and especially the ways he interacted with local rulers and sought to discipline his own staff, reveal a very different process at work. In fact, although Hastings sought greater powers for the governor-general over his own staff, he still fundamentally worked within the proximate, particularistic context of moral judgment that had characterized earlier company administration in Bengal. Indeed, disputes over the proper context of judgment proved to be an important source of conflict that would dominate the remainder of Hastings's life.

Hastings moved cautiously against Muhammad Reza Khan (the Mughal naib, or chief revenue officer, whom Clive had entrusted with collecting the company's *diwani*), essentially "employing Indian officials and Indian laws, while occasionally infusing English constitutional principles" in order to "[attach] the upstart sovereignty of the Company to some idea of stability and longevity."[38] Indeed, even though directly ordered to "stand forth" as the diwan and erase Clive's system of double government, over the course of 1772 and 1774, Hastings's movements toward reforming company administration and land revenue were tentative and sought to preserve the Nawab's "delicate" political position. Hastings's reforms were also calibrated to preserve company servants' precarious positions. Hastings feared that disrupting the indigenous Bengali political order would reveal that many wealthy Indians had "established an interest" among company servants,[39] and therefore, for example, he resisted prosecuting the company resident at Murshidabad because it would shed "more light than ought to be exposed" on officials' corruption,[40] especially when those under investigation were "so many Sons, Cousins, or élèves of Directors, and Intimates of Members of [the Bengal] Council."[41] And although his proposal was quickly overturned, Hastings appears to have looked backward for a solution to corruption—he sought to restrict company servants physically to Calcutta and EIC factories, thus promoting "harmony" and reducing "faction" by ensuring that junior servants stayed under the watchful eyes of their superiors.[42]

But reconstructing the company's old system of administrative order proved impossible, and Hastings's efforts instead generated more controversy. This was because, first, as a territorial sovereign restricting administration to company factories proved impracticable and simply prevented effective supervision of Indian revenue collectors and EIC political liaisons (as the example of the resident of Mushidabad illustrated). Second, the 1773 act established an English Supreme Court in Calcutta under the direct auspices of the British crown, creating an avenue of appeal to Britain that compromised the figure of the governor-general as the sole authority in the company's possessions. Third, and most important, the act also directly nominated a set of subordinate councilors to serve on a newly constituted Supreme Council in Bengal under Hastings. The composition of the council was a compromise between the Court of Directors and Frederick North's ministry, and ended up composed of Clavering, Monson, Richard Barwell (James' father), and Francis. Of the four, only Barwell was an "old India" hand like Hastings,[43] and Francis had already undertaken a public (although pseudonymous) career as the parliamentary-opposition pamphleteer "Junius" prior to his appointment by North.[44]

Although Francis had a prickly personality, his brand of oppositional behavior, particularly regarding Hastings's attempted reforms of land revenue administration in Bengal, proved especially chaotic. According to Francis, Hastings's proposed system of revenue farming "annihilated every idea of private property"[45] and instead ought to have been replaced by a system of fixed-tax private property in land that would replicate, in India, "a real nobility in the ancient and rational sense of the

English constitution."⁴⁶ Indeed, it was by invoking the abstract moral power of the company's state, conceived as "the political union of a Government with its subjects" and not "the oeconomical relation of master and slave."⁴⁷

This moral conception of the state as an abstract guarantor of private property stood in contrast to Hastings, whom Francis detested as "a busy, projecting, intricate politician of the lowest order, [and that] it is not in his nature to walk straight" who simultaneously "is not content with absolute power, but exercises it in the most arbitrary manner."⁴⁸ Above all, Francis appears to have detested Hastings for appearing to be disingenuous. As Francis wrote of Hastings to a friend:

> The qualification commonly called "parts," is in general too dangerous to be trusted in the management of public affairs. It requires firmness, integrity, and good sense, and it requires nothing else. Mr. Hastings is, literally and exclusively, a man of parts. This is not a single principle, moral or political, either in his head or his heart. One natural effect of this character is that, when he means best, he constantly begins his building at the top, or with some room that has an agreeable prospect, and never thinks of a foundation till the whole edifice falls to pieces for want of it. Another is, that he is uncommonly dexterous at extricating himself out of difficulties, which with a very moderate portion of common sense, and the tenth part of his microscopic sagacity, he might have averted. I am not sure that his vanity is not concerned in preferring the intricacy of a labyrinth to any plain road on which he must travel with the multitude. "I detest principles" is a common expression with him.⁴⁹

Hastings, in turn, appears to have attempted to manage Francis's prickly personality through politeness. As Hastings expressed his frustration to his friend (and successor) Macpherson, "I acted with the strictest Honor to Mr Francis even so far as to throw myself upon his Mercy by parting with Barwell. I bore his repeated Breaches of Treaty, and I bore his Insolences (I can not immediately find a softer Term for them) as long as I could do it without public and dangerous Consequences."[50] Yet as the enmity between the two worsened, Hastings eventually even accused the Court of Directors itself of stoking the conflict:

> For when this fair opportunity of restoring peace and Harmony in Bengal presented itself [of supporting Hastings fully]; When it was hoped that Party would have died with the Person who formed it; When the bad effects of it had been felt in every department; When the Fabric which had been raised by Mr H. had stood the repeated shocks that opposition of every kind had given it; And when nothing but Unanimity could repair the breaches which discord had made, the Court of Directors widened these breaches by keeping alive the embers of that Faction They ought to have smothered. They reviled and reprobated all the measures of Mr Hastings because Mr Francis objected to them. They praised Mr Francis because He was an enemy to Mr H. And they seemed to have kept the Governor General in the Chair purely for the sake of abusing him.[51]

The animosity between Hastings and Francis worsened to the point where the two even fought a duel in 1780 in which Francis was wounded but recovered. The duel appears to have revolved around Francis's defense of his own stand for principle and moral conviction because Francis challenged Hastings after the latter privately wrote to Francis that "I do not trust to Mr. Francis' promises of candour, convinced that he is incapable of it. I judge of his public conduct by his private, which

I have found to be void of truth and honour."[52] Thus, the conflict between the two was over the extent to which each could credibly be said to reflect their inner convictions in public matters. For Hastings the structure of the "honour" he represented meant a long-standing embeddedness in and deep experience of the company's administration in India, but for Francis, the goal was to represent "principles," especially that of a state guaranteeing its people's rights. Remarkably, both men were willing to die to protect these self-representations.

While the connection between abstract principles of state and moral conviction were crucial for Francis while in India, he could not sustain that connect upon his return to England in 1781. As soon as he returned, he set about projecting his favor with the North ministry and the risk that his political connections might mean to Hastings's allies in the Court of Directors (although those allies estimated that these connections were grossly exaggerated).[53] Francis's opponents, it seems, were capable of shutting off direct access to power and attacking Hastings directly, either from within the ministry or the court. Moreover, as a contemporary doggerel summarizes nearly, this was in part because Francis was made out to be acting on his own passions rather than on principle:

> No sooner on shore had our Phill set his feet,
> Than he drove, like a post boy, to Leadenhall Street;
> In the flames of his malice, he burnt to disclose
> A tale which had cost him some years to compose;
> But he got a rebuff from the Court of Directors;
> They were Hastings' friends; they were virtue's protectors;
> They paid just regard to their honour and glory;
> They read not Phill's papers, they heard not Phill's story.
> Tho' like lightning to England from India he came,

In speed he was greatly surpass'd by his fame;
They knew how the measures of Hastings he crost,
How near his advice Coromandel had lost;
By the Court of Directors, it clearly was seen
That the man was a compound of envy and spleen.
Then away to the mongers of boroughs went he,
To try, if with some one he could not agree;
And find a fit corner—for once—to his use
For speech unrestrained, and for licenc'd abuse.
But when he discovered that loud declaration
Could produce no effect on a sensible nation,
His attention was turn'd to the Quixote-like Burke,
Who is fond of engaging in Quixote-like work.[54]

But if Francis had no direct avenue of attack against Hastings, Francis turned, as the second stanza of the poem describes, to parliamentary opposition. Indeed, Francis cashed in on his "long-term insurance" policy—his friendship with Burke, begun before Francis sailed for India—and served as the key witness for Burke's reconstituted oppositional Select Committee of Parliament (in contrast to the ministerial "Secret Committee"),[55] which "smote [Hastings] hip and thigh."[56] These reports, moreover, are more important than the long-running parliamentary impeachment of Hastings itself because they decisively influenced the flavor and structure of Pitt's India Act of 1784 and especially its decision to place senior levels of EIC Indian governance under governmental supervision through the Board of Control.[57]

To sum up, between 1773, when Lord North's Regulating Act established Hastings as governor-general of Bengal, and 1784, when Pitt's India Act again altered the relationship between the EIC and the British state, the company's administration in

Bengal represented a clash of moral styles of self. Hastings, as an old India hand, represented a fragmentary, embedded way of judging the propriety of official action and hence of organizing the administration as a whole, which depended on servants' harmonious embedding within the company's larger patrimonial hierarchy. Francis, by contrast, came to India as an outsider and without the same kind of access to the company's network. Likely in part because of this exclusion, he depended on a form of decontextualized moral judgment that reflected (claims to) underlying "principles." At least part of Francis's failure to attack Hastings successfully and directly in London can be ascribed to his failure to maintain successfully the connection between his unitary, authentic personal belief and his political convictions. And as the next section describes, while his alliance with Burke may have pushed further structural transformation in the company's administration, Francis's fusillade against Hastings was hardly the last instance of perceived moral disorder in Bengal. Indeed, it would be carried to fruition by Charles Cornwallis.

AMBIGUOUS CORRUPTION AND THE MOVEMENT TO PITT'S INDIA ACT OF 1784

The EIC had been an important object of political struggle in England at the beginning of the eighteenth century because its regular charter renewal usually presented an excuse to extract money to pay for military adventures.[58] Because it was integrated as one of the "cogs" in the Whig political machine's dominance of eighteenth-century England, the company's internal affairs were left relatively undisturbed. In particular, the Court of Directors maintained control over patronage via appointments to both foreign and domestic administrative positions within the company, and thus contested elections were extremely rare, and an appointment to the Directorate came to be a de facto lifetime appointment.[59]

The company's new territorial holdings and how these holdings pulled the company into regional politics also had consequences for how the company operated internally. Those English and Scots serving in local factories or on presidency councils who supported a successful Indigenous claimant in a succession dispute now stood to gain enormous fortunes through the "presents" or favorable commercial concessions they received.[60] Local factional disputes among company officials broke out over how such emoluments were to be divided, and these disputes were carried back to London as returning "nabobs"[61] began bitterly contesting elections in the Directorate to protect their gains.[62] These contests energized and politicized the company's Court of Proprietors and drew increasing attention and interference from Parliament, whose members were also individually implicated more and more often.[63] This new, bitter political contention over the policies the company was pursuing resulted in repeated parliamentary investigation into Indian administration, especially as guaranteed company dividends of 12.5 percent played a role in a complex fiscal crisis in the company and threatened the health of British capital markets themselves.[64]

The newfound celebrity of company factional struggles in London brought widespread hostility to returned "nabobs"[65] and forced Parliament to intervene in the company's internal politics,[66] yet it did so with little detailed understanding of the issues at stake. Despite fears of growing Anglo-Indian influence in Parliament, in 1768, only nineteen members had ever been to India,[67] and few others had anything beyond a superficial acquaintance with the subject.[68] This did not prevent Parliament, despite fits and starts, one of which was the proximate

CONSEQUENTIAL REFORMS ⚭ 137

cause of the Charles James Fox-North coalition's fall in 1783, from drawing the company under increasingly tight oversight beginning in the late 1760s. This culminated in the passage of Pitt's India Act of 1784, which established a government board of control to monitor the company's foreign policy and established tighter administrative control among the company's subsidiary "presidencies" in India under the charge of a governor-general.[69]

Throughout this period of bitter struggle between the company and the British state and within the company itself, bitter insinuations of corruption flew back and forth. Yet even as more and more observers attended to company affairs in India, the discourse of corruption remained multivocal and confused. This can be seen clearly by political cartoons from the era (see figures 3.4, 3.5, and 3.6). The first cartoon (figure 3.4), "The India

FIGURE 3.4 "The India Directors in the Suds," 1772.
Source: Courtesy of The Lewis Walpole Library, Yale University.

138 ᴄᴏɴꜱᴇǫᴜᴇɴᴛɪᴀʟ ʀᴇꜰᴏʀᴍꜱ

FIGURE 3.5 "East India Reformers, or, New Ways & Means," 1783. Charles Fox, center, is portrayed defecating on the company's charter.

Source: Courtesy of The Lewis Walpole Library, Yale University.

Directors in the Suds,"[70] dates from 1772 and shows the directors presumably drinking at a shared table when "Black Merchants" confront a director, possibly the "Jaghire" (i.e., Clive), who reacts in fear as a note labeled "Apology" falls to his feet. Clearly, the insinuation is that the directors collectively (or the one director acting alone) feel guilt on their conscience over the origin of their fortune and that, by extension, they are themselves corrupt.

The second example (figure 3.5) dates from 1783, at the height of controversy over the Fox-North India Bill, which would have established (had it not failed) a much tighter grip over the affairs of the company than was achieved by the Board of Control after Pitt's India Act of 1784. But here, the insinuation of corruption runs in the opposite direction: Charles James Fox is portrayed in the center of the East India directors' chamber defecating on a copy of the EIC charter, while Burke shoos the directors out the door. Lord North stands beside Fox with stock certificates and money visible in his pockets, while Fox's pockets contain a "List of Commissions" (i.e., the company's patronage appointments to India) and the room itself is filled with money. The insinuation is that Fox and North have attempted to reform the company's administration in India not because of perceived mismanagement or even a desire to improve administration for the "Black Merchants" from the earlier cartoon but because of a corrupt desire to control the EIC's resources.

This ambivalent attitude toward corruption—whether it originated from the British state itself or resulted from company affairs in India—persisted even after Pitt's India Act established the Board of Control in 1784. Henry Dundas, a Scot, was the first chair and, as the 1787 cartoon (figure 3.6), "The Board of Controul, or, the Blessings of a Scotch Dictator," shows, a central worry was that he himself had won control of the company's patronage. Indeed, Dundas is literally doling out patronage to racist caricatures of Scots while behind him two pictures are labeled "Robbing" (in which Fox takes "India Patronage" at gunpoint) and "Stealing" (in which Pitt takes "India Patronage" from a sleeping man in Indian dress), and on the table are documents insinuating that the Board of Control will redirect India patronage to Scotland, prescribe the succession of the EIC directors and the senior levels of the presidencies, and circumscribe officials' behavior down to "The Length of their Letters."

140 CONSEQUENTIAL REFORMS

FIGURE 3.6 "The Board of Controul, or, the Blessings of a Scotch Dictator," 1787.

Source: General Collection, Beinecke Rare Book and Manuscript Library, Yale University.

EAST INDIA COMPANY PATRONAGE AS A TRANSMISSION BELT

The company's increasingly prominent geopolitical position, as well as the concomitant increase in the British state's attention to its affairs, brought significant changes to the way it staffed its emerging Indian empire. Commercial "writers" and military "cadets" had long been appointed by the Court of Directors, but because of high mortality in India and poor pay, these appointments were generally not sought after, and it was not unheard of for company servants to arrive in India as free agents and gain employment with the company there, expecting their appointments to be later ratified in London.⁷¹ But as hostilities escalated in India in the 1740s and especially after the personal fortunes won with the company's new territory after 1757, competition for appointments exploded and the directors instituted a strict rotation of their patronage. Appointments as writers were most prized, as cadets and assistant surgeons relatively less so.⁷² The Board of Control also participated in the disposition of patronage after 1784, and the appointment of governors, governors-general, and senior military officials in each presidency lay with the government despite being nominally approved by the directors.⁷³

As was the case for members of Parliament and state officials, East India Company directors found themselves at the center of a web of supplicants asking for appointments. The directors preferred their close kin most prominently (awarding them lucrative postings to the company's commercial station at Canton)⁷⁴ followed by more distant relatives and political supporters both inside and outside the company's Court of Proprietors.⁷⁵ As the court and the Board of Control fell into the hands of two Scots, David Scott and Dundas, the locus of patronage also shifted appreciably toward Scotland at the turn of the nineteenth century.⁷⁶ East India Company patronage therefore sent men to India who represented, in Bernard Cohn's words, "a very restricted group in Indian society and drawn from banking and commercial families and landed groups in Scotland and the southeast of England."⁷⁷ Or as Bourne more forcefully puts the point, East India Company servants were comprised of a class of "pseudo-gentry" who aspired to the distinction and markers of the gentleman but in reality came from "the ranks of successful husbandmen, yeomen and tradesmen and from the landless descendants of earlier landed families."⁷⁸ In sum, as the company was drawn into closer connection with and placed under increasing supervision by the British state, its servants were increasingly drawn from the tranche of the British petty elite, who aspired to gentility and carried with them to India the complex legacy of judging the moral propriety of action that had been so salient over the course of the eighteenth century.

The East India Company's patronage network was a function of its political position in Britain. Pitt's India Act transformed the terrain of struggle within the EIC's administration in India. One key index of this shift is the demography of the company's senior administration. Table 3.2 summarizes the relevant characteristics of the governors of each of the EIC's three presidencies immediately before and immediately after Pitt's Act—their age when first in India, how long they spent there, and what proportion of their lives that time was.

There are dramatic differences. Collectively, the governors immediately preceding Pitt's India Act spent nearly half their

TABLE 3.2 PRESIDENCY GOVERNORS BEFORE AND AFTER PITT'S INDIA ACT

Province	Name of presidency governor	Birth date	Death date	Age first in India	Years in India	Proportion of life spent in India
Bengal	John Macpherson	1745	1821	22	12	0.16
	Charles Cornwallis	1738	1805	48	10	0.14
Madras	Thomas Rumbold	1736	1791	16	29	0.53
	George Macartney	1737	1806	44	5	0.07
Bombay	Jonathan Duncan	1756	1811	16	39	0.71
	Evan Nepean	1752	1822	60	8	0.11
Average	Predecessor	1746	1808	18	26.7	0.46
	Successor	1742	1811	50.7	7.7	0.11

Source: Author created from the Dictionary of National Biography.

lives in India and, on average, arrived at the age of eighteen. By contrast, the successors arrived much later (at an average age of fifty) and spent only 11 percent of their lives in India. The source of such a dramatic divergence is not difficult to find: Pitt's India Act, in placing EIC affairs under the oversight of the Board of Control, specified that governors would now be appointed by that board, while all patronage below the level of presidency governor remained with the company. In the interest of both finding officers not already perceived to be stained by the notorious events in India since 1765 and also more firmly ensconcing the senior levels of Indian administration in the circuit of *government* (and not company) patronage, the board selected from among "known quantities" from elsewhere in the empire. Thus, in contrast to figures like Clive and Hastings, both of whom grew up from within the EIC's ranks, the terrain suddenly shifted so that Cornwallis became governor of Bengal after having surrendered to the Americans at Yorktown, George Macartney talked himself into the job after a diplomatic posting in Grenada and returned to the diplomatic circuit after his stint in Madras, and Evan Nepean was appointed governor of Bombay at the age of sixty.

CONCLUSION

Amid the chaos created by the East India Company's changing structural position, chapter 3 has shown how the process of reform was shaped by changing notions about how to define corruption. Aggrieved company officials had long complained to London about their conflicts with one another, but as the company's affairs drew interest from politicians (such as Burke) and others (such as company investors and the general public) who had never been to India and knew little about the state of affairs there, officials appealing for support began to draw on new arguments. They abandoned accounts of corruption that relied on the local context of company affairs and instead argued that their opponents were "corrupt" because they violated the ethical precepts of political economy, government duty, or fidelity to the public good.

4

MODERN SELVES

If a contextualist understanding of moral regulation (and an understanding of corruption as the loss of balance among competing passions) implied a fragmentary sense of self that could radically change its behavior and moral posture as social settings varied, the universalist understanding of morality and corruption ushered in by East India Company (EIC) reforms demanded a much more unitary self-presentation and consistent set of self-justifications. Thus, I address the self-presentation of company officials in the aftermath of EIC reforms and demonstrate that the EIC at the end of the eighteenth century was populated by both officials who followed the older system of moral regulation and those (primarily outsiders who needed to mobilize external support) who presented themselves in terms of the new one. By consequence, when officials struggled with one another in this period, the outcome was often misunderstanding, incoherence, and distrust. A key tool in these struggles, I argue, was the emergent moral biographies by which officials began to explain their seemingly aberrant behavior.

MADRAS: GEORGE MACARTNEY

The "revolution" in Madras reflected both continuity and change in company administration. Lord Pigot's downfall and death drew the attention of Parliament, the crown, and the British public to the "Nawab of Arcot's Debts" and gave spectacular ammunition to the company's domestic political opponents. When combined with the British state's first serious intervention into company affairs with the 1773 Regulating Act, increasingly intense political struggles surrounding the company as it sought its charter renewal, and the company's own internal factional conflict between Laurence Sulivan and his many opponents, this attention meant that a new class of senior administrators sailed for Madras beginning in the 1780s. These new men, especially George Macartney, were drawn from the larger British imperial patronage network, and although they arrived in Madras confident in their abilities to reform the administration, both encountered obstacles that had persisted through the Pigot scandal. Southern India remained an arena for multilateral military strife between Mughal successor states, to say nothing of French intrigues (whether real or imagined). Because the company's purge of the Madras administration had been half-hearted and unsuccessful, Macartney also dealt with the same recalcitrant men who had deposed and imprisoned Pigot.

Faced with these challenges, Macartney revolutionized the institutional logic of the Madras administration. Although he first tried to operate within the personalistic and patrimonial politics of the Madras administration and the situational moral order they represented, Macartney soon repudiated references to local peers, angering his cohorts in Madras. Macartney sought new foundations to justify his moral stances again the administration and eventually settled on an autonomous, if unsteady foundation in an authentic, consistent representation of himself across social settings. In other words, he used the story of his own life and past actions, combined with a claim to their consistency, as political ammunition against his own staff in Madras during administrative struggles.

In the aftermath of Pigot's death, the first governor sent to replace him was another quintessential company man, Sir Thomas Rumbold. The son of a former council member at Tellicherry and nephew of the former attorney of the Mayor's Court of Madras, Rumbold joined the company's civil service in India in 1752, eventually rising to sit on the council in Bengal between 1766 and 1769. Rumbold then returned to England and seats in both Parliament and the company's Court of Directors, but he sailed back out to Madras in 1778 at the court's behest.[1] Although his administration was a personal financial success—Rumbold returned to England in 1780 with around £750,000 in investment profits, salary, and bribes from the Nawab of Arcot—it was a political failure in both Madras and London.[2] In India, Rumbold struck out at the French, capturing Pondicherry from the French in October 1778 and Mahé in 1779, but he irritated both the Nizam of Hyderabad and the company's nominally superordinate council in Bengal by leasing the Northern Circars to the Nawab of Arcot in lieu of the Nizam's brother and likewise aggravated relations with Hyder Ali by violating Mysore's treaty protecting Mahé.[3] Even when he returned to England, Rumbold's political fate was no better. He had been elected a member of Parliament (MP) for Shaftesbury in absentia but was unseated by petition and returned a few days later from Yarmouth, Isle of Wight. He also was dismissed from the Court of

Directors and sued in Chancery for £60,000, in part because he was now acting directly as the London political agent for the Nawab of Arcot. Rumbold was even prosecuted in Parliament under a constitutionally unusual bill of pains and penalties for his conduct as governor. Although it failed on technical and political grounds,[4] Rumbold's prosecution drew more unwelcome attention to Madras administration from Parliament and the British public. This attention was compounded because Rumbold had clearly done little to settle the Madras administration: since Rumbold's departure, the governor pro tem, John Whitehill, had been suspended and recalled for incompetence and fled England under suspicion of supporting piracy;[5] three more senior company servants became embroiled in a public trial displaying Madras's factional infighting to an audience in London.[6] In sum, the company's efforts to contain the scandal of the Madras administration in the aftermath of Pigot's death using its own personnel proved an abject failure.

Part of the reason for this failure was that the company's London politics had been deeply unsettled through most of the 1770s. The Court of Proprietors had repeatedly fought to install directors who were hostile to the British government and who favored guaranteeing profits at the cost of company stability, while the government had sought to manipulate the company's internal affairs directly.[7] But in the company election of 1780, the North ministry forked the company's internal opposition by coopting Sulivan, with whom they forged a "curious alliance"[8] and began to collaborate on appointments for the governors of the presidencies while leaving lower-level appointments in the directors' hands.[9] The first fruit of this collaboration on appointments was to send Macartney, the "notoriously penniless"[10] former governor of Grenada (until it was captured by the French) and special crown envoy to Russia, and former chief secretary for

Ireland, to replace Rumbold as governor of Madras in 1780. Even though he was already an Irish peer, handsome, a skilled speaker, and embedded in the British elite (having married a daughter of the earl of Bute and friend of Edmund Burke's),[11] Macartney owed his appointment largely to the political disorder caused by Pigot's overthrow and the consequent political toxicity of his primary internal competitors, John Call and Claud Russell.[12] In other words, the first governor of a company presidency to take office without prior Indian experience was appointed, on the one hand, because of an awkward political coalition meant to stabilize the metropolitan relationship between the British state and the company, and on the other hand, because of an unusually favorable set of political circumstances caused by the company's colonial disorder. The fact that Macartney lacked Indian experience before his appointment is important. For a man like Rumbold, Macartney's predecessor as governor, Madras represented a well-known feature of the company's internal political landscape, its administration filled with known actors and its institutions relatively familiar. For Macartney, by contrast (and like Charles Cornwallis, who would become governor-general of Bengal over Macartney's candidacy in 1786), Madras was yet another stop on the perambulation of lower-tier British diplomatic-cum-military elites who circulated throughout the British Empire in the late eighteenth century.

Although he knew his status as an outsider would pique the jealousies of company administrators,[13] Macartney appears to have tried to turn that very status into an advantage. For example, he pitched himself in his letter of application to the directors as one who would not have applied "had not several of my friends [within the company], men of high character and large property, perfectly versed and deeply interested in Indian concerns, expressed a strong opinion that the situation on the

Coromandel Coast would probably require at this particular Juncture the appointment of one totally unconnected with any of the contending interests there, and absolutely free from local passion or prepossession."[14] Likewise a motion in the Court of Proprietors for Macartney's appointment declared, in part, "that integrity unshaken by the example of plunder and corruption, a character to lose and consequently one to save by shunning the faults of former governors, were to be considered as the fittest qualifications in their new governor of Madras."[15] Above all, Macartney promised to turn this very lack of local knowledge into a tool for disinterested administration in Madras:

> [Macartney] was aware, he said, of the popular and interested objection of his want of local knowledge [as voiced by a court motion]. . . . He found that prudence and integrity, temper and perseverance seldom failed to surmount the difficulties of public stations, and those difficulties for which they are established; that local knowledge, which is necessary to men in eminent offices, is indeed either quickly acquired or easily supplied by inferior persons on the spot; not the report of an individual, bur compared and collected from many. Any one man's local knowledge must be so corrected, or it will be found both lame and blind. The public man becomes the impartial judge, who gathers from the witnesses of the facts, the truth of the evidence.[16]

Thus, Macartney portrayed himself to the Court of Directors as a figure that closely mirrored Adam Smith's ideal of the impartial spectator. While he provided essentially no details of what policies he would pursue or of the substantive principles that would guide his conduct, Macartney instead offered a strong formal description of how he would broker and synthesize competing sources of local knowledge, acting with "prudence and integrity" as an "impartial judge" to obtain the "truth of the evidence."

Because his avowed role as governor of Madras was thus to balance competing political actions within the administration on the basis of his own objective distance from the stakes of the conflicts, Macartney claimed he was well-suited to the task because of his affable personality and the consequent "independence" it afforded him. John Barrow emphasized how Macartney's personality, for example, made him one of the few men who "could temper the impetuous eloquence" and "silence the wild and democratic effusions" of parliamentary opponents while chief secretary of Ireland,[17] and as Macartney himself told the Court of Proprietors during his election campaign for the governorship, he hoped to apply these skills in India:

> [He declared himself] possessed of the friendship and good opinion of all parties, but resolutely fixed on continuing unconnected with any party. . . . You do not, I hope, suppose that enormous wealth alone can warrant independence. That happy spirit proceeds from a disposition of the mind, which is not governed by the accidents of life; and, I hope, I have what is the surest pledge of honorable independence, the independence of honest and moderate desires. My aim will ever be so to conduct myself, on all occasions, as to be able to appear before you in this court, on my return from India, with as little necessity of apology for any part of my proceedings there in your employ, as I have ever had in those other stations with which I have had elsewhere the honor to be entrusted.[18]

Macartney appears indeed to have tried to rely on his personality and ability to persuade even the most intransigent of opponents when he took up his post in Madras on June 22, 1781. Just four days later, for example, he wrote his immediate superior in Bengal, Governor-General Warren Hastings. The tone of Macartney's private correspondence closely echoed his earlier speech in London:

> Sir,
>
> The prospect of a satisfactory connection and communication with you in my present Station, which I derived from the high Character you bear in the World, was confirmed to me and heightened, if possible, by our common friend Mr. [Samuel] Pechell, from whom I have the honor to transmit a couple of Letters to you. It is my good fortune to be supported by the same Persons who are attached to your Welfare; a coincidence which I trust will lay a foundation of Friendship and Confidence between Us. In this reliance it should be my constant Aim to give you my best Assistance in forwarding the public Business; and I flatter myself with finding every facility on your part. I trust you will please to open yourself to me, without reserve, on the present State of Affairs.[19]

Macartney also wrote to Sir Eyre Coote, the commander of the company's military forces in Madras, in November of the same year, declaring that "Though with an exact knowledge of facts, I combined the observations of several capable persons, I was very cautious in forming my own judgment; but after taking these precautions, it appears to me a laudable exertion of duty to become responsible in following the dictates of such a judgment."[20]

In the same letter to Coote, Macartney displays frustration with Coote's intransigence—a frustration that was generated by the repeated challenges Macartney faced from both his own staff and his superiors in Bengal as he attempted to govern Madras.

In 1781, the company suffered grave military defeats at the hands of the sultan of Mysore, had yet to reconcile and settle its political relationship with the Nawab of Arcot (whose extraordinary debts were still being pursued aggressively by Madras civil servants), was at war with the French, and was dependent on cash from Bengal to meet its military's payroll. (See Barrow and Macartney for a good summary.)[21] Yet whenever Macartney attempted to coordinate civil operations with the company's military in Madras, negotiate effectively with Arcot, or leverage new revenues from local merchants or Bengal, he found himself, to his surprise, thwarted by some of the same men he had expected to be his allies.

Consider the course of Macartney's relationship with Coote. In October 1781, Macartney wrote to Coote upon hearing that Coote felt disrespected by Macartney. Concerning Coote's "Dissatisfaction and disappointment," Macartney was "Totally at a Loss to guess from whence it arises: I know It ought not to arise from any part of my Conduct, which I am conscious has been not only perfectly blameless towards You; But I should flatter myself in some degree meritorious."[22] A month later, Macartney still expressed optimism that his diplomacy and affability would win over Coote, writing to John MacPherson that

> Sir Eyre Coote and I are, as far as I know, upon good terms. If every mark of Regard, and even of Respect towards him personally, and an implicit and immediate Compliance with all his Wishes in his public Situation, can ensure his Satisfaction and Good Will, I must consider myself in possession of them; nor shall I be induced to think otherwise from any momentary Sallies of ill humour which disappointments, Hastiness of temper, or ill health may occasion; his cooler and fixed Sentiments will lead him to do me justice.[23]

Later that same month, Macartney was even blunter, writing to Macpherson that "The General and I are at bottom the best of friends that can be. . . . I have courted him like a Mistress, and humoured him like a Child."[24]

But these attempts to woo Coote failed, and especially when Coote appealed to Hastings in Bengal over Macartney's head, Macartney's descriptions grew increasingly negative. At first, Macartney blamed Coote's behavior on sycophants taking advantage of his passions. In January 1782, Macartney complained that Coote had been "made ridiculous by those who ought to make him respectable; made miserable by those who ought to make him happy; and from a great public Character worked into the little instrument of private Malignity and disappointed Avarice."[25] Finally, when Hastings ratified Coote's counterclaims against Macartney and declared that Macartney was to obey Coote's orders on military matters in the summer of 1782, Macartney was incensed enough to question Hastings's conduct, albeit with great circumspection:

> I know the public importance of concert and confidence between us [Macartney and Hastings]. On this ground I have implicitly followed all his ideas since his return to Calcutta, and wherever my Opinions have been communicated to him, I have delivered them with as much delicacy and deference as possible. I own to you [Macpherson] they some times differ much from his, but he having been long resident in India, and I being new in it, I distrust my own Judgment, except where the points appear impossible to mistake. I think for instance that the recommendation of gratifying *Sir Eyre Coote* [emphasis in the original] in his Command "to the utmost possible extent of his wishes," and entrusting to him the other unusual Powers, may be attended with very serious inconveniences, but what can we say, what can we do?[26]

Even though Coote died in 1783, the course of his relationship with Macartney was hardly unique. The same pattern—in which Macartney initially showed high hopes that his persuasiveness could bring recalcitrant administrators around but then gave way to bitterness and confusion—was repeated with Anthony Sadlier on the Madras council; Paul Benfield, who resumed attempts to recover the Nawab's debts illicitly; James Stuart, who replaced Coote and who Macartney eventually had forcibly deported; Hastings, over whose affections Macartney incessantly agonized; and even John Macpherson himself, who proved to be more loyal to Hastings than Macartney.

Disconnected from politics in Madras, these interactions between Macartney and his superiors and inferiors could be mistaken for personality conflicts or as artifacts of the crises that dogged company servants in India at the time. Yet it is important to remember that what looks, on the surface, like epiphenomena in fact had important consequences for the EIC's organization and its policies in South India. The conflict between Coote and Macartney, for example, is thought to have led to several of the military disasters against Hyder Ali in the early 1780s; the fate of whole Indian districts (in this case, the Northern Circars) rested on the extent to which Macartney and Hastings felt their careers to be threatened by each other. And as Pigot discovered (along with Macartney, as shall be discussed below) what began as breakdowns in decorum could have violent consequences.

In the face of these conflicts and the failure of his original strategy—to combine politeness, persuasiveness, and impartiality—Macartney combined three approaches into a novel way of governing in Madras. First, in both his private and public correspondence, he shifted his appeals from primarily appeals to personal ties and his particular relationships with other administrators to broad, abstract justifications. As late as September 1781, Macartney included long passages in his public correspondence with Bengal that justified his behavior in terms of personal relationships, writing, for example, that "our personal respect and esteem for the Governor-general and other members of your board, on all occasions have naturally excited in our minds to yield implicitly to every direction we receive from you" even when protesting that "the dictates of duty" prevented him from executing the specific policy.[27] But by 1784, when Hastings was about to be recalled to London, Macartney took pains to distinguish between his public and private roles even in his private correspondence, writing to Hastings that "I am conscious in my own Mind of a wide distinction between public, and personal differences and am not without hopes of finding the same distinction in the liberality of your sentiments."[28] Thus, at the beginning of his administration, Macartney closely intertwined personal and public sentiments and duties, but by the end he held them carefully separate.

Even as he held these two dimensions of himself—his role as a company official and his private likes and dislikes—Macartney reconnected them powerfully. If men like Benfield had "endeavored to give false impressions," Macartney, by contrast, claimed credibility on the grounds that he was "open and undisguised" in his declarations.[29] In other words, by separating his personality from his public duty and then reconnecting them while using the consistency of his desire to perform that duty as evidence of his truthfulness and authenticity, Macartney added new force to statements like "One thing depend on, I never will deceive your Government in the slightest point. I would sooner cut off my right hand."[30]

But if Macartney turned away from personalistic ties and instead relied on a narrative of his own consistent representations of inner desire to his official duty, what ends was he to serve? Macartney found footing in service to "the public" and, by applying it to Madras, transformed it from an aggregation of his close peers (i.e., other Indian administrators) into an amorphous domain of social life. As he put the point to Macpherson: "Amidst all the difficulties which Surround Me I hope to stand firm. Indeed nothing but Integrity can support a man against the universal Intrigue and Duplicity which prevail here thro' every department. It is to guard the public in these circumstances that I am under the necessity of attending perhaps too much to inferior affairs."[31] Or even more bluntly, "If I have done ill, let me suffer, if I have done well, I will trust to the Public for my reward."[32] Thus, by Macartney's own account, he stood as a protector of a slippery thing: a "public" in Madras, which was composed of virtually none of the administrators or private merchants he encountered but which had the capacity to command his duty and judge his behavior.

Although it emerged as a rhetorical strategy to justify his personal integrity, authority, and policy claims in Madras, Macartney directly defended the public in two spectacular incidents. The first occurred in 1784, when Macartney was still governor of Madras, with Anthony Sadlier, a long-time and senior company servant who Macartney's biographer castigates for his "petulance, unsteadiness, and timidity."[33] Their dispute arose, by all accounts, because Sadlier reversed himself on a matter before the council and refused to withdraw his lone opposition to the technical matter at hand. Macartney then accused Sadlier of lying, and although he immediately apologized, Macartney let the accusation stand in the council's minutes, writing to the Court of Directors that he did so because "I never will attempt to conceal from you any thing, however unimportant, which the meanest member of this community might wish to be laid before you. Every gentleman of feeling knows that there is a species of audacious contradiction which can only be stopped by a particular mode of expression. In the case no alluded to, that expression, although arising from absolute necessity, was no sooner used but apologized for to the board."[34] In the subsequent duel in Madras, Macartney was wounded in the chest but recovered.[35]

The second incident was also a duel, and while it stemmed from conflicts over the administration of Madras, it took place in London. While governor, Macartney also clashed with the replacement for Eyre Coote, Major General James Stuart. Macartney, who was dissatisfied by what he perceived to be Stuart's continuing insubordination, had him dismissed, and when Stuart (he had lost a leg in military action in 1781) refused to board a ship home, Macartney had him forcibly carried on board.[36] This (somewhat understandably) enraged Stuart, and when Macartney returned to London in 1786, Stuart challenged him to a duel. Again, in responding to Stuart's challenge, Macartney carefully distinguished his private and official roles:

> [W]hen Major-general Stuart thought fit in January last . . . to send a letter . . . censuring, in unqualified expressions, my public conduct in relation to him, and contradicting my assertions, I held it sufficient to observe, that those persons to whom I was accountable for my public conduct, if any such there were, who entertained a doubt of it, would ever find me ready to explain it to their satisfaction; but that I was long resigned to the consequences of having fulfilled the duties of my station, and to be exposed to the contradiction and opposition of those individuals, of whose misconduct in my official capacity I had been obliged to take notice.[37]

The two men fought in Kensington Park in 1786—Stuart having to be propped against a tree and an aging Macartney suffering from poor eyesight—Macartney was again wounded but survived, declaring that Stuart had "called upon me to give him satisfaction in my private capacity, for offence [sic] taken at my public conduct, and to evince that personal safety is no consideration with me, I have nothing personal, the General will proceed as he thinks fit."[38]

In contrast to the Madras governors who had proceeded him (and some who would succeed him), Macartney resigned his post of his own will and returned to England with his reputation at least relatively unscathed. He declined to be made governor-general of India when it was offered without a British peerage and was subsequently made an envoy to China and governor of the Cape Colony in modern-day South Africa.[39] In other words, after his stint in Madras, his reputation was intact enough that he continued his perambulation around the British Empire.

While to him it represented only one step in his career, Macartney transformed the way Madras was governed. By divorcing his public and private roles, reintroducing his private self as a source of motivation for his official conduct, and then turning to a consistent account of his private desires toward an amorphous "public," Macartney introduced a powerful new institutional logic into Madras administration. While the notion of an autonomous public making moral demands on officials' duty was still ambiguous, the subsequent cohort of Madras governors (most notably William Bentinck and Thomas Munro) attached Macartney's notion of public to Indian society itself.[40] But again, this society did not correspond to any specific Indian social group or particular class of society but rather stood as an imaginary form that justified the actions of the colonial state.

BENGAL: CHARLES CORNWALLIS AND JOHN MACPHERSON

Cornwallis returned to England a French parolee (his transport from America having been captured), but he was somehow free from blame for his surrender at Yorktown. While most of the blame for the American misadventure may have fallen on Cornwallis's superior, General Clinton,[41] Cornwallis still found himself in debt and in search of government employment. Considering that Cornwallis was friendly with the incoming government after Lord North's first vote of no confidence in 1782, it made sense that the incoming parliamentary leader, Lord Shelburne, proposed to repay Cornwallis's political support by nominating him to be governor-general of India. The position would be lucrative for Cornwallis, and he eagerly accepted.

But the instability of British politics in the early 1780s blocked Cornwallis's way. When the elderly marquis of Rockingham died in July 1782, Shelburne's ministry lost a key bastion of support because Rockingham's parliamentary faction was taken over by Charles Fox, who personally opposed Shelburne. Fox allied with the previously ousted Lord North, and formed a coalition that replaced Shelburne after the Peace of Paris with America in 1783. Although they were detested by George III, Fox and North nonetheless proposed a sweeping East India bill in 1783 that would have meant radical state intervention into the affairs of the company and would have placed all of the EIC's administrative appointments under the crown's control. However, as noted in the last chapter, the act proved to be the wedge necessary to bring down the coalition, and when parliamentary opposition, backed by the EIC itself, approached George III and proposed a government headed by William Pitt the Younger (son of the earl of Chatham, first minister from 1766 to 1768), the king withdrew his support for Fox and North, and their coalition quickly fell.

To reward the company for its support and in keeping with its line of attack against the 1783 India bill as a sign of ministerial corruption and usurpation of the company's rights to patronage appointments, Pitt proposed a considerably more compromise-minded India Act. The 1784 act established a ministerial board of control over India appointments and claimed a right to propose the governor-general and subsidiary governors (although in practice, these were agreed-upon by the Court of Directors) yet left all appointments below that in the hands of the directors themselves.[42]

Amid this intersection of colonial and national politics, Cornwallis bargained his political support for the best appointment he could obtain. He first supported Fox and North, but when they appeared to have passed him over for the Indian appointment, he followed the king's lead and threw his support behind Pitt. He was rewarded for his newfound support first with an offer to be lord lieutenant of Ireland (he discreetly refused) and then by a renewed offer to go to India. Cornwallis sought a military command, and the terms of Pitt's 1784 India act kept the governor-generalship a civil appointment. Cornwallis subsequently was slighted for domestic military appointments (as the governor of Plymouth and in the king's Grenadiers) and bounced among a series of government posts, including as an envoy to Russia. But by 1785, his indignation at having been denied proper terms for the post in India had reached Pitt's ears, and the India Act was modified in 1786 not only to unify military and civil command in the person of the governor-general but also to boost the post's salary to £25,000 a year. This time, Cornwallis took the job.

During his administration in Calcutta, Cornwallis faced pressure from above and resistance from below. From above, the

Court of Directors constantly applied pressure to reduce territorial charges for the administration of Bengal so that Cornwallis had to assure them repeatedly that he was motivated by an "earnest desire to avoid and discourage in every shape all kinds of superfluous expenditure of the public money."[43] This became extremely difficult, however, because renewed hostilities with the Maratha confederacy in Bombay and Tipu sultan in Madras loomed. Cornwallis was also under pressure from the newly constituted Board of Control to reign in perceived corruption and fraud throughout the company's administration in Bengal. As Cornwallis wrote to the Court of Directors, "I am doing everything I can to reform the Company's servants, to teach them to be more economical in their mode of living, and to look forward to a moderate competency; and I flatter myself I have not hitherto laboured in vain."[44] And in these efforts, Cornwallis hoped to preserve his own integrity and reputation because "[t]he reasonable object of ambition to a man is to have his name transmitted to posterity for eminent services rendered to his country and to mankind."[45] More publicly, to the marquis of Lansdowne, this self-presentation translated into the declaration that "I am not conscious that I have, in any one instance, sacrificed the public good to any private consideration."[46]

While these pressures worked on Cornwallis from London, he faced stiff resistance to his reforms from long-established company servants in Bengal. Cornwallis expressed shock, for example, at how brazenly taking bribes—and giving them to EIC directors in exchange for patronage appointments within the company's service—was discussed, to the point that he stormed out of a conversation with a colonel who was describing the practices. Likewise, his correspondence is peppered with admonishments to redacted inferiors for appealing to him for relief from punishment for corruption,[47] and he was particularly galled by the behavior of the company's political residents at the courts of the Wazir of Avadh and the Nawab of Bengal, the latter of whom Cornwallis described as having "enjoyed the almost absolute government of the country without control."[48] In spite of the harsh diagnosis of the company's administration in Bengal, Cornwallis resisted ascribing its sources to the individual characters of the servants involved. He resisted the directors' orders to dismiss and prosecute the entire Bengal Board of Trade for dabbling in silk speculation, telling Henry Dundas that to do so would mean "cruelty to some of their best and most deserving servants, and . . . mischief to the public service."[49] Instead, Cornwallis ascribed their corruption to systemic sources: "[Company servants targeted for prosecution] have committed no fault but that of submitting to the extortion of their superiors; they had no other means of getting their bread, and they had no reason to expect support if they had complained."[50]

Instead of relying on his own moral example or on the proximate actors' judgment of administrators' behavior, Cornwallis instead proposed an ambitious plan that at once would raise their regular salaries beyond the temptation of perquisites while substituting an abstracted sense of duty for earlier forms of ensuring administrative order:

> When you consider the situations of your servants in this country, the very high responsibility now more particularly annexed to the office of a collector, the temptations of the situation, the incessant labours of his office, and the zeal which must be exerted to promote the prosperity of the revenues and the country at large,—when on the other hand, you advert to the solemn restrictions imposed upon him by the Legislature, as well as those in the Public Regulations, and the separate orders already noticed absolutely precluding him from any emolument whatever, excepting

such as are publicly allowed,—and when you are further pleased to consider, that excepting instances of extraordinary merit, your servants cannot in future expect to obtain the office of a collector under a period of twelve years spent in your service,—we trust that we shall be found to have consulted your true interests with every compatible attention to economy, and that you will approve the allowances and commission fixed by us for your servants in the revenue department.[51]

In Cornwallis's formulation, immediate superiors provided no fatherly moral example of conduct to their inferiors, nor did peers help to rein in administrative corruption through their virtuous gaze. Instead, corruption was a matter of sheer incentive, wrought by ill-considered policy, to deviate from the remote imperatives of the "Legislature" and of "the Public Regulations." In other words, the logic of administrative organization in Bengal differed from Madras—rather than standing as part of an amorphous, abstract "society," the organization of the company's officials in Bengal was meant to free them from the "temptations of the situation" they faced and allow them to express their obedience and "zeal" to a set of morally compulsory regulations.

In implementing these changes, however, Cornwallis had not only to contest with the Court of Directors and Board of Control in London but also jealous competitors on his own council. Chief among these was Macpherson, who had sat on the council when Pigot was overthrown, acted directly as a political agent-for-hire for the Nawab of Arcot in London, was a close confidant of Benfield and Hastings, and yet somehow survived the direct purge of such "undesirables" to serve as governor-general pro tem in the interim between Hastings's resignation and Cornwallis's arrival. Macpherson was a longtime India hand and, along with Macartney, he canvassed to replace Hastings[52] and then again to succeed Cornwallis.[53] Although he was not chosen either time, during his governor-generalship, he proposed a sweeping set of reforms to the company's administration that attempted to ratify implicitly many of William Bolts's criticisms and assuage the directors' worries about rising expenses in Bengal. The proposal is worth quoting at length because it reflects an important counterfactual path for mitigating corruption within the EIC:

> [2] The opposition, which, in all Government, resist every attempt to reduce the Public Expence, have their peculiar Force in this Presidency; and the doubtful light, in which the Advocates [3] and Leaders of extraordinary Efforts of Public Reforms, are generally considered, is more discouraging in India, than in any other Country. Here, the voice of the People is not heard, to confer praise, or animate to Perseverance. (Every advantage, that is retrenched in favor of the Company, is lost to an Individual; of, perhaps, extensive Connections, and ultimately creates an Enemy.) But, to take a decided Lead in a general and bold Controul of the inveterate Abuses in Office, is to rush upon general dislike. The Governor, or Councilor, who attempts such a Duty, ought to possess the Confidence of permanent support. He should be assured that his Character and Office are protected, by the Justice and Influence of his Employers: His best Labours may, otherwise, meet with an ungracious return.
>
> (Even Punishment, which should be the Penalty of Misconduct, may await him in the Career of his Merit; and it may be his Lot, to see his threatened, or actual recall, turned into a Subject of public triumph, or secret ridicule, by those whom he was restraining from Peculation. To give a further Trial to his Philosophy, it is not unlikely, that, on his Return to Britain, he may find himself neglected, if not distressed; while those who are grown powerful

at the Expence of your propriety, are treated with Respect) and congratulate themselves upon the Boldness of their rapacity, amidst Impunity.

In offering these Truths to your Notice, I mean to impress their force in Favour of your Future agents. I disclaim any Application of them to my own particular Situation; my Obligation to the Company have been great, and uncommon: they more than counterbalance and disappointment I can experience in your service.

[4] Zeal, determination, and Unanimity in your Executive administration, are not alone sufficient to complete a public reform. The temper of your service must be managed; and the exigencies of the public Distress, with an exemplary Conduct on the part of every Member of your Government, must be brought to operate in Concert, to carry through a reforming System.

[...]

From you, who are charged with the supreme Administration of our Affairs, we demand the unqualified execution of our Orders: and to convince all our Servants, Civil and Military, that we consider their real Welfare as justly connected with the prosperity of the Company; we renew, and repeat more explicitly in their favor, our former Regulations and Orders, which direct that no Civil Servant is to be removed from our Service, but by our final Orders and that the power of Suspension from our Service, is only granted to our Government, under the Reserve of their giving the accused, a [22] Copy of the Charge against him in writing, and time for making his defense; which by being recorded, must wait our final Judgement. In like manner, we order that no Officer, holding a military commission in our Service, shall be deprived of that Commission, or removed from our Service, but by the Sentence of his Brother Officers, in Regular Court Martial. After securing, in this manner, the Rights of our Servants, we doubt not but they will, unitedly and unanimously, strive to assist in the Execution of Orders, which have an equal Tendency to secure their own general Benefits, as they seem indispensible to preserve the Existence of the Power which employs them. They will, upon the least Reflection discover, that those who by Peculation, or abusing the great Trusts of our Service, have brought the Company to a distress, which incapacitates them from paying their Current Expences, so as to throw them Months in Arrears, have been the greatest Enemies of the Service in General.

[...]

To such a Consideration of the Subject, are you indebted for those immense Supplies of Goods, which are now pouring upon you from Bengal. Such an extraordinary number of Cargoes must arrive with you seasonably, when a general Peace has opened the Doors of Commerce, and to every Market. The Bills which provided the prime Cost of these Goods, are rendered convenient to your Ability to discharge them. They are British Property, which pay the Duties of Commerce to the Parent State; and in preventing it from passing as a remittance into the hands of Foreigners, to undersell you at the Market, with [28] goods provided upon your own Estate; a real Service is rendered to the Company; and an extensive one, to Great Britain. Upon a liberal Extension of this Commercial Plan, you turn any Peculations of your own Service, to a Public use: You perhaps establish some lights by which they may be brought to your knowledge. At all Events, I rejoice in having given my Voice for a Resolution, which, at the close of a destructive War, dispatches for England fifteen Indiaman, loaded with the Manufactures of Bengal, of an improved Quality, and at a reduced original Cost!

Should you fortunately approve of the Plan, upon which your Commerce has been lately extended, and which enables your Ships to return with Advantage; and should you further have it in your Power, to adopt, and enforce Regulations, which, by a frugal and just application of your Revenues, may perpetuate your Tenure of your Asiatic Possessions; You will render the India Company a Medium, for administering the British Empire all the Blessings, without the disadvantages, of great and distant Colonies: It may be observed with equal truth, and without Prejudice, or Flattery, that there is no Medium, but that of the various Checks of the Company's institutions, thro' which, Britain can receive the same Benefit in a constant flow, and without Danger to the Equilibrium in the Constitution; on that order in the State which leaves Room for the Operation of every good, while it resists improper Influence.[54]

Macpherson thus called for a broad-based reform rooted in, first, a recognition of company servants' rights to appeal charges against them and, second, a fundamentally economic appeal to the alignment of their pecuniary interests with those of the EIC itself. But his appeal for how exactly a connection was to be made between affirming servants' commercial rights and administrative order rested on a personalistic conception of moral judgment. This is evident in both Macpherson's pleas for support from the directors—however much he may have disclaimed "any Application to my own particular Situation," he was most concerned about the "general dislike" reforming efforts might provoke and hence wished that his "Character and Office are protected"—and also how Macpherson imagined EIC officials would react were his reforms to be implemented. The key to the plan was "Concert" in the operations of "every Member of your Government," which was to be achieved not, as in Cornwallis's formation, to the universal sense of public duty to the administration that existed in every honorable official but rather by securing "the Rights of our Servants," which would "convince all our Servants, Civil and Military, that we consider their real Welfare as justly connected to the prosperity of the Company."

Above all, then, in the name of turning "any Peculations of your own Service, to a Public use," Macpherson's proposed reforms called for persuasion, harmony, and moral example—all watchwords of an embedded, proximate form of moral judgment.

What happened when Cornwallis's and Macpherson's views of the proper administrative order in Bengal, and especially the underlying abstract and proximate foundations for these views, collided? Although Macpherson's administration was, in the estimation of one eminent Indian historian, "an example of vacillation [with] no parallel in the history of the omnipotent governor-generalships of the eighteenth century,"[55] Macpherson still served as the most senior member of the Bengal Council on Conrwallis's arrival and began, at least, as a key adviser. But over the course of the next three years, their relationship soured as Cornwallis discovered Macpherson's efforts to outmaneuver him both on the Bengal Council and in London.

A sample of Cornwallis's changing opinion of Macpherson from his correspondence illustrates the deterioration of their relationship:

> Sept. 1786: "Macpherson is perfectly cordial, and all promise a most hearty support" (Cornwallis to Dundas).[56]
>
> Aug. 1789: "His flimsy cunning and shameless falsehoods seem to have taken in all parties; believe me that those who trust the most in him will be the most deceived" (Cornwallis to Dundas).[57]
>
> Nov. 1789: "[H]e is a very good-humored fellow; but I think him weak and false to a degree, and he certainly was the most contemptible and the most contemned Governor that ever pretended to govern" (Cornwallis to Dundas).[58]

But Macpherson not only lost credit with Cornwallis personally; upon his return to England, he also aggravated the Court of Directors and Board of Control. In essence, Macpherson simultaneously campaigned to be reappointed as governor-general and challenged the legal grounds for replacing him with Cornwallis to begin with. The case has been seen as a spurious attempt to extort a pension from the court[59] but, from the perspective of Macpherson's style of proximate moral judgment, the case also represents the failure of Macpherson's political strategy to accomplish its stated goals in London. Although Macpherson was successful with the court, his claim to the Board of Control rested on sets of personal correspondence,[60] and even his assertions about personal conversations with Cornwallis, that carried little weight with Dundas.

A CHOICE OF ADMINISTRATIVE ALTERNATIVES: CORNWALLIS, MACPHERSON, AND ADMINISTRATIVE REFORM

Viewed from London, Bolts's ejection from Bengal and the Nawab of Arcot's debt scandal together generated a crisis for Indian governance. The effects of previous corruption scandals had been confined to the company's internal factional politics, but thanks to Clive's efforts to keep his jagir and returning servants' increasingly public profiles, both scandals had become domestic political phenomena. These newly interested observers in England also found four answers to the dual questions of what corruption was and how to organize the seeming bedlam among company administrators in India. Pigot presented a seemingly conservative option—the company could simply affirm the governor's power to discipline his staff like they were unruly children, seeking to restore the paternal organization of power and moral order that had been the company's approach since the seventeenth century. But the other three appealed to abstract ideas about what was right and wrong and, by consequence, how society and the company's administration of India ought to be organized. Two options—the economic order proposed by Bolts and the system of constitutional checks offered by the conspirators in the Nawab of Arcot's debt scandal—saw corruption in tyrannical administrators interfering with the natural operation of society and the economy. But the third option—championed most directly by Harry Verelst—appealed to an empowered, abstract state and as the only means to discipline subalterns tempted by avarice. Which answer would metropolitan authorities choose?

In this section, I suggest that administrative reformers, particularly Cornwallis, chose the empowered state as the option to tame a corrupt administration.[61] To understand how this happened, I review the reforms that took place within the domestic apparatus of British colonial rule in the 1770s and 1780s. By revisiting MacPherson's brief tenure as governor-general, I suggest that the choice of the state as the supra-individual, stabilizing entity of EIC administration was contingent on Cornwallis's selection as governor-general.

Thus, the structural changes that took place in the company in the 1770s and 1780s represented a compromise that partially ratified the empowered state form Verelst advocated. The new governor-general in India was entrusted with wide authority—however circumscribed by retrospective comment and censure by the government and directors in London—over administrators and the Indian economy and society more broadly. In practice, these powers included the power to make war and peace, and to decide matters of taxation, jurisprudence, and the training and progress of civil servants. Thus, after 1784, London could determine who ruled India but could not determine just how they would do it.

The question of who was to be the new governor-general hung over the head of the Board of Control in London. On the passage of Pitt's India Act in 1784 and the recall of Hastings in February 1785, MacPherson became governor-general as the next most senior member of the Bengal council. MacPherson, the son of a Scottish minister, had been in India on and off since 1767 and had played a central role in the events precipitating the overthrow of Pigot in Madras. (Pigot had suspended MacPherson from the council there shortly before he was overthrown.) MacPherson had acted as the agent for the Nawab of Arcot in London and briefly served in Parliament, but he returned to India to serve under Hastings on the Bengal council in 1781.[62]

MacPherson's abilities have generally been frowned on by historians—B. B. Misra calls him "devoid of any insight and ability"[63]—but his policies reveal attempts to stabilize EIC administration through economic exchange. MacPherson appeared committed to the EIC's charge for retrenchment and economies of rule,[64] indeed criticizing British administrators in Bengal for "certain abuses,"[65] but he pursued a very different route than Cornwallis would after him. Upon assuming office, MacPherson abolished monopolies held by the company on country trade (which had much exercised Bolts in Considerations on Indian Affairs) and suspended duties and tariffs on country trade on British Indian ports.[66] He also attempted to cut military and civil budgets, and was even able to make up arrears in military pay of almost fifty lakhs of rupees (about £50,000) over the twenty months of administration, although the EIC's overall debt remained staggeringly large.[67] Moreover, "as an inducement for them to serve the Company," MacPherson relaxed restrictions on remitting goods home on company ships for civil servants.[68]

Cornwallis's reforms and policies presented a stark contrast and the further empowerment of the state and the office of the governor-general in particular. A "Whig aristocrat and military officer who . . . had somehow avoided taking the blame for defeat in America,"[69] Cornwallis held several positions within the domestic British government, including constable of the Tower of London. However much he may have coveted its newly increased salary of £25,000 a year, Cornwallis refused to accept the governor-generalship in India without powers beyond the 1784 India Act. In particular, he wished for the ability to overrule his council—a key issue that had precipitated Pigot's overthrow in Madras—and for definitive control over Madras and Bombay's foreign policy. Pitt and Dundas, the new chair of the Board of Control, were eager to have an unimpeachable character and a firm hand in India and granted Cornwallis's request in the Amending Act of 1786, and Cornwallis sailed for Calcutta.[70]

Cornwallis used his newly ratified powers upon arrival to enact sweeping reforms of British administration in India. Rather than the enticements of economic exchange offered by MacPherson, Cornwallis aggressively prosecuted exemplary cases of corruption, especially with regard to members of the Board of Trade who had profited from silk contracts.[71] Interestingly, however, Cornwallis did not advocate a wholesale prosecution of every offender in the administration; he only wished to see them reined in from future offenses. And he blamed their conduct on the corruption of their superiors in government, especially his predecessor, MacPherson:

> In this system [of poor remuneration under the previous administration and fear of dismissal from the Board of Trade in Calcutta] they were reduced to the singular predicament of acquiescing in the terms prescribed to them, or of forfeiting, by a refusal, their

present appointments & future expectations . . . the circumstances of their situation admit of some palliation for submitting to propositions which afforded present & future advantage, under the countenance of that authority, which the commercial servants were bound to obey.[72]

Through Cornwallis's reforms, a critical shift in how corruption was viewed took place: corruption was chased from the ranks of European administrators and into Indian society. Although Indians' exclusion from some revenue posts began before Cornwallis arrived,[73] one of his complaints to superiors in London in 1786 was the reticence of Indians—because of their "customs and prejudices"—to provide evidence against European administrators.[74] By 1787, his attitude hardened into the assertion that "every native of Hindoostan (I really believe) [is] corrupt."[75] These attitudes coalesced in regulations, from 1793, that excluded Indians completely from the senior ranks of administration for twenty years and more generally in a campaign to "create a wall of regulations separating the Indian and European worlds."[76] As Travers neatly summarizes the result: "A major way the new empire of 'British India' sought to distance itself from its troubled past was to redefine corruption as an Indian disease, and posit the reformed Company service, now differentiated into commercial, revenue, and judicial lines, as the necessary agents of political virtue."[77] This politically virtuous administration, cleansed of what was now defined more clearly as "native corruption," acted as the arm of a newly empowered state. Of course, this state was not yet a supra-individual entity.[78] But it had taken important steps toward becoming a space at once separated from domestic Britain and yet home to a powerful state apparatus. Most important for our study of corruption, the alternative sources of order for the administration proposed by those accused of corruption, and one actually briefly put into practice by MacPherson as governor-general, had been decisively foreclosed.

What effect did this have on corruption? Defendants within the administration were reduced to railing against the new, oppressive and divisive character of the empowered company state. As Edward Colebrooke, brother of noted Sanskrit scholar Henry Colebrooke, EIC servant of nearly fifty years, and resident at Delhi, complained when accused of corruption by a young Charles Trevelyan in 1830,

> I am sacrifice to the resolution of putting an end to all interchange of courtesy between the British functionaries and our Native subjects and allies. After the example which has been made of me, mangoes and oranges will be sacred from the profane hands of every Political Resident to the great savings of the Natives in pice and annas [small Indian coins] nor will any Englishman dare to accept the entertainment from a Native gentleman who will thus be spared the expense of dinners, nautches [Indian dances] and firework, and the new reformers will have to congratulate themselves on the thorough establishment of the favorite system of total estrangement and alienation.[79]

5

MODERN MORAL SPACES

This chapter weaves together the themes explored so far in *Modernity's Corruption*. It begins by showing how company reforms extended beyond merely regulating the moral self-presentation of its officials differently. Justifying behavior in terms of Universal moral spaces meant also that those spaces—"the state," "society," and "the economy"—had to be disentangled from one another. Thus, officials defined their behavior no longer in terms of concrete commercial exchanges, the imperatives of particular state treaties, or their concrete peers (whether Indian or British) but instead spoke in terms of abstracted social spaces that could compel their senses of duty. "Corruption" came to mean not the loss of balance among these moral spaces but rather their entanglement. This chapter also explores the practical bases of administrative life and argues that they display three main phases: one heavily Situational, another representing a confusing blend of Situational and Universal imperatives, and a third much more recognizably Universal—and modern because it deployed the "Rule of Colonial Difference"[1] to distinguish company and Indigenous moral orders.

DISENTANGLING MORAL WORLDS: CORRUPTION AND THE GREAT DISEMBEDDING[2]

We begin by examining two episodes from the height of the East India Company's (EIC) organizational chaos in the 1760s and 1770s, which have already been introduced in previous chapters: the debate between William Bolts and Harry Verelst in Bengal, and the overthrow of Lord Pigot in Madras. But whereas previous chapters emphasized the different understandings of corruption at play in these debates, this chapter probes those understandings to show how they represent radically different moral orders and supply a scaffolding to understand how the moral comparisons that undergird "corruption" were to be made.

WILLIAM BOLTS IN BENGAL: "WHERE INTEREST AND PASSION UNITE TO CONFOUND ALL ORDER"

The first case of imperial corruption occurred in Bengal, where the British first and most rapidly acquired territorial power by intervening in complex dynastic disputes among the Nawabs of Bengal. The Nawab Alivardi Khan died in 1756 having named his grandson, Siraj-ud-Daula, as his successor. Siraj-ud-Daula aimed to reduce European privileges in Bengal, and upon the company's refusal to cooperate in 1756, his army sacked Calcutta. In response, the British transferred a European-style army from Madras and, under the command of Robert Clive, defeated and deposed the Nawab in favor of one of his own generals, Mir Jafar, at the battle of Plassey in 1757. From Plassey forward, the British were regional political players and began to demand special commercial privileges and eventually territorial revenues to pay indemnifications and the cost of military operations.

This demonstration of military prowess (although victory at Plassey actually rested on the Nawab's betrayal by his key lieutenant, Mir Jafar) served to involve the British further in complex succession disputes and meant large emoluments for "service" to those who supported a successful claimant.[3] Disputes over whom to support and how to divide "presents" sparked rounds of factional conflict within the EIC's Bengal council: Mir Jafar was deposed in favor of a rival, Mir Qasim, in 1760, but reinstalled in 1763 as power turned over on the council. Each round of conflict brought more gifts and ever-increasing demands for revenues to mount military campaigns and satisfy the pensions of political allies. As these revenue demands increased, both the EIC and the Nawabs of Bengal pursued mercantilist strategies, monopolizing and carefully regulating trade within their territories. For example, Mir Qasim, in an effort to restrict growing EIC influence outside lower Bengal, attempted to restrict private commercial activity by company servants and free-traders, while in EIC territory, Clive and his successors sought to monopolize salt production.[4]

It was against this backdrop of territorialization and economic retrenchment that Bolts, probably born somewhere in Germany as Willem Bolst,[5] arrived in 1759. One of ten factors sent by the company to manage trading posts in the Bengali interior, Bolts was soon a valuable asset as one of the few servants to learn Bengali and parlayed his political connection on the Bengal council into extensive private trade, mainly in salt, throughout Bengal. However, his increasingly brazen commercial activities—carried on in open defiance of the company's policy and the Nawab's wishes— and his declining factional support on the Bengal council meant Bolts was reprimanded and recalled from his station, and then eventually arrested and deported by the Governor Verelst after resigning from the service in 1768.

Whatever the real reasons he had been ejected from India, Bolts set to work suing the Court of Directors and Verelst everywhere he could and campaigning for his cause to the British public. Toward the latter end, he published *Considerations on Indian Affairs* in 1772. Verelst, having by then returned from Bengal, published his response in *A View of the Rise, Progress, and Present State of the English Government in Bengal* in 1773, which was in turn answered by a second edition of Bolts's book in 1775.

In one sense, both books were noteworthy simply because both were very long. In other respects—their polemical rhetoric, repeated defenses of the author's character and aspersions on his opponent's, and openly political quality—they fit into a genre of pamphleteering that was typical of mid- to late-eighteenth-century British politics, the same environment into which East India politics had been drawn since directors' elections had become politicized after Plassey. Thus, while the works were little distinguished from countless similar pamphlets, their novelty lay in the fact that they discussed specific aspects of Indian administration.

The books mount this discussion similarly. Both begin with introductions directly attacking the specific actions of the other and attempt to refute the specific charges against them. But both also quickly escalate to point-by-point analyses of the history of India, detailed examinations of the legal framework of the company's monopoly privilege and legal rights in India, its economic and monetary policy, and the organizational structure of its administration and court system in India, and they conclude with broad, rhetorically infused assessments of the British presence in India and its future.

But just what was the problem that needed to be addressed? For both Bolts and Verelst, the problem stemmed from the mixture of political and economic power in the EIC's unreconstructed administration. Bolts, quoting the 1770 pamphlet "The True Alarm," wrote, "That the Company is a Sovereign in the capacity of a merchant, and accordingly acts there in that double capacity; and that those who act under them are despots and merchants, as well for themselves as the Company: which are circumstances that must prove destructive to a commercial country. That, being a subject, depending on the government of the country in which it resides for its own protection and existence, it is totally devoid of that quality which constitutes the very end and being of government, which is protection."[6] Bolts thus drew a clear line from the macro-ambiguity of the company's statutory position in Bengal—being both a sovereign and merchant—and the confusion of its officers, drawn to act simultaneously for themselves and for the company as both merchant and ruler. Bolts directly equated the company's monopoly, the quality of its government—despotism—and commercial immiseration. As he put it, "The loaves and fishes are the grand, almost the sole object. The questions, How many lacks shall I put in my pocket? or, How many sons, nephews, or dependents shall I provide for, at the expence of the miserable inhabitnats of the subjected dominions? are those which of late have been the foremost that be propounded by the Chiefs of the Company on both sides [of] the ocean."[7]

Verelst, meanwhile, had a similar indictment to make about the character of the Bengal council in its decision to depose Mir Jafar in favor of Mir Qasim: "[A] majority of the council viewed with jealous eyes every act of government. They considered all resistance to the privilege they claimed, as a settled determination to subvert the power of the company; and passion thus uniting with interest, they urged a measure of national policy with the little peevish petulance of a personal quarrel. In truth it very early became such."[8] For Bolts, the most important outcome of the collision of "passion and interest" had been the commercial degradation for Bengal and despotic reign by officials, but Verelst just as closely equated the collision with the subversion of "the power of the company." He amplified these complaints when discussing the consequences of territorialization:

> The dissolution of government in Calcutta kept pace with that of the country. A general contempt of superiors, a habit of equality among all orders of men had obliterated every idea of subjection. To reclaim men from dissipation, to revive a general spirit of industry, to lead the minds of all from gaudy dreams of suddenacquired wealth to a patient expectation of growing fortunes, were no less difficult in execution than necessary to the existence of the company. Large sums of money, obtained by various means, had enabled many gentlemen to return to Europe. This cause . . . occasioned a very quick succession in the service, which encouraged a forward spirit of independency, and produced a total contempt of public orders, whenever obedience was found incompatible with private interest.[9]

While both men saw the same problem—the confusion of the administration following its territorial conquest—they saw the disorder stemming from different sources. For Bolts, it was the despotism of senior company officials, drunk with power and feeding their own avarice while impeding the development of commerce and industry among both Europeans and Indians. For Verelst, the problem was lower-level officials claiming privileges above their station and jeopardizing the company's vitality while themselves oppressing Indian society.

Their different diagnoses led to different prescriptions. For Bolts, the solution was to remove the company from the role of commercial interest in Bengal (he did not yet advocate the outright abolition of its monopoly on trade to London) and the formal integration of Bengal into the domestic British state, particularly its system of justice and protection afforded its citizens.[10] For Verelst, meanwhile, the solution was to ratify the company's position as the government of India and its power to deport disruptive characters like Bolts. Thus, Bengal was to have separate courts, and indeed a wholly separate system of government monitored from London, but it was considered a separate entity from Britain itself.

The difference in policy prescriptions for Bengal reveals different assumptions about the sources of social order. For Bolts, whose opinions must largely be inferred by inverting his repeated attacks on monopoly, order flowed from the market and free exchange between merchants—Black and white, British and European—and was being distorted by the EIC's monopolistic intervention. He seems to have thought that, if industry and exchange were allowed to operate unimpeded, the social disruption that he thought characterized late-eighteenth-century Bengal would evaporate. In a typical passage, Bolts criticized the influence of the EIC's monopoly on the market's efficient operation:

> [I]t may with truth be now said, that the whole inland trade of the country, as at present conducted . . . has been one continued scene of oppression: the baneful effects of which are severely felt by every weaver and manufacturer in the country, every article produced being made a monopoly; in which the English, with [collaboration from Indian middlemen] arbitrarily decide what quantities of goods each manufacturer shall deliver, and the prices

he shall receive for them . . . to Increase the amount of the Company's investment of goods for Europe . . . has been the constant endeavour of every succeeding Governor of Bengal, in order to acquire reputation with the Company. To obtain this increase great strictness has been used with, and great hardships have been exercised on the manufacturers, who are in general now monopolized by the English Company and their servants, as so many slaves . . .

However excusable the oppressing of manufacturers might have appeared in the Company, as merchants while the country belonged to another power, and the profit arising from trade was their only object in view, now, when they are become the Sovereigns of Bengal, the continuation of such a practice can no [*sic*] otherwise be considered than like the idiot-practice of killing the prolific hen to get her golden eggs all at once.[11]

This passage neatly summarizes Bolts's view of the danger of the company's monopoly once it held real territorial power. According to Bolts, oppression sprung from scheming senior officers within the EIC competing for favor within the ranks of the company and disrupting the natural level of prices and manufacturers' ability to market their products freely. The state's role was to guarantee and protect the market, which would itself stabilize colonial society. As he neatly summarized at the beginning of his conclusion, "It may be deemed ridiculous in any man to suppose, that a far-distant country will be long kept in peaceable subjection by any other ties than justice, humanity and convenience."[12] Justice, humanity and convenience stemmed in turn from "encouraging manufactures and free trade."[13] Thus, for Bolts, corruption lay in the mixture of commerce and sovereignty, which in the process of disentanglement came to rest on abstract foundations.

While Bolts thought that markets would ultimately stabilize colonial society and administration, Verelst thought that the state was the ultimate source of order. The answer, Verelst thought, was not more civil protections for "fellow-subjects" of the EIC but more power for the government:

> [T]he evils complained of in Bengal, have arisen rather from the inability of the governor and council to restrain the daring and pernicious projects of private interest in others, than from a rapacious spirit in themselves. Had the higher servants of the company, as the author of Considerations would wish us to believe, been alone the oppressors of Bengal, the evil could not have extended far. But when the rapacity of all who assume the English name, is let loose upon a harmless and inoffensive race of men; when every attempt of the governor and council to restrain these lawless traders, is represented as a violation of property, and infringement of those laws by which only Europeans can be governed; and when this spirit, supported by interested men, proceeds so far, that the governor, council, and commander in chief, are presented to the grand jury as conspirators against the life and fortune of an individual; we must not be surprised if gentlemen relax somewhat in the exercise of new, unknown, and questionable powers, however, necessary to the welfare or safety of the province.[14]

According to Verelst, to mend the social fabric of Bengal and the reckless administration of the company's servants—their "relaxed" use of newfound power—the company must be entrusted to punish firmly and coerce right behavior from all of its subjects.

Another phrase in Verelst's passage above—his description of "lawless traders" set loose upon the Indians, whom he describes as "a harmless and inoffensive race of men"—hints at another key distinction between his and Bolts's thought. While Bolts is ambiguous about precisely who the "fellow-subjects" of the EIC were, it's also clear he thought that the inhabitants of Bengal—English and Indian—would be respond similarly to English institutions—even bluntly declaring that "the same causes will ever produce like effects in all countries."[15] He thought, that is, that the institutional foundations of English justice, law, and social relations could be transported to Bengal without major modification.

For Verelst, however, it was the state, in the form of the EIC, that would be a source of social order, tutoring the inhabitants of Bengal in the different habits, laws, and institutions of the West until they would similarly join Britain in a state of commercial prosperity. By this view, the Indians were, at least for the present, decisively different people from domestic British subjects insofar as they would not be responsive to the wholesale transposition of domestic British institutions to India:

> Our notions of man are two [sic] frequently taken from the polished citizen of Britain; and we rudely imagine him to be the same creature in every state. We forget that society has a progress, as well as the individual. Man may exist, where the citizen is unknown. With growing laws the latter gradually unfolds, until, assured of protection, each individual looks around with confidence for the objects of his separate pursuit, and becomes unmolested the artificer of his own fortunes. But as well might we expect the frivolous gallantry of a Frenchman in the wilds of America, as hope that minds depressed by despotism can embrace the idea of a common interest, or conceive the dominion of laws.[16]

To be sure, both men thought that the fact that British rule in India was colonial introduced obstacles and difficulties to its prosperity and stability. But while Bolts argued, almost certainly from self-interest, that overcoming the disparity was a matter of creating a relationship between state, society, and economy that functioned like he thought it did in Britain, Verelst argued vehemently that such an act would produce further distortions in Bengal's society. The answer, said Verelst, was an empowerment of the company's state to control Indian society and its economy far beyond what was thought appropriate in Britain.

To sum up, a dispute that arose out of cross-accusations of corruption in the administration of the EIC in Bengal quickly escalated into competing justifications of British rule when the debate was transported back to London. These justifications in turn were founded on different understandings of social order. Bolts thought that order ultimately derived from the market, while Verelst thought that it ultimately flowed from the strong, just hand of the state. Both lodged their arguments in terms of perceived benefits to English and Indian subjects in Bengal. But on the one hand, Bolts made his arguments in terms of the protections that should be afforded to all subjects of the crown, which he thought included both English and Indian subjects of the company in Bengal. On the other hand, Verelst's argument rested on differentiating the political state in Bengal as much as possible from that of Britain. He thought that Bengal in the late eighteenth century was a land where "the citizen was unknown"—that is, where the institutions known in Britain could only be applied after the strong hand of the state had disciplined its own administration and society to receive them.

The corruption scandal in Bengal surrounding Bolts was spectacular but not isolated. Indeed, the same blending of personal and private interest among company servants, as well as the public mixture of the EIC's older commercial and newer territorial functions, existed throughout its burgeoning Indian empire. And while Bolts's expulsion from India had been spectacular and a point of contention in England, it was dwarfed by the brouhaha surrounding the Nawab of Arcot's debts in Madras; indeed, only eight years after Bolts was deported, a similar set of circumstances would lead to the overthrow and death of the governor there.

"HONOUR FOR THE NATION AND ADVANTAGE TO THE COMPANY": THE NAWAB OF ARCOT'S DEBTS IN MADRAS

Located south of Calcutta in an eastern coastal region of India then known as the Carnatic (in the present-day state of Tamil Nadu), the Madras presidency developed under circumstances both similar to and different from Bengal. The differences were important. Madras was smaller and considered less commercially important than Bengal.[17] During the 1770s, there were fewer than one hundred fifty British administrators in the presidency (the community in Bengal was then several times larger), and Madras was seen mainly as a check on French territorial ambitions. The French factory in South India, at Pondicherry, was captured in 1761, but their regional threat was thought to persist for decades.

Madras's development was also different because, in south India, the influence of the Mughal Empire had been much weaker. In the south, the Mughals' expansion was sternly resisted by the Hindu Vijayanagar dynasty, and as the Mughal Empire weakened, its successor states—Arcot and Mysore—asserted independence from Delhi sooner. These successor states were militarily tenacious and repeatedly dealt setbacks to the EIC armies, nearly capturing Madras city in the Second

Anglo-Mysore War of 1780. The last major Indigenous Mughal successor state in South India, Mysore, remained a major military threat until 1799. Thus, in the late eighteenth century, southern India was a cauldron of fiscal-military competition, with increasingly expensive campaigns fought among the sultan of Mysore, the French, the Nawab of Arcot, the EIC, and all of their various subordinates.

While the context of British administration may have been different, the way the British system functioned internally was fundamentally the same. Madras was also ruled by a governor with unclear powers over his council; promotion within the administration was also a function of seniority; and, most important, officials were also expected to supplement their income in the country trade. And as in Bengal (although with different consequences) one way that British officials made money was by investing in the Indigenous credit networks that formed the backbone of both capitalist and state finance.

The origins of the administrative crisis in Madras lay in this system of Indigenous credit. The Nawab of Arcot, Muhammad Ali Khan al Walajah, ascended to the throne with British support against a French-backed rival in 1755. He lavishly distributed presents, including cash, jewels, and the promise of pensions, to his British supporters, including the governor at that time, George Pigot, and promised to repay the British for military support against local Indian rivals. This generated a large debt that he financed by borrowing money throughout the 1760s.

The Nawab's increasing debt quickly became a stake in his struggle for independence from the British. Fearing that he would become an ornamental sovereign like the Nawab of Bengal after the grant of the *diwani*, the Nawab of Arcot refused to assign revenues directly from his territories over to the company. Instead, he unsuccessfully attempted to reform his revue administration by trying to gain a tighter hold over his system of tax farmers. Meanwhile, the EIC was wracked by its own fiscal crisis as a result of expensive wars with the French and Mysore, and hence wanted quick repayment of its military expenses. In particular, the British eyed the rich coastal province of Tanjore, which was thought to be one of the richest in Madras. It was held by the rajah of Tanjore, nominally a subordinate to the Nawab of Arcot but in reality a semi-independent ruler.[18]

The Nawab of Arcot's escalating debts—in the form of bonds with interest rates as high as 30 to 40 percent—were problematic for the EIC's administration because the Nawab owed money to the EIC as a public entity and to administrators as private individuals engaged in the country trade. Indeed, at the height of his indebtedness, almost every European in Madras—including officials like George Stratton on the Madras council and free merchants like Paul Benfield, who organized a coalition of the Nawab's European debtors—had some stake in his debts.[19] Throughout the 1760s and early 1770s, negotiations between the Nawab, coalitions of creditors led by Benfield, and an increasingly alarmed EIC administration in London tried unsuccessfully to resolve the issue. The Nawab himself even dispatched a European, John MacPherson, to London to appeal to the crown for relief on his behalf. MacPherson, however, was only able to obtain a writership in the company for himself and returned to serve on the Madras council.

Lord Pigot, former governor of Madras and hero of its resistance against the French in the 1760s, returned to this tense environment from London in 1775. He immediately clashed with his subordinates on the Madras council over the issue of Tanjore. Although a 1762 treaty between the company and the rajah had guaranteed his autonomy, the Nawab of Arcot had been given the territory after the EIC conquered it in 1773. Of course, the

EIC administrators' ulterior motive was that it would have been nearly impossible for the Nawab to repay his debt to them without the revenues of Tanjore. Beyond simply following the EIC's treaty obligations, Pigot also moved to have the Nawab's debts owed to administration members classified as private and ranked for repayment behind debts to the company as a whole.

These matters came to a head in June 1776, when Pigot moved that members of the Madras council be suspended for insubordination over the appointment of an administrative representative to the court of the rajah. This led to motions and countermotions that quickly ground the council to a halt. When dissenting members of the council began circulating their objections to the wider public, including military officers in the garrison, Pigot attempted to arrest them. The commander of the British forces, Colonel James Stuart, instead arrested Pigot in August. The governor-general in Bengal, Warren Hastings, refused to intervene on Pigot's behalf, and the Bengal supreme court (thought to be the supreme English legal institution in India) also refused to issue an opinion on the legality of the council's action. The council thus wrote to London in September 1776 attempting to explain their actions and including depositions from both sides. It took almost a year—until August 1777—for the answer to come from London. Pigot was to be reinstated but immediately recalled, along with Benfield and other dissenting members of the council. But by the time the news arrived, Pigot had fallen ill and died while gardening under his house arrest.

Immediately after Pigot died, his allies in Madras convened a coroner's inquest, which returned a verdict of willful murder against the architects of the "revolution." The findings were invalidated, however, by the Bengal supreme court. Upon the conspirators' return to London, the death of Lord Pigot and the broader issue of the "Nawab of Arcot's debts" influenced British political consciousness over the late 1770s and early 1780s. Pamphlets containing accusations, defenses, and counteraccusations were published by returning participants and their defenders. Pigot's narrative of the events was also published posthumously, as were the depositions taken immediately after the incident and by the coroner's inquest and the correspondence within the company surrounding his impeachment. But perhaps most famously, the issue was taken up by Edmund Burke against Benfield in a 1785 speech before parliament.[20] The incident was rhetorically important and certainly dramatized the issue of political control of the EIC's administration that was eventually placed on firmer footing with Lord North's Regulating Act of 1773, but the consequences for the conspirators themselves were comparatively muted. Four of the civil conspirators, including Stratton, were eventually convicted of misdemeanor in England and fined £1,000 each. Benfield returned to India as a member of Parliament, and although he was eventually permanently ejected from India in 1788, he eventually became an important member of the London finance sector.[21] Most important, William Pitt's ministry decided in the 1784 India Act that all of the Nawab's debts, including private ones, would be repaid.[22]

Examining the content of the claims made by both parties in the "revolution" in Madras is more difficult than in Bolts's case in Bengal. This is partially because the surviving justifications and arguments are much more fragmentary. Neither side produced sweeping, coherent justifications of their behavior, which is unfortunate from the perspective of this analysis. Rather, understanding the logic behind their arguments requires piecing together perspectives from statements and actions scattered in several documents. But when this is done, a no less coherent picture of the problem and sources of social order emerges. As in Bengal, both sides of the debate agreed that corruption was eating away at the effectiveness of EIC administration in India, but they disagreed about the sources of that corruption and consequently the origins of the forces that would stabilize it. While Bolts saw economic relations as the fundamental stabilizing force that would ensure the prosperity of Bengal and the surety of its administration, those recalled for overthrowing Pigot consistently argued that they were acting as constitutional checks against Pigot's corrupt, dictatorial government and, as such, were creating just administration from the stable source of an effective society.

The language of constitutional defense against tyranny—from the majority's perspective—and the forces of disorder—from Pigot's perspective—are clear from the beginning of the episode. Pigot's specific order indicted dissenting members of council for "an act subversive of the authority of government and tending to introduce anarchy."[23] In his view, the governor had direct and unmediated authority to legislate directly in Madras, and that, given the language of his orders from the Court of Directors in London, "the name of the President [of the Madras council, i.e., the governor] was necessary to make an act of Government."[24] Consequently, the decision by the dissenting members of council—who formed a slim majority—to appoint their candidate to the residency of Tanjore anyway formed, in Pigot's mind, an insubordinate act by servants.

This was likewise how Pigot viewed his interactions with British military officers as he attempted to move aggressively against the dissenting members of his council. As soon as the dissenting members of council began circulating critical materials throughout the town, Pigot called Stuart, the commander in chief of military forces in the settlement, ordering him to arrest the two leaders of the dissenting faction. Stuart, however, "wanted to see all the proceedings, that he might judge as an honest man, and a free agent. It was replied by one of the Council, that this doctrine, of a military officer's being a free agent, and entitled to know on what grounds orders were given, could not be admitted; that a military officer was bound to obey the legal orders he received from the proper authority issued in due form, and had no claim to know whether those orders were for good reasons or not."[25] Pigot thus seems to have found Stuart's assertion that he was acting as a "free agent," capable of making decisions about orders outside the authority of the governor, particularly galling. Indeed, his diagnosis of the problem, which implies his means of stabilizing the administration, was to recognize what he considered to be the governor's traditional power and authority within the presidency, both over its military and civilian branches.[26] (Pigot's impeachment occurred in part because he had already interpreted his powers in such terms, but his clear desire was to have them affirmed and ratified either by the governor-general in Bengal or the Court of Directors in London.)

Of course, this is hardly how the majority justified itself to other members of the Madras community or to the company in London. The letter circulated by the conspirators in Madras, which originally led to Pigot's move to arrest them, stated their case in strongly constitutionalist language. They complained of Pigot that

> the unexampled outrage offered to the constitution, and arbitrary behavior towards two of our members, by an illegal attempt to suspend them . . . the public safety is in danger by the conduct of Lord Pigot, and you gentlemen, who have supported, and by every person, who shall continue to support such measures; and we shall hold you therefore responsible for all the consequences that may ensue. *We the majority of the board do consider ourselves as*

the only legal representatives of the Honourable Company under this presidency, and as such we have no doubt but all the servants of the Company will regard us."[27]

The majority of the council amplified this assertion in a proclamation to Madras town after arresting Pigot. They argued that Pigot's "arbitrary behavior" stemmed from his attempts to overturn the will of his council. They imagined an unlikely scenario, but one that nevertheless reveals the basis of their argument: "If an enemy invaded this settlement, and the President chose to oppose preparations for the public defense, it is evident, that the loss of the settlement might attend such power in the hands of an ill-disposed President; and further, if such a system was supported, and that a President, vested with such powers, was detected in sacrificing the public interest to his own, it is clear, that no measure of detection or punishment could be carried out against him."[28] This passage is interesting because the bugaboo of a power-mad tyrant acting in his own interest against the community's captures two pieces of the disorder of the Madras administration. For the majority, the danger seemed to be both that Pigot carried tyrannical powers and that he himself was corrupt. They justified their actions as a defense of the community against tyrannical behavior, but in the process, they transformed the English community of Madras from an administration subordinate to the will of a hierarchical leadership into a quasi-constitutional polity capable of overthrowing its rulers. After arresting Pigot, Stuart summarized the majority's justification: "I cannot close this narrative without adding my satisfaction at having had an opportunity . . . to declare my Sentiments upon the nature of a free Government under the Auspices of the British Constitution, that it consisted in the due Subordination of the Military to the Civil Power. . . . [Stuart's toast at a public banquet held shortly after Pigot's arrest was] 'Justice to the Army while Subordinate to the Civil Power.'"[29]

For Pigot, meanwhile, the diagnosis was the same—corrupted, insolent administrators acting out of their own interest—but the source of order could not be any kind of polity in Madras outside the government. This is obvious in his reasoning rejecting the majority's claim to legitimacy in his absence because they, having not been ratified by his presence, as governor in council, "were incapable of any public act, and could be nothing but mere private individuals."[30] Order was only possible, according to Pigot, with his personal representation of authority capable of bringing his unruly servants to heel. However, the problem in Madras seems to have been that they did not think of themselves strictly as servants but rather as fellow citizens.

Of course, such a claim—to being a citizen before a servant of the company—was a peculiar one to make and certainly was only one part of the majority's defense in deposing Pigot. But it is also an important and interesting one because it highlights another possible source of social order in the growing British Empire in India. Bolts in Bengal had suggested the abolition of the EIC's monopoly and extension of British justice systems to India so that economic order could be freed from the yoke of a tyrannical government. The conspirators in Madras seem to have thought something similar—or at least seem to have justified themselves in a similar way. It was only if the Indian empire could be more tightly integrated into the British state—only if, that is, company servants or Europeans in company territory could be granted protections similar to what they thought they deserved at home—the scourge of corruption—which they took to mean tyrannical government—could be expunged.

Unsurprisingly, the superior company officers in Bengal and Madras—Verelst and Pigot—had little sympathy for such a perspective and suggested an alternative analysis. For them, corruption meant the disruption of traditional systems of patronage and political authority within the company's administration—effectively, precocious subalterns grasping for fortunes beyond their station.[31] Far from being the source of corruption, the state, empowered to discipline its own servants by censure, arrest, or expulsion, and protected from their legal challenges to its authority, was the only hope for tranquility and prosperity in India. Of course, these claims for such an empowered state—so different from what they believed existed in England—meant that the EIC's circumstances in India must have been different than in England. For Pigot, the difference was statutory, and all that was needed was for the Court of Directors to ratify what he believed to be his personal power to discipline his subordinates, but for Verelst, the difference lay in deep-seated habit that rendered English institutions useless (at least for the time being) on Indian soil, and by consequence order required an empowered state and the firm articulation of difference between India and Britain.

THREE PHASES: MORAL BACKGROUNDS, ADMINISTRATIVE LIFE, AND CORRUPTION

The perspective of administrators in the EIC can be seen as flowing through three primary moments: one clearly rooted in a Situational moral order; a second where the bases of moral judgment, the modes of abstraction, the paths of escalation, and the styles of self were confused; and a third where they had much more recognizably achieved their "modern" valence of a Universalist understanding. In this chapter, I focus not on the totality of each of these moments but rather on how they demonstrate each of the features of the model of corruption.

As we saw in chapter 2 and throughout *Modernity's Corruption*, nearly as soon as the EIC founded its factories in India, its officials there began quarreling with one another. Yet until the middle of the eighteenth century, even when those quarrels and their cross-accusations of corruption managed to reach all the way back to England, they still expressed a fundamentally Situational moral order.

The First Phase: Situational Moral Claims

It is not hard to find Situational moral claims among EIC servants before the middle of the eighteenth century.

Consider the case of one Richard Boothby. Boothby joined the EIC's service around 1630 and immediately began to cause problems when he arrived in Surat.[32] While Boothby's job in Surat was to sit in Council and manage the company's accounts, "conceiving he was a better man in England than [another councilor at Surat, George Page], he quickly fell into open enmity with him." After the president of Surat, Richard Wilde,[33] failed to "reconcile" the two, Boothby was assigned to the subsidiary factory at Baroda but initially refused to go. But just over two weeks after he finally went, Boothby left without permission, conducting unauthorized trading (probably on his own account as a private trader) which disrupted the company's efforts to purchase indigo in the region. Boothby then reappeared at Baroda and was called to Surat, where he publicly accused Wilde of plotting against his life. The Council at Surat backed Wilde, and because this suggested that Boothby was falling out favor with the company, Gujarati banians emerged to call on credit that they had extended to Boothby, claiming to think that his private trading was on behalf of the company. To protect the company's own reputation, the Council took over the debt and seized Boothby's assets to liquidate them and sought to deport him to England. Boothby first answered the charges against him within the framework of Council proceedings, but then asked that a special tribunal be constructed among the English "sea commanders" in and around Surat to judge his conduct; and while the Council grudgingly agreed, the commanders first refused to participate unless they were given binding authority to arbitrate, and then refused to mediate because they thought Boothby was so obviously guilty. Accordingly, Boothby was deported (first to Persia) and eventually returned to England.

Upon his return to London in 1644, Boothby published a pamphlet called "A True Declaration of the Intolerable Wrongs Done to Richard Boothby by Two Lewd Servants."[34] The point of the document was to demonstrate "the intollerable wrongs which I, Richard Boothby, an honest poor member of the India Company, and your trusty servant, hath undergone both in India, by lewd, malicious, tyrannicall, fraudulent, jugling fellow-servants; and also at home, by partiall, injust, ingratefull, unconsionable, corrupt Governours, and timeserving Committees in the India Courts,"[35] and it was addressed as a petition simultaneously to Parliament and "the Generality of the honorable East India Corporation" (the latter presumably refers to the General Court of the EIC).

While it is true (and unusual for the time) that Boothby directly escalated his claims all the way to the London reading public and the EIC's general court (as evidenced by Boothby's exhortations that EIC shareholders actually attend General Court meetings),[36] it is also clear that the very structure of his long "Epistle Dedicatory" (which takes up nearly half the pamphlet) reveals a deeply Situational, direct connection between the moral structure of EIC servants and their behavior. For instance, Boothby said his appeal to the company's General Court came from two conjoined reasons. One was to exhort the Committees to appoint "men of good repute and credit in life and conversation, as well as of men of ability and understanding to manage their affairs" in India. This was to replace the current practice, so that

> no lewd, debauched, ill-livers, prodigall unthirfty persons, prophane swearers, drunkards, and lascivious persons, of which sort too many have been entertained, by favour and friendship in Court, even of their own sonnes, kindred or friends, and by letters from great men of pleasure them, (sent out as the phrase hath been, for sacrifice, or by such voyages to reclaim them, which is rather the next way to thrust such persons into the Devils mouth, and to make them ten time worse then [*sic*] ere they were before) which turneth to the dishonour of God, the prejudice of the honourable Company, and their own souls hazard, countenanced by example of superiors there, given to all excess of ryot, and delighting to make others children of Belial as themselves.[37]

To Boothby, the population of company ranks in India with such corruptible specimens meant that, in the absence of clear declarations of the rights of officials' private trade and succession through the company's ranks in the (frequent) case of mortality in India, the president of a factory could easily corrupt the entire apparatus and establish a sort of despotism:

> A wicked President, and his packed main part of Councell, can easily in India make malicious shew of great crimes fained to be committed, against an honest man, and to arraigne him, condemne him to prison, suspend the salary, and ship him home a delinquent, before ever he make his purgation to the Court

at home, and so he and all his are inpossibly [*sic*] to be ruined unjustly . . . it seems strange to me, that a government in India by a President and Councell, should be established by a privat Commission[38] never seen to any in my time . . . who under colour of that power and authority, rules as a Tyrant, according to his own wicked disposition . . . which whoever shall question, is in dager ipso facto to be arraigned for his life as a trayter or mutineer.[39]

If his introductory epistle virtually screams "Situational moral background," the substance of his account is even more concrete. In Boothby's telling, soon after his arrival as a member of council at Surat,

> I took good notice of the great dishonour done to Gods glory by the lewd lives and conversations of all the English in generall, and the chief heads in particular; the dishonour also therein to my gracious King and native Countrey, and the deep juglings and impostures of the President Richard Wild, and George Page of the Councell: to the defraudment of their Honorable Imployers, which first brought me in envie and bad suspition of a Spie, a Puritan, and Informer (and so called) because I did not run in the same excesse of riot with them.[40]

Of course, Boothby is casting himself as a god-fearing, moral, upright, and duty-bound agent faced with a dissipated factory led by corrupt officials who turned on him when he refused to sink to their moral level. By consequence, at first this looks like the kind of (dis)embedded claims making we would expect to see in a Universal style of moral appeal. But while this appearance must be counterweighed by the documentary back-and-forth of which it is a part, as we shall see, it is also contradicted within the declaration itself as the narrative evolves. Consider, for example, the fragmentary moral presentation Boothby seemed willing to undertake when White and Page assigned him to be chief merchant at an unpalatable subsidiary station and Boothby learned that they were trying to "lay traps to insnare me":

> A day before my departure, George Page, notwithstanding his said wicked plot, with my second to betray me, insinuated himself into sudden familiarity with me, excusing himself for having a hand to put me out of the Factory at Surrat to be sent to [Baroda], laying all the malice on Richard Wilde the President; And to make me more blind then [sic] a Beetle, or sencerely ignorant of the play, would need bestow upon me a Michivile Brile [sic; perhaps "Bridle"] or poysoned Piscash,[41] like the traiterous kisse of Judas to our Saviour Christ . . . I made fair shew of complement with him, and accepted his Piscash or gift, rather then shew distaste, or to give any notice that I had any intelligence of the plot against me, by discovering the secret imparted unto me by my second to his detriment.[42]

Additionally, contrary to what we would expect if Boothby expressed a Universal moral order in his corruption accusations and accounting for his own virtue, when he left Baroda without permission[43] and returned to Surat, Boothby was subject to an indignity that only made sense as an indignity in the first place within a Situational order:

> At my arrivall at Surrat, I was presently put out of my chamber, and thrust into the worst lodging in the house, adjoyning the Porters lodge, commanded to take my diet at the second table, among Counting-house Scrivans, Pursers, Mates, and Cabbin-boyes taken ashore for inferior services, and they commanded to take place at table above me, whose parents, or themselves,

if I had been ambitious or malicious, I would have scorned with Job, to have set with the Heardsmen of my flock, having at home at that present, a family living in reputation, and having had men of better quality then the best of them, I mean the chiefe, to wait at home upon my Trencher, Knights, Gentlemen, and Citizens.[44]

Boothby's claims are unusual insofar as they were documented extensively and rose to the attention of company authorities in London, but his outlook and tactics appear commonplace. Indeed, it is easy to see how Boothby's contentious tactics led to the embedded style of moral regulation described (and derided) by Alexander Hamilton at the start of the eighteenth century.

The first illustration of the moral background of administrative claims making is John Braddyll's "Vindication," published in 1746 as an open letter to the Court of Directors.[45] The "Vindication" sought to clear Braddyll's name from the aspersions cast by Henry Lowther, the chief factor at Surat whom Braddyll had dismissed from his post for corruption. It is remarkable for its time, first, because it was published at all because this sort of direct, and public, appeal became far more common after the 1760s. But the text is also unusual for how clearly it expressed both embedded moral claims making and the embedded nature of social relationships within the company's trading posts along the Indian coast.[46]

In his defense (complete, as was common eighteenth-century pamphleteering practice, with appendixes reproducing correspondence and official reports) against Lowther's corruption accusations, Braddyll sought above all to rebut what he called Lowther's "serious objection to my moral character."[47] Braddyll dismissed outright as "a curious anecdote" Lowther's accusation that he had plotted to assassinate a previous governor but went on more specifically to rebut another charge:

> But where he taxes [i.e., accuses] me with being recalled by the Governor and Council of Bombay, from the Chiefship of Tellicherry, for the disagreement with the rest of my fellow-servants, and pusillanimity, I shall in brief remark, that his celebrated Friend and Patron Mr. Cowan [probably Sir Robert Cowan, governor of Bombay from 1729 to 1734] had resolved my remove, purely because I was not as ductile and pliant, as fond of being his dupe and money-cully, as this worth Gentleman. This was the true reason of my recal [sic]. For as to my pretended disagreement with my fellow-servants, Mr. Cowan, who never scrupled what disorders he occasion'd in the Service, so they promoted his private ends, or satisfy'd his private passions, had underhand stirred up, and encouraged my inferiors in the Factory, to breaches of discipline and subordination, which I never would suffer in any Post committed to my charge; and which they, it seems, depended on being supported in by the Governor, as they accordingly were.[48]

Cowan was not the only governor of Bombay against whom Braddyll had to defend himself. Part of Lowther's complaint relied on the testimony of the superior of both men, John Horne, who served as governor from 1734 to 1739. In response to Horne's apparent questioning of Braddyll's "veracity," Braddyll noted that:

> As to the other personal points, especially where [Lowther] quotes Mr. Horne for his Author, I can only say, that Mr. Horne, as he well may, stedfastly [sic] denies his ever having made use of those false and scandalous expressions attributed to him, relating to my want of veracity, to "my being a dangerous man, and

one that no one could safely associate with."—I hope, and believe, Mr. Horne was neither weak nor wicked enough to propagate a character of me so inconsistent with the important Trust he actually reposed in me; and indeed such abuse carries with it more of the Lowther-stamp than that of a very civil Gentleman, with whom I had never any dissention, nor to whom I ever gave the least reason to traduce me in so cruel and unjust a light; neither, admitting that Mr. Horne spoke thus injuriously of me, will I allow that my character is to stand or fall by what Mr. Lowther, or he either, says of it. That the enemies to the Company, with whom I never would associate, have along found me dangerous to them, and that the innocent Friends, with whom only I chose to associate, have never experienced any injury from this "well known talent of mine for being romanticly [sic] historical," or from any part of my private conduct, is a justice, I presume, they will not refuse me, and for which I fairly appeal to them, and, above all, to matter [sic] of Fact.[49]

Braddyll's defense of his own character was still deeply embedded in a network of concrete and specific relations in Bombay and Surat. Reports of his "moral character" reflected his capacity to be an effective agent for the Court of Directors, and to establish that credibility, he had to use reports of superiors that could be ambiguous or even shift outright. To this, of course, he had recourse to "matter of Fact," but only after appealing to his association with "innocent friends."

This contextual style of moral reasoning had powerful influences on the content of judgments made in India, Braddyll explained. The core of his "Vindication" recounts his commission to investigate and suspend Lowther from his post as chief factor at Bombay's subsidiary station in Surat. When Braddyll arrived in Surat with his commission from the governor of Bombay, however, Lowther fled to the local "Moorish" factory and refused to return. As he attempted to establish a regular council with the remaining company servants and investigate Lowther's malfeasance, however, Braddyll discovered that most of the council had been "effectually seduced from their duty and fidelity to your Honours, [and] that they acted in all respects more like Lowther's Champions, than like YOUR Servants."[50]

Braddyll quickly clashed with the most senior remaining servant and banished him to Bombay for insubordination. Two more junior members of the council next resigned in protest, and while Lowther later accused Braddyll of dangling the carrot of reinstatement before them in exchange for condemning Lowther, Braddyll justified his leniency through the importance of contextual moral judgment. As he wrote:

> That they had no right to protest against a step to which their assent was not so much as ask'd, and taken entirely upon myself, in virtue of the commission I acted by, is, I presume, a little too plain for even Mr. Lowther to deny. However, as they were young Gentlemen, otherwise of fair characters, and whom I have since so plentifully loaded with (positively no other) calumny and slander, than imputing their seduction from their Duty to Mr. Lowther's practices and ascendant over them; I compassionated [*sic*] extremely with their misguidance, and would, with great pleasure, have seen them retract a step which clenched their (N.B.) self-dismission, or rather Desertion of the Service: and the Proposal to them of re-instating them on the very Proviso so manifestly misconstrued by Lowther, was surely not the ridiculous reason he gives of our not caring that this Testimony against my violent Proceedings, should stand upon our Registers, but purely lenity [*sic*] and compassion for two Gentlemen, whom he had so perfectly misled, and whose breaches of duty, and order were reproaches to

himself, and undeniable proofs of the eighteenth Article charging him with the seduction of his fellow-servants from their fidelity and subordination.

Your Honours cannot but observe, with indignation, what an use is attempted to be made of our unwillingness to pursue any rigour, or to take advantages of the weakness and precipitancy of those two Gentlemen, and how far I was, in the execution of my Commission, from stretching it to ill-natured extremes; consequently, how little the proceedings I was forced into, to maintain the order and discipline of the Service, and, above all, for example sake, the respect due to YOUR authority, deserved the name violent.[51]

In other words, according to Braddyll, Lowther's influence as a company superior was so strong that he could "seduce" two junior servants, corrupting their moral judgment. Yet Braddyll hastens to add that, even though his own leniency toward the two might be construed as corruption in its own right (namely, an effort to secure false testimony against Lowther and to disguise his "violent" treatment), in fact it was a judgment made in the particular situation of the particular social relations he found in Surat. In other words, Braddyll justified himself using moral claims and in light of social relations, both of which were embedded in local context.

Tom Raw

If the first phase of the moral background of India officials was embedded in both the mode of its claims making and the social relationships sustaining it, the second phase was characterized by a breakdown and chaotic ambiguity along both these dimensions. Among the representations available to the British public of this transition,[52] one that encapsulates this breakdown best is *Tom Raw*, a satirical poem published in 1828 by an EIC official, Charles D'Oyly.[53] The fictional poem is illustrated with beautiful color illustrations of Anglo life in India (see one example in figure 5.1) and is clearly written for an unfamiliar audience (each canto is annotated with explanations of Anglo-Indian pidgin vocabulary). It recounts the career of a young cadet in the EIC's army as he sails to India, experiences social life in Calcutta, makes his way to his eventual army post, fights in a battle, and eventually marries the daughter of his commanding officer.

A central theme of *Tom Raw* is the ambiguity of the moral background of the Anglo-Indians, especially the question of whether it should be rooted in local circumstances or in more

FIGURE 5.1 "Tom Raw Presents Letters of Introduction."

Source: General Collection, Beinecke Rare Book and Manuscript Library, Yale University.

abstract ground. In the verse preface to one of the cantos, for example, D'Oyly complains about British perceptions of company officials in India:

> It's often struck us a curious thing,
> That England knows so little about India,
> Consid'ring we return, and, with us bring
> The wealth of Poona and the lacks of Scindia;
> Still speaking in our native tongue,—our Hindee, or
> Persian discarded quite, and—given the chatter:
> But Laplanders, their sledges, dogs, and rein-deer,
> Khaskatkans, or Americans, no matter,
> Are more known than your Hindoo, Muslim, or Mahratta
> We've heard it traced to envying and jealousies
> Of our rupees, and characters of Nabobs,
> Obtained by acts that richly merit gallowses.
> Our vulgar fondness for pillows and cabobs,
> Snatching the shawls and jewels, as the tray bobs
> Under our noses at a grand Durbar;
> In short, that every Indian every way robs.
> We've heard that folks often have gone so far,
> As to place 'gainst all Indian company a Bar!
> And yet with all this ignorance and scoffing,
> On Eastern things, they of the truth come short;
> For instance—there's a dutchess who went off, in
> An Indian coarse silk petticoat, to court,
> Which Khidmutgars a buckishism vote,
> And are seen strutting in, of grandeur plenary:
> There's Ackermann, a bank of England note
> Of some amount work give—the sinner he—
> For twelve good drawings of our lovely Indian scenery.[54]

In this passage, D'Oyly defends against the condemnation of the British audience content to judge the "acts that richly merit gallowses" undertaken by company officials. Yet the terms of this defense are themselves ambiguous. On the one hand, D'Oyly suggests a universalistic moral background, in the sense that both the British audience and Indian officials are equally subject to seduction and corruption by luxuries imported from India (from the "dutchess" in her petticoat to those seeking to buy artwork about India, to "the lacks [large amounts of money] of Poona or the wealth of Scindia"). On the other hand, there is still a fundamental difference between Indian (and even Anglo-Indian) culture and British culture, even elsewhere in the imperial diaspora ("Laplanders . . . or Americans").

This ambiguity is reflected several times in *Tom Raw*'s main narrative and, in each instance, the narrator mocks traditional embedded and contextual modes of moral stabilization. Thus, when Tom Raw arrives in Calcutta, he carries with him a series of patronage letters meant to embed him in favorable networks in Anglo-Indian society. But Raw's contact proves practically useless—refusing Raw further connection or a place to stay—after quizzing him on distant relations in Britain.[55] This Anglo-Indian official, whom Raw finds clouded with hookah smoke in his office, is a symbol for decay:

> There, seated, was a most cadav'rous figure,
> With sallow visage, long and wrinkley too,
> A large hooked nose, and twinkling eyes—no bigger
> Than gooseberries, with just their greenish hue;
> His spindle shanks were twined with treble screw;
> And the think hoary honours of his head
> Fell long and lank, and scraped into a queue;

> His clothes might o'er him and his wife have spread,
> And shoes of red nankeen he wore—stitched with white thread.[56]

But if any character is singled out for excoriation in *Tom Raw*, it is "Churbee Doss," an Indian elite who "from his infancy/ Had been 'mong Europeans, who had traded/And had acquired their taste."[57] Doss represented an upward mobility possible for those who allied themselves to British officials as "banians" or "dubashes"[58]—middlemen overseeing commercial affairs. While this role had been essential in the eighteenth century, by the nineteenth, it had taken on a far less savory cast:

> To any family of wealth or pride.
> Forth issued in the world,—a hack sircar [head servant]
> Wrote passes at the Custom House, where hied [*sic*]
> Intriguers in abundance—on a Par,
> With them he cheated, stole, deceived, and—cleared the bar
> Of penury—then; at the Ghauts [hills] he plies
> For country Captains and tehri keen nipcheeses [goat cheese],
> Passes scot-free their secret merchandise,
> For a good bribe, which mutually pleases.
> Then, acting as an arutdar [financial agent] he eases
> His clients of their cash—the state, of duties,
> Lends Speculists some hundreds of rupees he's
> Accumulated, for the most acute is
> In interest usurious, which will nobly suit his
> End, and—then passing to a higher grade,
> He doffs his coarse habiliments for muslin,
> Lolls in his palkee,—talks of ships and trade,
> Buys large investments—thrusts his ugly muzzle in

Th' Exchange Rooms, and commences ampler guzzling,
Drinks ghee [clarified butter], which smells him for a bag of bones
To blubber cheeks and paunch enormous—puzzling
To all but those who know much men's zones
May be expanded by the bhyn's [cattle's] buttery loans.[59]

However offensive a portrait may be drawn of Doss in *Tom Raw*, the most remarkable passage from the standpoint of the moral background of administration comes when Raw meets another elite Indian, this time the Nawab (or Indigenous governor) of Bengal, in audience with the British resident, or political supervisor. When the Nawab seeks to embrace Raw, "To give him— par usage—th' embrace fraternal,"[60] he is disgusted, shouting in front of the Court:

"I hug the filthy fellow?—no, not I",
Cried Tom—"I think it—hang me—a disgrace;
"And if he says another word on 't,—by
"The Lord!—I'll spit in the black rascal's face!"
"Hush! hush!" Said Mr. B., "regard the place
"And consequence of doing foolish things."
"Nay"—murmured Tom—"I am not of a race
"That will be slobbered o'er by native kings,
"Despite his cloth of gold and all his sparkling rings."[61]

Thus, in *Tom Raw*, there is an evident ambiguity in the moral background of official behavior. Should it be contextual, reflecting "the place" and local ties to both Anglo-Indian society and Indian elites? Or should it reflect a more universal grounding in the potential seduction of luxury (that could affect Britons, Anglo-Indians, and Indian elites equally) and in racial distinctions between "black rascals" and company servants? By at once narratively portraying Raw's outrage against an established elite network that includes both Anglo-Indians and Indians, by portraying his disembedded (racist) moral claims to difference as violations of local norms recognized by both Indians and Anglo-Indian officials, and by itself reiterating the cultural gulf separating Britain and India even as it seeks to portray a universal moral seduction of luxury, *Tom Raw* never provides a clear answer.

The Competition Wallah

If Braddyll's "Vindication" presented a moral background that was unambiguously embedded in local social relations and made embedded moral claims, and *Tom Raw* presented an ambiguous picture that struggled with the disembedding of both dimensions, the final illustration presents an unambiguously disembedded style of claims making and social relations among Anglo-Indian officials. *The Competition Wallah* was published in 1864, as the company was being unwound and folded into the larger British Empire in the aftermath of the Sepoy Rebellion of 1857.[62] The rebellion coincided with major reforms to the EIC's civil service and especially the introduction of competitive exams. The author of *The Competition Wallah*, George Trevelyan, thus presents the work as the fictionalized correspondence between two Cambridge school friends—Henry Broughton, who joins the company's service as a junior official, and Charles Simpkins, who remains in England.

The bulk of *The Competition Wallah* is taken up with wry observations about Anglo-Indian and Indian social, economic, and religious life. But from the standpoint of the changing moral background of imperial administration, two passages are key. First, the narrator, Broughton, presents a long description of the moral posture of company servants:

> Any one who wishes to preserve a high tone of thought, and a mind constantly open to new impressions, must look for a calling which is an education in itself—that is, a calling which presents a succession of generous and elevating interests. And such is pre-eminently the career of a civil servant in India. There is no career which so surely inspires men with the desire to do something useful, in their generation—leave their mark upon the world for good, and not for evil. The public spirit among the servants of the Government at home is faint compared with the fire and zeal which glows in every vein of an Indian official. It is a rare phenomenon this of a race of statesmen and judges scattered throughout a conquered land, ruling it, not with an eye to private profit, but even in the selfish interests of the mother country, but in single-minded solicitude for the happiness and improvement of the children of the soil.
>
> Whence comes this high standard of efficiency and public virtue among men taken at random, and then exposed to the temptations of unbounded power and unlimited facilities for illicit gain? It cannot be peculiarly the result of Haileybury [the training facility for EIC servants], for that institution, from its very nature, united the worst faults of school and college. The real education of a civil servant consists in the responsibility that devolves on him at an early age, which brings out whatever good there is in a man; the obligation to do nothing that can reflect dishonour on the service; the varied and attractive character of his duties; and the example of precept of his superiors, who regard him rather as a younger brother than as a subordinate official.[63]

Beyond the final collegial reference to fraternity among officials, Treveylan's account of the moral life and motivation of company officials is pitched in the register of moral universalism. People have inherent good within them, and the early, enormous responsibility of service coupled with the "obligation to do nothing that can reflect dishonour on the service" brings out "whatever good there is in a man," whoever he may be.

While the civil service was cast in selfless terms, Trevelyan established a strong contrast with elite Indian society. Broughton is invited to a tumasha (a ball or entertainment) by a local zemindar (or Indian elite landowner). The tumasha itself is portrayed as boring and bizarrely wasteful, but as Trevelyan notes,

> The motive for this profusion is evident enough. All the world within a hundred miles will hear that the Futtehgung man has induced the sahibs [Anglo-Indians] of Moffussilpore to be present at a tumasha; and the Rajah of Doodiah,[64] his dearest enemy, will not know a moment's peace until he has achieved the same honour. Under the feeble rule of the Mogul, these great landholders exercised an absolute authority within their own borders, and made war upon each other with considerably gusto. Since we have been in the country they have been forced to confine their rivalry to quarrels concerning precedence, and endless litigation about every imaginable subject.[65]

Thus, the moral background of modern imperialism in India allowed officials to separate themselves from local entanglements and make moral claims to govern in the name of downtrodden Indian subjects. This allowed them to universalize their moral claims. After all, according to Trevelyan, the spirit of public service, rather than a particular personal interest, called one to service in India. Yet universalizing moral claims also depended on decisively severing social relations from Indian society; embedded social relations seemed to be a space of rivalry, political entanglements, and corruption, and they were therefore confined to neutered, elite Indians from whom everyday Indian subjects needed to be protected by Anglo-Indian officials. Put differently, it was a recognizably modern apparatus of colonial administration, dependent on an essentializing, objectifying differentiation of ruler and subject.

CONCLUSION

The point of this chapter can be stated simply: "corruption" is not merely a name for an objective behavior but rather a rich moral signifier that constructs and fractures political and administrative coalitions and supplies moralized understandings of appropriate social order. In the case of the East India Company, these shifted from understandings embedded in Situational moral orders to Universal ones by the nineteenth century, but these, in turn, depended on the existence of a gulf between colonizers and colonized. In a phrase, Universal understandings of corruption implied an imperial administrative imagination.

CONCLUSION

REPRISE

Throughout *Modernity's Corruption*, my argument has interwoven historical, theoretical, and analytic aspects. Historically, it is rooted in the case of the English East India Company's (EIC) transformation, between the middle of the eighteenth century and the middle of the nineteenth, from being a state-like commercial entity to a more or less direct subsidiary of the "second" British Empire.[1] To make sense of this shift, I have argued that the EIC is best seen as a complex organization riven by internal disputes among its officials and embedded in both British and South-Asian political contexts. And as my analysis of the case has demonstrated, the transformation of "corruption," and the company's administrative apparatus with it, are at least partly the stories of how conflicts taking place within and involving the EIC telegraphed back and forth between South Asia and Britain, and how this process of transmission altered the positions of officials, almost all of whom would seem self-evidently corrupt if judged by modern standards. And I have suggested that the language of corruption, especially as it became modern (in the sense that I revisit below) was a crucial part of the "rule of colonial difference" insofar as it simultaneously came to represent a modern ideal of the separation of society, the economy, and the state from one another yet also pushed the source of corrupting influence into Indigenous, "othered" populations.

This historical analysis relied on a particular substantive and theoretical understanding of what corruption is, which I articulated in the introduction and in chapter 1. Corruption is a phenomenon that depends on moralized accusations that abstract from particular circumstances; depend on biographical narratives of the accusers and accused; and, via their appeals, escalate the conflict between at least two parties to involve an audience—together, I have called this the model of corruption. A central theme of *Modernity's Corruption* has been that the different features of the model can be drawn into at least two configurations: one Situational, in the sense that "corruption" is woven into familiar circumstances, that conflict and escalation usually flow along networks of those familiar with the details of those circumstances, and that there is comparatively little emphasis on an actor's need to act with moral consistency as circumstances vary; and one Universal, which depends for the force of its criticism on the purported existence of "disembedded" moral spheres that span human societies and provide a convenient shorthand to escalate corruption conflicts to unfamiliar audiences. From this vantage point, the story of *Modernity's Corruption* is about the shift within the EIC from a predominantly Situational to a mainly Universal way of viewing corruption, the forces that drove it, and some of its consequences.

These historical and theoretical insights have been expressed with a particular style of analysis. Instead of searching for a vocabulary that maintains its stability over time—which can often leave a scholar chasing shadows[2]—I have instead explored how shifts in the very categories of what corruption was understood to be intertwined with other processes, like the expansion of British imperial power, modes of thinking about virtue and obligation, the dilemmas of complex organizations in the early modern world, and the changing prosopography of colonial administrators. I hope that this effort has at least been empirically generative, even if it may leave some expecting more straightforward conclusions unsatisfied.

I hasten to add, however, that this last point about the analytical style I have employed does not mean that I have either abandoned social science in the preceding pages or think that the case of the EIC is so unique and singular as to prohibit generalization. To the contrary: its very complexity and intensity—the ways it is at once so very familiar and startlingly alien—supply a host of profitable "deep analogies"[3] that apply not only to general investigations of corruption but also to the crises afflicting us today. In the remainder of this conclusion, I will draw out some of these implications.

CORRUPTION IS RELATIVE, BUT MODERN CORRUPTION PROCEEDS AS THOUGH IT IS UNIVERSAL

A central theme of this book has been that "corruption" is not *just* a material behavior or a universal kind of action but instead is always also bound up with institutions, situations, and understandings that supply the content to the forms of moral accusation it represents. Thus, part of what makes the Situational configuration of corruption seem at once familiar and alien is that, while we can certainly understand judging, for instance, the propriety of behavior through reference to social context or appealing to those most familiar with the circumstances we describe, the institutions within which these judgments are embedded have decisively changed. In particular, there is now a widespread legal and academic consensus on what "counts" as corruption and can be treated as such.[4] By consequence of that consensus, a variety of other behaviors—addiction, licentiousness, swearing, violence—have come under the jurisdiction of other institutions. Put differently, under the Situational mode of corruption I have analyzed in this book, other behaviors we now think of as personal troubles were quite public companions of behaviors we now call corrupt—after all, men fought duels and risked their lives not just over whether they had been convicted in a court or administrative judgment of accepting bribes but whether they had been accused of lying by their colleagues.

This view follows excellent contemporary work that is critical of orthodox corruption studies,[5] and one avenue along which it could continue is to turn to explanations of the jurisdictional conflict among various disciplines over the categories of corruption themselves.[6] In this approach, the study of "first-order" effects of corruption—the negative consequences it has, under its modern definition, on health, welfare, and development—are still important, but it must be coupled with careful, reflexive analysis of how the categories of corruption themselves fit into a wider network of politics, institutions, and organizational struggle.[7] For instance, if corruption stands as an "empty signifier"[8] and as part of a complex "moral economy"[9] including categories and behaviors, how can we explain the dominance of economic reasoning—the holdover rational-choice language of incentives to pursue well-understood and relatively unchanging goals—to understand it?

This first general insight about the nature of corruption carries a risk with it: if we recognize that corruption is embedded in and sustained by a web of institutions that might vary considerably, doesn't that simply replicate the original problem of variation in norms that troubled social analysts back to John Locke and beyond? Here, I hope another major theme of *Modernity's Corruption* can help steer away from danger. I have argued that, while there are two major configurations of corruption and its moral background, which I have called Situational and Universal, there has historically (at least within the EIC) been a shift in the relative predominance from the former to the latter. The dominance of the Universal understanding of corruption meant in turn the narrowing, in one sense, of what counted as corruption and a radical expansion, in another sense, of the concept's scope of reference. Situational understandings ran along the lines of those familiar with a given social situation or circumstance, but because the Universal mode referred to domains like "the economy" and "society" with seemingly self-evident internal rules governing propriety and behavior no matter where it was taking place,[10] an accusation rooted in the Universal understanding lifted behavior out of concrete circumstances and framed it within social spaces meant to cover all possibilities.

This paradoxical feature of the Universal understanding of corruption, I believe, is a key feature of "modernity" itself. A wide variety of scholars have argued that modern life is characterized by using cultural and moral distinctions to draw boundaries among different social domains, like economic, political, public, and private life,[11] and that economic and political modernity, in particular, has been organized into states and markets that simultaneously project an image of unity while being composed of endlessly fragmented components and diffuse boundaries.[12] Along with these excellent works, I hope that *Modernity's Corruption* has emphasized that whatever we might call "modernity," it is an organizational and social *accomplishment* that was hardly inevitable but instead was constructed by concrete actors in specific places, albeit not always intentionally.[13]

In addition to observing that modernity is the outcome of specific social processes, I also think that *Modernity's Corruption* offers another insight. There is endless debate about the definition and timing of "modernity,"[14] but if we stipulate that it at least partly features the dynamics of differentiation noted above, the careful study of the shift from one category of corruption to another suggests that there is no inherent reason that the Universal mode of corruption, and the social domains it defines, sustains, and reinforces, are themselves inevitable or permanent. Put differently, *Modernity's Corruption* has argued that structural transformations in imperial administration resituated organizational conflict such that a Universal category of corruption could predominate, but structural circumstances could also easily allow the category to return to a more Situational understanding or transform into some other configuration of the model of corruption. This transforms "modernity" to the description of a potentially recurring constellation of social arrangements rather than a historical period and, as such, invites continuing work into these modernities without the weight of inevitability hanging over them.[15]

CORRUPTION IS FRACTAL AND SCALAR

Beyond these broader points about the nature of modernity and the peculiar power of *modern* corruption, the model of corruption itself supplies some insights that may also be worth pursuing. One set of insights deals with the abstract properties of corruption when we think of it, as I have argued we should, as a style of moral accusation. This shift emphasizes how corruption is a property of social interactions between at least two parties struggling with one another from recognition and advantage within a given social setting, and draws our attention to two unusual dynamics in corruption studies. The first is that corruption is *fractal*.[16] This means that corruption dynamics are self-similar at different scales; whether one studies two colonial administrators stationed together in an outpost, the different branches of the colonial service (judicial, military, or mercantile), the different provinces they serve, and on and on, the distinction between "corrupt" and "virtuous" is an available distinction for organizational struggle. It is tempting to reduce this point to the triviality that however one defines corruption, behaviors that meet that definition will vary among individuals and groups, but I mean something more: because corruption is an *empty* signifier that simultaneously moralizes struggles by virtue of its employment, it can be applied in surprising places and times that seem to exceed any "objective" criterion.

Thinking of corruption as a fractal potential in any setting that is also enormously powerful when invoked (and recognized) implies, and the analysis in this book has demonstrated, that control over the scale of conflict surrounding corruption accusations matters a great deal. Following some of the work discussed in greater detail in the introduction,[17] organizational struggles can be divided into incumbents, who have more local power and resources in a given setting, and challengers to their position within that setting. Because social settings for organizational struggle exist as parts of wider "ecologies"[18] of other settings and struggles, the incumbent in any given setting has a powerful interest in keeping the conflict localized if they can successfully defeat the challenge; likewise, whoever "loses" the local conflict has an interest in appealing for support outside that local setting.

The addition I would suggest to this general imagery of organizational struggle is that this dynamic of escalation and localization is intertwined with the Situational/Universal distinction at the heart of *Modernity's Corruption*. After all, the Situational understanding of corruption depends on reference to circumstances similar to the one at stake, which in turn is usually recognized when claims using it are escalated along networks of familiar observers. (In the central argument of *Modernity's Corruption*, these were primarily members of the EIC in London who had long experience in India before retiring—in other words, familiar from years "on the ground" with the details of company life and procedures in India.) By contrast, Universal claims tend to work when appealing to those who are *un*familiar with local settings because they provide a convenient—and nominally impersonal—moral shorthand to understand often quite esoteric circumstances. (In the preceding chapters, this unfamiliar audience was first a London public anxious about the company's increasingly precarious position in India and Britain, then administrators like George Macartney and Charles Cornwallis who "parachuted in" to senior roles in the EIC subsequent to Pitt's India Act of 1784.)

This dynamic suggests that the ecological structure of the audience to corruption disputes deserves careful attention. This structure could range from one extreme in which the entire audience is unfamiliar with a local setting—that is, in which the wall between a setting and the institutions in which it is embedded is quite "sheer." In this circumstance, we might expect to see a dynamic of experts and apostate insiders "translating" local circumstance into Universal terms for the benefit of their audience. (These acts of translation were at the heart of the debate between William Bolts and Harry Verelst that I explored in chapter 5.) At the other, some local settings might be structured so that both incumbents and challengers have extensive audiences deeply familiar with local circumstances, which would in turn suggest that corruption claims would be deeply Situational and rely on highly specialized knowledge of local circumstances. Here, corruption disputes would involve raw factional mobilization. Of course, neither of these extremes is likely to obtain for very long—in the former extreme, eventually a group of brokers would form an adjacent ecology to the specialized area (as with, for instance, expert witnesses or forensic accountants in fraud cases); and in the latter case, the "local setting" is likely to grow by incorporating its neighbors until, given the specialization of complex society, it encounters something like the "carrying capacity" of familiarity for any given actor. Instead, actually existing cases lie somewhere in between, but the dynamics of their organizational struggle over corruption within and beyond them are likely to revolve around the dynamics of the social distance the claims must traverse, and the kinds of difference (of any salient form) they encounter along the way.

A PERSONAL SUMMARY

This discussion of the extensions of the argument of *Modernity's Corruption* feels abstract, so let me personalize it. I mentioned in the introduction that I came to the study of corruption laterally, through the study of empires and the moral worldviews of their administrators. One of the reasons I didn't originally recognize the urgency of studying corruption is because I have an extraordinarily privileged experience relative to it: I grew up in an upper-middle-class white family in Baltimore, and I have not (nor, to my knowledge, has anyone in my family) had to pay a bribe to attend school, obtain vital health or public services, or avoid unjust punishments. Instead, all my encounters with corruption were superficial: a political reporter visiting my elementary school and talking about the governor of Maryland being convicted for corruption;[19] I was struck by an episode of *The Simpson's* which revolved around corruption;[20] and I was exposed by osmosis to the ambient sense that "quite a lot" or "almost all" politicians were corrupt in some way, even in America.[21]

Yet thinking through the meaning of corruption has given me a different perspective from what one might expect given these superficial encounters. For one thing, I am now a reasonably comfortable and certainly privileged university professor, and, as such, I inhabit a remarkably specialized "local setting"—that of the classroom, the conference presentation, and the "invisible college"[22] of colleagues around the globe on whom my intellectual career directly relies. I have grown aware that, even though I have tried to maintain my "moral compass" and consider myself to have behaved virtuously, there are still a multitude of practices common to this setting that a reasonable outsider could consider corrupt. Some of these are trivial violations of the letter of New York State anticorruption regulations: I have occasionally taken office supplies home, and I have not always strictly accounted for my sick time. But others are more important: as a white man who is the child of academics, I have a tacit familiarity with academia that at once embeds me in the "right" networks of colleagues and lends me a kind of ease that people from different backgrounds might reasonably see as a violation of the spirit, if not the letter, of the meritocratic order that academia claims to represent.

The example of my own biography suggests two points. The first is that, no matter how carefully I try to "keep my nose clean," and the extent to which I actually do so relative to others, there is still *something* about the life I live that a reasonable outsider, unfamiliar with its dynamics, could label corrupt. The fact that this has not yet happened is a function, on the one hand, of the sheer fact that no one has seen fit to accuse me of anything, probably because of my relative obscurity.[23] But on the other hand, it is because the local setting I inhabit is insulated by laws, norms, and conventions that contain the scale of conflict about corruption within it. By consequence of my own deep, ongoing familiarity, in other words, when I wonder whether a given act is proper, I don't look at the letter of the law as prescribed by my human resources department for all New York State employees; I look to a concrete example within my department or to a friend or family member with experience.

The second point I draw from my own experience qualifies the first. While I inhabit an insulated world that could, in many ways, be characterized as having some features of a Situational order, I still live in a time and place where a Universal understanding of corruption predominates. Because of that, I feel convinced that bribery is wrong; that it is at a minimum inauthentic, and can even be a sign of mental disturbance, for someone to set their ethical compass by whatever social circumstance they encounter; and that public institutions ought to be as impartial as possible. I try to follow these convictions as though they transcend given circumstances, even as I see them as a product of those very circumstances. For me, this tension is at the heart of modernity's corruption.

CORRUPTION AND TRUMPISM

It's very important to talk about corruption. If you don't talk about corruption, why would you give money to a country that you think is corrupt?

—Donald Trump, September 23, 2019[24]

On January 6, 2021, like many others, I was ready to feel relief. A little over four years before that, I sat ready with fellow sociologists and a bottle of champagne for what we thought would be the election of the first female president of the United States, to follow the first Black president.[25] Of course, that did not happen, and like many others in positions of relative privilege, I endured the ensuing four years (the failed impeachments; racist cruelty and brutality; and economic, social, and health disasters) with an eye to making Donald Trump a one-term president. And while I was disappointed that Joe Biden's electoral victory was not larger—and especially that many down-ballot elections showed that Trumpism was far from exhausted—I approached January 6 with a kind of giddy excitement that Trump would *finally* be out of political power.

I learned from news broadcasts that January 6 would feature the hitherto-obscure process of Congress certifying the election results and that it was likely to be a sort of Alamo moment for Trumpist hardliners in the House and Senate to draw out the process in the service of political theater. I imagined myself biting my fingernails in fury or drinking too much beer (or both) while listening to speeches by Josh Hawley or Ted Cruz, so instead, I decided to go grocery shopping while listening to the proceedings on Cable-Satellite Public Affairs Network (C-SPAN) radio. On the way back, at 2:15 p.m., I heard first the Senate then the House abruptly gavel out of session as rioters, egged on by Trump, broke into the Capitol.[26]

Modernity's Corruption is a work of historical social-science, and so I cannot use its findings to predict what will become of the political forces empowered and flourishing through Trump's presidency. Yet I *do* think the framework I have proposed to think about corruption supplies some important, and hopefully generative, insights into the "general crisis in the field of power" we are now living through.[27]

A first observation is that the Universal understanding of corruption spectacularly failed to describe or restrain the activity of Trump and his underlings. Among other things, Trump's presidency offered a nauseating demonstration that many structures and procedures (privileged, white, highly educated) Americans took for granted were themselves simply conventions. For example, because the Supreme Court has progressively narrowed the legal definition of "corruption" from an *appearance* of a conflict of interest to the cumbersome demonstration of a concrete *quid pro quo*,[28] there was little recourse for those who wanted to restrain a president who simply ignored worries about conflicts of interest. During Trump's first impeachment,[29] for attempting to extort a political investigation into the son (Hunter Biden) of a political rival (Joe Biden) from the president of Ukraine in exchange for foreign aid, the managers of the impeachment consciously chose to shed other potential criteria for impeachment (like Trump's manifest violations of the Emoluments Clause of the Constitution). Instead, they focused on the narrow (and, they thought, legally and politically compelling) issue of the Ukraine call as a quid pro quo because they hoped it would have "clarity and understanding in the eyes of the American people."[30]

This move to narrow the focus of impeachment, of course, represented an effort to control the scope of the conflict over corruption and was clearly done in the hopes, if not of actually convicting Trump, of at least exacting the greatest political toll possible from him during his trial. Yet this strategy was equaled by Mitch McConnell, who controlled the Senate's schedule for the impeachment. From compressing the timeline of the trial, to whipping his Republican caucus into opposition to conviction, to successfully suppressing efforts to call witnesses, McConnell deflated and localized the conflict over Trump's corruption as much as possible.[31] These tactics, of course, produced the grotesque spectacle of Senators asleep or playing with fidget spinners during the trial,[32] and Adam Schiff delivering his closing remarks at 7:30 at night.

These tactics to localize or extend the scale of the corruption accusations against Trump, of course, did not exist in a vacuum. They were carefully calibrated to translate well beyond the cloister of Washington, DC, politics, but in narrowing their focus they ironically opened themselves to symmetrical claims of corruption that obscured Trump's uniquely disturbing behavior. After all, if what was at stake was the use of public office for private gain, is it not manifestly true that, at a minimum, Hunter Biden's appointment to the board of Burisma was clearly meant to gain access to or influence his father,[33] or that while Hillary Clinton may have obeyed the letter of conflict-of-interest laws in her speeches, she was paid an average of $210,795 per speech by the likes of Goldman Sachs before she began her run against Trump?[34] Of course, there are distinctions: Trump acted *while in office* and potentially *against U.S. foreign-policy interests*, but my point is rather that there is a reasonable case to be made that his behavior was simply a more extreme and cynical expression of a common pattern among elite politicians.[35]

Of course, Trump's presidency, by virtue of its corrupt extremes, was hardly more of the same. Indeed, it was remarkable in how it deftly exceeded the narrow confines of contemporary understandings of corruption: where some constitutional scholars hoped that an Emoluments Clause might restrain Trump, others argued that the clause was being interpreted too widely;[36] some hoped that financial regulations of and criminal probes into Trump's business empire would expose his wrongdoing, but they are still ongoing and have yet to yield decisive judgments.[37] Trump surrounded himself with a cast of grifting adventurers like Paul Manafort in a way that seemed it would surely collapse under the weight of scandal,[38] but Trump pardoned Manafort (and Steve Bannon and Roger Stone and Michael Flynn) with seemingly little consequence, and while one might expect Trump's corruption to intensify "political gravity," shortly after the 2020 election, nearly three-quarters of Republicans doubted that the election itself was "free and fair."[39]

The serial failure of these institutional anticorruption mechanisms in the face of Trump's presidency, combined with the wildly different views of who is corrupt and in which circumstances, together suggest that an era of straightforward Universal understandings of corruption may be passing. Because this book has been a study of the *emergence and institutionalization* of such a Universal understanding of corruption, the lesson to draw must only be analogical. It is common in the face of this disorder to call for a return to "first principles" to guide our understanding, but if we attempt to reconstruct a common sense of corruption, a new Universal view, we must also attend, on the one hand, to the structure of the moral backgrounds on which any understanding of corruption depends, and, on the other hand, to the risks of excluding other understandings (and thus, other people) in the process of constructing it.

NOTES

INTRODUCTION: MODERNITY'S CORRUPTION AND THE ART OF SEPARATION

1. The origin of Clive's "astonished at my own moderation" statement is obscure. In personal correspondence, the historian Mark Knights said he could not find its source, but it has been referenced extensively in the literature on Clive. The most direct citation I can find is Bence-Jones (1974, 350n24), who cites this statement and refers to "Powis Collection, Box VI, anonymous testimony to Clive." Unfortunately, because of the COVID pandemic, I have not been able to travel to Wales to verify this source.
2. A convenient source for Clive's life is the *Dictionary of National Biography* (H. V. Bowen 2008), and the most reputable of his biographies was written by Bence-Jones (1974). P. J. Marhall (1976, 236), meanwhile, reports that by 1767 Clive estimated his own fortune at over £400,000.
3. *Report from the Select Committee Appointed by the House of Commons . . . to Enquire Into the Nature, State and Condition of the East India Company and of the British Affairs in the East Indies* (1773).
4. While familiar to American readers mostly because of Spiro Agnew's reference to the "nattering nabobs of negativism," the term is a bastardization of the Hindi word *nawab* and was used as a pejorative for returned Anglo-Indians in Britain. See Nechtman (2010) and P. Lawson and Phillips (1984).

5. Clive himself used the term, and it is cited in Sutherland (1952).
6. Macaulay's famous essay on Clive (Macaulay and Scudder 1889) puzzles over this point somewhat apologetically, and more recent biographies have wondered over the structure of his psychology (for example, Harvey 1998).
7. For the sake of brevity, throughout *Modernity's Corruption* I use "EIC" or "company" to refer to the United Company of Merchants Trading to the East Indies, or the English East India Company.
8. J. E. Wilson (2007); J. E. Wilson (2011).
9. Rose-Ackerman (1999); Rose-Ackerman (1978).
10. Rothstein, B., and Torsello, D. (2014).
11. Pierce (2016).
12. Johnston (2005).
13. Abend (2014); Wuthnow (1987).
14. Most famously, modernization theory broadly argued that corruption was a phenomenon of "transitional" moments in society and would resolve as societies became more democratic and capitalist. See, for example, Hungtington (2002).
15. Muir and Gupta (2018).
16. Becker (1973); see also Adut (2008) and Adut (2004).
17. Polanyi (1944); Block and Somers (2016).
18. Taylor (2004).
19. Migdal (2001); Mitchell (1999).
20. Notably, even those procedurals and memoirs take place in front of an audience—of viewers and readers!
21. This distinction is inspired by Hirschman's classic (1997).
22. Bobonich and Destrée (2007, xv) note that *akrasia* means either "lack of knowledge" or "weakness of will" and that it reached its apotheosis in Aristotle's *Nicomachean Ethics*, book 7. Dixon (2003, esp. chaps. 1–3) analyzes the "afterlife" of the passions in the nineteenth century: They get converted into "emotions" and a "secular psychological category."
23. See the extraordinary collection of essays in Kahn, Saccamano, and Coli (2006).
24. Hirschman (1997).
25. See Heidenheimer et al. (1989) for a standard-setting compendium of social-scientific research on corruption.
26. Ryan (2013, 978).

27. See Osrecki (2017), Prasad, Martins da Silva, and Nickow (2019), and Jancsics (2014) for useful reviews.
28. Fukuyama (1992).
29. Mauro (1995).
30. Nye (1967, 459). As of this writing, the article has been cited nearly 3,000 times.
31. For example, Fisman and Golden (2017).
32. See Heidenheimer et al. (1989, introduction) for a discussion of these questions.
33. Nye (1967, 419).
34. See Chakrabarty (2000), Go (2013), Mehta (1999), G. Bhambra (2007), and G. K. Bhambra (2011), among many others.
35. From the view of *Modernity's Corruption*, Nye's concept of corruption is unworkable, but it was enormously empirical productivity. Nye yanked "corruption" from concrete political circumstances and into abstract "general linear reality" (Abbott 1988b) because he imagined doing so would yield a universal understanding of corruption's causes and consequences. Indeed, his 1967 article ends with a speculative regression table to kick-start investigation (Nye 1967, 976).
36. Scott (1972, 6).
37. Scott (1972, 7–8).
38. Scott (1972, esp. chap. 2).
39. Scott (1972, 34), emphasis added.
40. Rose-Ackerman (1999, 9) defines bribery as "payments . . . illegally made to public agents with the goal of obtaining a benefit or avoiding a cost."
41. As Julia Adams says (1999), rational-choice theory is often an excellent "first cut" at analysis!
42. Rose-Ackerman (1999, 2).
43. That is, while it is only a single chapter, "Culture" is given a whole "part" of the book!
44. Rose-Ackerman (1999, 5).
45. Rose-Ackerman (1999, 110).
46. McDonnell (2020).
47. Rothstein (2011).
48. Rothstein (2011, 13).
49. Rothstein (2011, 12–30).

50. Rothstein (2011, 14–15).
51. Rothstein (2011, 19).
52. Rothstein (2011, 19).
53. Rothstein and Torsello (2014, 265, see also 279–280).
54. See Gupta (1995), Gupta (2012), Koechlin (2013), and Harrison (1999) for excellent examples of this work.
55. Muir and Gupta (2018, S6).
56. The term was coined in de Sardan (1999).
57. In particular, along with Muir and Gupta (2018), I emphasize the importance of corruption's inevitable valence of moral judgment, and the importance of its discussion before an audience.
58. Gupta (2012).
59. Pierce (2016, 196).
60. Bourdieu (1998).
61. Emirbayer (1997); Erikson (2013); Hacking (2004); Mische (2011); Vandenberghe (1999).
62. As Rorty puts the point (1999, 47), the goal is "to replace the world pictures constructed with the aid of . . . Greek [philosophical] oppositions with a picture of a flux of continually changing relations." Or, as Mohr describes Bourdieu's approach, "objects under investigation are seen in context, as a part of a whole. Their meaningfulness is determined not by their characteristic properties, attributes, or essences of the thing itself, but rather with reference to the field of objects, practices, or activities within which they are embedded" (2013, 101–102).
63. This is the risk I have outlined above in anthropological critiques of the corruption literature's mainstream.
64. Here, I have in mind Lukes' idea (2003, 22) of "detachment" when considering questions of "justice" and the attachments required of practical ethical conduct. "Corruption" seems to me to be such a powerful concept because it inevitably bridges the two domains when invoked.
65. Particularly Jancsics (2014) and Granovetter (2007).
66. Hacking calls this approach "dynamic nominalism." See Hacking (2004).
67. Geertz (1983, 157).
68. Broadly, this style of analysis follows Levine's description of Simmel's method (1971, xxxii–xxxv). This approach is also indebted to Tavory (2011).
69. This section draws from Bargheer and Wilson (2018), Bargheer (2018), Krause (2014), and Keane (2015).

INTRODUCTION ☙ 237

70. This sense is indebted to Durkheim's sense of the dualism between "scared" and "profane," and is an example of their mutual constitution.
71. Abend (2014, table 1.1).
72. Abend (2014, chap. 1).
73. Taylor (1989, 27); see also Taylor (1985).
74. Goffman (1974); Geertz (1983); Schutz (1967).
75. In political sociology, the modern articulation of such organization has been masterfully explored by Scott (1998) and mapped onto colonial relations by Wyrtzen (2016).
76. Becker (1973).
77. Abbott (1995); Lamont and Molnár (2002).
78. Austin (1975).
79. Teachout (2016).
80. White (2008); McLean (2007).
81. Padgett and Powell (2012).
82. As we shall see, there have indeed been many such variations. In the domain of the individual, classics include Elias (2000), Greenblatt (1980), and Taylor (1989).
83. This discussion is indebted to Schattschneider (1975), as well as the discussion of incumbents and insurgents in, among others, Fligstein and McAdam (2012).
84. See, for example, Abbott (2005), Fligstein and McAdam (2012), and Bourdieu, Wacquant, and Farage (1994).
85. The term comes from Thomas Aquinas, referring broadly to the "great chain of being" supposedly linking all entities together and decreed by God. See Jerome B. Schneewind (1998, 19).
86. The classic discussion of this differentiation in sociology is Weber (1946), and my invocation of it, and especially the term "disembedding," is owed to Polanyi (1944).
87. See Barkey (2008), Adams (1994), and Adams and Charrad (2011).
88. Steinmetz (2007).
89. Chakrabarty (2000), Go (2016), and G. Bhambra (2007), among others.
90. Bourdieu (2000, 109).
91. Walzer (1984).
92. Chatterjee (1993).
93. Mehta (1999).
94. See N. H. Wilson (2011).

95. Adams, Clemens, and Orloff (2005).
96. Seeley (1891).
97. See, for instance, Pincus (2009), Brewer (1990), and Dirks (2009).
98. Corrigan and Sayer (1985), Vernon (2014), and Harling (1996), among others.
99. See Graham (n.d.), Stern (2011), Vaughn (2019), Leonard (2014), Gilding (2022), and Knights (2021).
100. See Sewell (2005, 112–113). Elsewhere in *Logics of History*, Sewell also advocates for a metaphor of "the built environment" (2005, 362–369) but I favor this paleontological analogy because it more centrally focuses on the scholar's activity.
101. Sewell (1996); Lieberson (1991); but cf. Ragin (1987).
102. See George and Bennett (2005, 222–223 and chap. 6).
103. Migdal (2001); Fligstein and McAdam (2012).
104. I here enclose both terms in scare quotes because, as we shall see, in one sense those distant spectators to EIC affairs *in India* were *deeply* interested in its affairs *in Britain*.
105. N. H. Wilson (2011).
106. Cohn (1987).
107. Gorski (2004, 28).
108. See Mayrl and Wilson (n.d.).
109. Frickel and Gross (2005); Gieryn (1983).
110. Abbott (1988b); D. Hirschman and Reed (2014).
111. Goldthorpe (2000, esp. chap. 2).

1. CORRUPTION AND MORAL ORDERS IN EIGHTEENTH-CENTURY BRITAIN AND INDIA

1. Adams (2007, chap. 6).
2. See Adams, Clemens, and Orloff (2005).
3. See Abend (2014).
4. An excellent recent effort on this front is Knights (2021), which has greatly influenced my thinking and argument later in the chapter.
5. Thus, for example, I deal with the questions of corruption in religion and philosophical debate only insofar as they figure directly into my account of moral regulation within the East India Company (EIC).

I. CORRUPTION AND MORAL ORDERS ○R 239

6. Recall also from the introduction that I am drawing a distinction between the most appropriate mode to *analyze* corruption, and *empirical* manifestations of the category. More specifically, I am trying to say that "corruption" is best analyzed contextually, but that contextual analysis can sometimes reveal (as here) people who thought that corruption expressed universals. For a parallel distinction about "modernity," see Chakrabarty (2011).
7. Johnson (1755).
8. The contemporary *Oxford English Dictionary* (OED) contains a roughly congruent list of meanings for "corruption," but adds "[p]erversion or destruction of integrity in the discharge of public duties by bribery or favour; the use or existence of corrupt practices, esp. in a state, public corporation, etc." (OED n.d.).
9. This is, of course, an old point in the sociology of culture, dating from Dukheim's emphasis on the arbitrariness of sacred symbols, running through the structural linguistics of Levi-Strauss, and recognized in Bourdieu's analysis of the meaning accorded to cultural goods. I prefer the language of relationalism though (e.g., Emirbayer 1997), because it stresses that these relations are not merely contained in symbols or our labels for things but in the concepts and qualities of the things themselves.
10. As Alan Ryan puts it, "in order to decide what is and what is not corrupt behavior, we need an antecedent view about what good behavior is like and how it comes to be corrupted" (2013, 978).
11. "Moral orders" are defined and developed by Wuthnow (1987, 14*ff*) as "a set of definitions about what is proper to do and what is reasonable to expect." My specific analysis is also deeply inspired by Abend's concept of the "moral background" (2014).
12. Throughout my discussion, I favor prepending references to the systems with an indefinite article. This is because I do not think that there is a single, definitive, coherent entity with stable boundaries constituting *the* Situational or Universal moral order. Instead, I believe that the distinction I make throughout *Modernity's Corruption* is between the central tendencies of two moral orders that shape the course of historical events in very different ways.
13. Hobbes (2009, 184), emphasis in the original.

14. If the language in this passage were modernized, it would not feel out of place in a film about urban corruption in America, like Christopher Nolan's *The Dark Knight* (2008) or one of Donald Trump's screeds against "activist judges"!
15. Schneewind (1998, 145).
16. Schneewind (1994).
17. "Nothing but consciousness can unite remote Existences into the same Person, the Identity of Substance will not do it" (Locke 2008, 216).
18. Locke (2008, 214), emphasis in the original.
19. "[I]f it be possible for the same Man to have distinct incommunicable consciousness at different times, it is past doubt the same Man would at different times make different Persons" (Locke 2008, 215).
20. Locke (2008, 215).
21. Locke (2008, 216).
22. Charles Taylor emphasizes the self's "disengagement" during his masterful analysis of Locke. See Taylor (1989, 173–176).
23. Locke (2008, 223–224).
24. The repeated encounter of cultural variation with a purportedly universal moral standard, and its long shadow on the social sciences, is something Stefan Bargheer and I have explored (2018). This tension, moreover, has been recognized as a key sign of "the failure of the Grotian project" to provide a theory of morality in terms of natural law that simultaneously defended a nonvoluntarist account of Christianity (Schneewind 1994, 222; see also Forde 2011). For a theological attempt to reconcile these paradoxes, see Rossiter (2016).
25. Locke (1693, sec. 34).
26. "[T]he great principle and foundation of all virtue and worth is placed in this, that a man is able to deny himself his own desires, cross his own inclinations, and purely follow what reason directs as best, though the appetite lean the other way" (Locke 1693, sec. 33).
27. Locke (1693, sec. 35).
28. James (1997, 2); see Dixon (2003) for a treatment of the transition between "passions" and (secular, psychologized) "emotions."
29. James (1997, 5).
30. Aristotle (2009, 28).
31. Hirschman (1997, 9).

1. CORRUPTION AND MORAL ORDERS ⚭ 241

32. Miner (2009, 59–63). The distinction between irascible and concupiscible passions is Platonic.
33. Descartes (1985, 353).
34. Machiavelli (1984, 462).
35. For many social scientists, this intellectual terrain was mapped by Hirschman (1997), who argued that greed or self-interest was adapted to a "safe" passion that could successfully dampen others that more directly threatened social order.
36. The discussion occupies all of Book VII of Aristotle (2009).
37. Aristotle (2009, 123).
38. Aristotle (2009, 132).
39. Aristotle (2009, 131).
40. See Lear (1988, 154–158) for a felicitous discussion of how this contrasts with the Kantian/Universal moral background discussed in the previous section.
41. Aristotle (2009, 182).
42. See especially the *Discourses*, book I, chap. 2. Pocock (2003) is the classic discussion of Machiavelli's wide-ranging, and sometimes subtle, influence on eighteenth-century Atlantic political thought.
43. Machiavelli (2005, 61).
44. See, for example, Fiddes (1724).
45. See Hundert (2005) for a masterful treatment of Mandeville's thought.
46. As Mandeville put it, "Thus Sagacious Moralists draw Men like Angels, in hopes that the pride at least of some will put 'em upon copying after the beautiful Originals which they are represented to be" (Mandeville 1970, 88).
47. Mandeville (1970, 337).
48. Mandeville (1970, 85).
49. Mandeville (1970, 85).
50. Mandeville (1970, 88).
51. While I am treating these as distinct axes for the sake of clarity and summary, they are of course deeply intertwined with one another. Intellectual debate was often geared toward practical cultural navigation and politics; political conflict drew from intellectual resources and cultural sensibilities; and culture is, of course, reciprocally affected by political events and intellectual developments.

52. Hayton (2002, 36); see also Pincus (2009).
53. Clark (2000, 43–66).
54. Quoted in Klein (1996, 48); see also Colley (1992, 196–204).
55. Owen (1976, 94–96).
56. Brewer (1976).
57. Bourne (1986); Brewer (1990); Kramnick (1968, chap. 3).
58. Kramnick (1968, 63–83); Langford (1992, 58–70). Langford notes that this disagreement remained within the bounds of a discourse on liberty and property; what was at stake was the *kind* of property that best secured elites' political independence and virtue.
59. Graham (2015); Brewer (1990).
60. Knights (2014).
61. Pocock (2003); on the deployment of this discourse in the American Revolution, see Wood (2009) and Bailyn and Bailyn (1992).
62. Black (1990, 48–51); Perkin (1969, 38–56).
63. Namier (1957); O'Gorman (1989); Owen (1976, chap. 5); Plumb (1967).
64. Namier (1957, 2–4); Owen (1976).
65. Porter (1990, 56).
66. For example, Edmund Burke's cousin William served briefly in India and acted as an agent in London on behalf of the Rajah of Tanjore; see Burke (1981, 5–11).
67. This patronage network reached so deep that the "massacre of the Pelhamite innocents" (an administrative purge in 1762) revealed that the Duke of Newcastle's patronage extended down to the official position of "Hawker and Pedlar," occupied by a Mr. Coates in Sussex (see Namier 1961, 408). For examples of incessant requests for patronage, see Namier (1957, 402–425).
68. Brewer (1990, 114–126).
69. Owen (1976).
70. Marshall (2005, chaps. 3–4).
71. Langford (1992, 3).
72. For these events, the three best narratives are Brewer (1976), Namier (1961), and Owen (1976, 169–234).
73. Namier (1961, 403–415).
74. Brewer (1976, 44).
75. Namier (1961, 412–413).
76. Brewer (1976, 4).

1. CORRUPTION AND MORAL ORDERS ∞ 243

77. Lord John Cavendish, quoted in Brewer (1976, 71).
78. Quoted in Brewer (1976, 93).
79. Quoted in Brewer (1976, 108).
80. Harling (1996); Rubinstein (1983); Hellmuth (1999); Corrigan and Sayer (1985, chap. 5).
81. See Thompson (1991; 1978) for key statements of this perspective.
82. See Adams (2007) and Adams and Charrad (2011).
83. See Rothschild (2011) for a magnificent biography of the whole family. See also Davidoff and Hall (1987), especially part II.
84. Klein (1989).
85. Quoted in Klein (1996, 48). See also Shaftesbury (2012).
86. This break with Locke is especially noteworthy given that Locke had been Shaftesbury's tutor and remained a correspondent.
87. Politeness and manners have been the subject of important studies in historical sociology, such as Elias (2000) and Arditi (1998).
88. Langford (1992, 71).
89. Clark (2000, 53–54, 37–42); Thompson (1991); Langford (1992, 3); but see also Wahrman (1992).
90. Carter (2001; 2002).
91. LaRouchfoucald, via Boyer, quoted in Klein (1984, 190).
92. Carter (2002, 341).
93. Stanhope (1992, 106).
94. Wahrman (2004).
95. Hirschman (1997, 32).
96. See, for example, Buchan and Hill (2014).
97. I believe this point to be in contrast to those who search for the genealogies of modern intellectual formations to their earliest possible origins. Thus, I do *not* think that the receptions of Smith, Locke, Hobbes, or any other contemporary can be easily disembedded from their intellectual contexts or read as self-evident precursors to utilitarianism, romanticism, or totalitarianism, at least not if our goal is to account for the course of contemporary historical events themselves.
98. Brewer (1976, chaps. 8–9, 11).
99. Pocock (1985, 97–99).
100. Wilson (1995).
101. Phillipson (1989, chap. 2).
102. Phillipson (1989, 29).

244 ◆ 1. CORRUPTION AND MORAL ORDERS

103. Phillipson (1989, chap. 3).
104. Phillipson (1989, 330).
105. Carter (2002, 345–346).
106. Phillipson (1983, 179).
107. Smith (2002), introduction.
108. Smith (2002, 12).
109. Smith (2002, 11); Raphael (2007, chaps. 2–3).
110. Smith (2002, 129).
111. Smith (2002, 150).
112. Smith (2002, 131).
113. Smith (2002, 169–170).
114. Smith (2002, 167–168).
115. Smith (2002, 158).
116. Phillipson (1983, 181).
117. Phillipson (1983, 198–202).

2. SHIFTING GROUNDS: THE TRANSFORMATION OF THE EAST INDIA COMPANY

1. A full review of the East India Company's (EIC) historiography is beyond the scope of this book, but see Stern (2009) for a useful review. Standard sources on the EIC's overall history include Lawson (1993) and, more recently, Wilson (2016). For excellent recent accounts of the EIC prior to its territorial expansion in the middle of the eighteenth century, Stern (2011) and Erikson (2014) excel.
2. As I discuss later in chapter 2, one key point of struggle among officials in India was what exactly the relationship among the factories and presidencies was.
3. This reference to the southern tip of Africa was no straightforward geographic reference. Like many other "composite" (Elliott 1992) authorities at the time, the reference served more as a foundation for claims making than a rigid demarcation. The company, for instance, claimed that St. Helena, in the Atlantic, was subject to the charter's provisions (Stern 2011, 42), and, as we shall see, the precise status of English "interlopers" in India was a matter of nearly permanent dispute.

2. SHIFTING GROUNDS ○ 245

4. For a detailed discussion of these matters, see especially Stern (2011, chaps. 1–2).
5. These affairs are recounted with excellent clarity in Stern (2011, chap. 7).
6. For the Glorious Revolution and its aftermath, see Pincus (2009) and the discussion in chapter 1 of this book.
7. This is an ambiguous label because it was a rallying cry not only for those who thought that trade between India and England should be thrown open to all but also for those who simply wanted the ability to purchase EIC stock (Stern 2011, 144–145).
8. This was compounded by the fact that the Scottish Parliament had chartered its own East India Company in 1695.
9. Sutherland (1952).
10. Stern (2011, 166).
11. Spear (1963, 11). "Child's War" (1686–1690), named for a powerful director of the EIC, Josiah Child, involved Mughal retaliation for company aggression in Bengal and resulted in the humiliating defeat of the EIC and yearlong siege of Bombay. Stern (2011, 37) reports Bombay's European population to be ninety when it first came under company control and 252 in 1675.
12. For a discussion of Indian intermediaries, see Neild-Basu (1984).
13. Crooke (1915 [1733], 216–218).
14. Bank of England Historical Inflation Calculator, accessed March 27, 2021.
15. For a discussion of the private trade's origins as a "pragmatic response" by EIC authorities, see Erikson (2014, 63–65). Until at least the middle of the eighteenth century, the "country trade" was explicitly tolerated by the Court of Directors.
16. After 1709, the company's executive body would be styled "the Court of Directors."
17. Alternatively, deceit and fraud or items of no value.
18. A bundle or package of goods.
19. Yule (1888, v. 2, cxvi).
20. The passage *does* seem to imply a unitary sense of moral character because it acknowledges the motivation to deceive through false attestations and the potential of enduring corruption, but as we shall see later in the chapter, struggles within the company in the era reveal this assertion to be wishful thinking.

21. Master (1911, v. 1, 202, 204).
22. The council complained of Hall: "He has Constantly, ever since his arrivall in Bengala, binn a Contemner of the Honourable Companyes Chiefs, slighting their persons, and a great Incendiary, aggravating small differences amonge their servants, endeavouring by clandestine meanes to animate and Creat factions and partyes to their disquiete" (Master 1911, v. I, 459).
23. Master (1911, v. I, 453).
24. Master (1911, v. I, 463).
25. Master (1911, v. I, 489).
26. Ogborn (2006, 141).
27. Master (1911, v. 1, 247).
28. Ovington (1929, 230–231).
29. Hedges (1887, v. II, cccvi).
30. Henry Yule commented that Master had an "evident desire to controvert the impression . . . of the irregular and heathenish habits into which the servants were supposed to fall, and . . . under this feeling he painted such matters as nearly of rose-colour as his conscience would permit" (Hedges 1887, v. II, cccv).
31. Winter had extensive Indian experience, having been an assistant at Masulipatam and a senior factor at Viravasaram (Watson 2004). Lawson identifies Winter as being from a family of "staunch Royalists" whose family had been "ruined" when "his estate was confiscated by vote of the House of Commons in 1648 . . . and it was left for Mr. [Thomas] Winter to repair its fortunes by means of the wealth that he acquired during twenty years of exile in India" (Lawson 1905, 14). Lawson guesses that Edward Winter was Thomas's brother. Leighton, moreover, declares that Winter was "personally known to Charles II" (Leighton 1902, 8).
32. Penny (1900, 24).
33. Penny (1900, 24). Leighton (1902) describes an incident in which, in order to enforce the payment of some money due to the company by an Indian broker named Bera Timana, "[Winter] erected a gallows and prepared to have him hanged. This had the desired effect, and if the action be condemned as unjustifiable, it must be remembered that in those days drastic measures were necessary towards people who

outraged the rules of society. Bera Timana was re-admitted into the Company's service, and probably lived to feel grateful for the means taken to reform his life." Leighton also notes, "Even Winter, though he recovered the money, retained it for his own use."

34. Leighton (1902, 9) describes him as "a Roundhead, as were probably many of the younger servants of the Company, for the City of London, whence they were drawn, had been solidly Parliamentarian." Foxcroft had no Indian experience at the time he sailed for Madras (Watson 2004).
35. Penny (1900, 24).
36. Penny (1900, 25).
37. Penny (1900, 25).
38. Hedges (1887, v. II, cclxvii–cclxxxi); Penny (1900, 25–26).
39. Hedges (1887, v. II, cxcix).
40. Hedges (1887, v. II, cclxxx).
41. Hedges (1887, v. II, cclxxxi).
42. Hedges (1887, v. II, cccxxv).
43. Hedges (1887, v. II, cccxxv).
44. Nightingale (1970).
45. Perlin (1985); Stein (1985).
46. Phillips (1983).
47. Peers (1995).
48. Hui (2005).
49. Dodwell (1920).
50. Gurney (1968, 1–2, 9).
51. Gurney (1968, 4).
52. Phillips (1985, 368–370).
53. Gurney (1968, 28).
54. Phillips (1985, 375*ff*).
55. Gurney (1968, 33).
56. Gurney (1968, 31–32).
57. Gurney (1968, 33).
58. Gurney (1968, 36).
59. Gurney (1968, 37).
60. Gurney (1968, 45).
61. Gurney (1968, 37–45).

62. Gurney (1968, 52).
63. Gurney (1968, 56).
64. Gurney (1968, 64).
65. Gurney (1968, 66).
66. Gurney (1968, 67–93); on Benfield, see Moles (2000).
67. Marshall (1987, 49).
68. While the annual tribute to Delhi under Murshid Kuli Khan and Shuja Khan was allegedly 10,000,000 rupees annually, an audit in 1758 showed that only 4,000,000 to 5,000,000 had been paid over the last fifteen years of Alivardi Khan's rule (Marshall 1987, 51–52).
69. Marshall (1987, 71).
70. Marshall (1987, 76).
71. Marshall (1987, 76–77).
72. Marshall (1987, 77).
73. Marshall (1987, 77–78).
74. Hill (1905, v. II, 442); Dodwell (1920, 133).
75. Hill (1905, v. II, 451–452).
76. Dodwell (1920).
77. Watts (1760, 131–132), emphasis in the original.
78. Dodwell (1920).
79. Marshall (1976, 163).
80. Marshall (1976, 164).
81. Dodwell (1920, 185); Marshall (1976, 164).
82. Marshall (1976, 166–167).
83. Marshall (1976, 165).
84. Marshall (1976, 256).
85. Marshall (1987, 87–89).
86. Sutherland (1952).
87. National Archives of India (1958, v. IV, 330–331).
88. Dodwell (1920, 186).
89. See the correspondence on July 2, 1757. Number 493 in Hill (1905, v. II, 444).
90. Watts (1760, 83, 87).
91. To John Payne. Quoted in Forrest (1918, v. II, 10).
92. Sutherland (1952, 53).
93. Verelst (1772, 56–57).
94. National Archives of India (1958, v. IV, 337).

3. CONSEQUENTIAL REFORMS AND CHANGING CORRUPTION

1. Leonard (2014).
2. See Semmel (1993).
3. National Archives of India (1958, v. 5, 268).
4. Quoted in Bowen (1991, 13).
5. I could not have navigated the intricate politics of this period without the able guidance of Sutherland (1952), Bowen (1991), and most recently the masterful Vaughn (2019).
6. Bowen (1991); Sutherland (1952).
7. Bowen (1989); Bowen (2006).
8. The data comes from the indispensable bibliography in Pickett (2011).
9. The two primary sources for this data are Philips (1961) and Bourne (1977). I take the language of incumbency and insurgency from Fligstein and McAdam (2012).
10. This was at the height of the first stock-splitting battle between the ministry and powerful shareholders for control of the directorate; see figure 3.2.
11. Bowen (1991, 55).
12. Bowen (1991, 1).
13. Bowen (1988, 51).
14. National Archives of India (1958, v. IV, 337–338).
15. Bowen (1988, 64–65).
16. Bowen (1988); Sutherland (1952).
17. Furber (1997); Kuiters (2002).
18. While I briefly overview the arguments here, I probe the exchange between Bolts and Verelst in greater depth in chapter 5.
19. Sutherland (1952, 260).
20. Sutherland (1952, 254).
21. See Sutherland (1952, 295) for the quoted descriptions.
22. Phillips (1983) and Love (1988, v. II, 82–122) are good summaries of this complicated episode. The controlling although curiously unpublished source for the Nawab's perspective is Gurney (1968), and the diaries of the Nawab's English secretary provide more perspective (Nightingale 1985). As with the confrontation between Bolts and Verelst, I return to these matters in greater detail in chapter 5.

250 • 3. CONSEQUENTIAL REFORMS

23. Burke (1981).
24. Indeed, East India servants were permitted to hold seats in Parliament while simultaneously on duty until 1830 (Philips 1961, 260, n. 4).
25. Marshall (2004a); Moles (2000). Benfield's fortunes waned, however, and he died in France hiding from his creditors.
26. Philips (1961, 36–41).
27. Dalrymple (1776, 8).
28. Dalrymple (1776, 7), emphasis in the original.
29. Dalrymple (1776, 13).
30. Dalrymple (1776, 17).
31. Dalrymple (1776, 9).
32. Dalrymple (1776, 21).
33. Critics argued that Pigot had received large gifts from the Nawab after his succession. See Marshall (2004b).
34. Love (1988, v. II, 93).
35. Dalrymple (1776, 25).
36. Marshall (1999).
37. Travers (2005).
38. Travers (2007, 106–107).
39. Quoted in Travers (2007, 108).
40. Quoted in Marshall (1976, 176).
41. Quoted in Travers (2007, 115).
42. Travers (2007, 112–115).
43. Sutherland (1952).
44. Bowyer (1995).
45. Quoted in Guha (1982, 111).
46. Quoted in Guha (1982, 111).
47. Quoted in Guha (1982, 111).
48. Parkes and Merivale (1867, v. II, 82).
49. Quoted in Parkes and Merivale (1867, v. II, 81).
50. Hastings and Macpherson (1927, 93). Correspondence dated October 15, 1781.
51. Hastings (1786, "Abstract").
52. Quoted in Impey (1846, 211–212).
53. Lawson (1895, 80).
54. *Letters of Simpkin the Second to his dear brother in Wales* in Lawson (1895, 87).

3. CONSEQUENTIAL REFORMS ↔ 251

55. Marshall (1965, 16).
56. Marshall (1965, 14).
57. Sutherland (1952, 362–364).
58. For example, in 1744, the EIC loaned the British State £1,000,000 during the War of Austrian Succession in exchange for a longer charter renewal (Sutherland 1952, 30).
59. Sutherland (1952, 18–19).
60. Lawson and Phillips (1984); Marshall (1976).
61. The term "nabob" was an Anglicization of the Urdu nawab (usually used to refer to a native prince) and became a pejorative for returning, wealthy former East India officials (Holzman 1926; Nechtman 2010; Dodwell 1926).
62. Sutherland (1952, chaps. 4–5).
63. It is especially noteworthy that, following Bowen (1989a, 192), "campaigns for the reinstatement of dismissed Company servants became a common occurrence in General Court politics . . . [as] a steady stream of discontented ex-Company servants returned to Britain from India. They all sought redress of various grievances in the General Court, and virtually all of them endeavoured to regain access to the source of the newly acquired wealth through reappointment to the Company's service."
64. Bowen (1991, chap. 8).
65. Lawson and Phillips (1984).
66. Lenman and Lawson (1983, 810–812).
67. Bowen (1991).
68. Bowen (1998, 536).
69. The political causes of these shifts are quite complex and are covered in detail by Sutherland (1952), Bowen (1991), and Philips (1961). Although the post of governor-general had existed since 1773, Pitt's act and subsequent legislation strengthened the governor-general's hold over his subsidiary presidencies.
70. "In the suds" is an idiom meaning "to be in difficulty."
71. Sutherland (1952, 60).
72. This is evident not only because writerships were openly advertised for sale but also because directors' own patronage notebooks declare the priority: David Scott was asked to nominate Samuel Martin's nephew to a cadetship "in case he should not be able to get a Bombay writership" (British Library, IOR/MSS EUR/D 1087).

73. Philips (1961, 14–16).
74. See Philips (1961, 14, n. 6).
75. See Bourne (1977, 83–108).
76. This turn in the company's patronage practice led to a so-called "Scottish school" of imperial administration. See McGilvary (2008).
77. Cohn (1987, 502). See also Cohn (1962), particularly table II on page 175, which reveals a similar breakdown of collectors and judges in the Benares district from 1795 to 1850.
78. Bourne (1986, 89).

4. MODERN SELVES

1. Kuiters (2004).
2. Phillips (1988, 82).
3. Summarized in Love (1988, v. III, 141–149), Kuiters (2004), and Rumbold (1868).
4. A Bill of Pains and Penalties was a special class of parliamentary act that allowed extraordinary prosecution for behavior that was not technically illegal but deemed morally or politically outrageous. In other words, it was a means for Parliament to retroactively legislate. Members of Parliament were concerned that prosecuting Rumbold in this way would expose them to similar prosecution for corruption and worried about the constitutional propriety of Parliament acting as both judge and jury. Moreover, Rumbold's prosecution stretched until the fall of the Rockingham ministry in 1782, and the succeeding Shelburne ministry was much closer to Laurence Sulivan and Robert Palk (a former Madras governor) and hence was less eager to pursue the prosecution. For Rumbold's fate in London after his return, see Phillips (1988).
5. Love (1988, v. III, 195).
6. See Anon (1793).
7. Sutherland (1952, 240–290).
8. Dodwell (1925, 376) describes the coalition this way: "They were a curiously mixed body of men. Some, like Pechell or Palk [long-standing Company Directors], were respectable enough; others, like Laurence Sulivan or Paul Benfield, were men whose ideas of policy were deeply coloured by financial interests of various kinds." It was especially unusual for North's ministry to ally with Sulivan because it had spent

five years (between 1773 and 1778) trying to exclude Sulivan from the Directorate (Sutherland 1952, 346).

9. Sutherland suggests elsewhere that this political coalition was brokered by none other than John Macpherson, who had "close links [with] his friend and collaborator James Macpherson (North's ablest political pamphleteer) and John Robinson [the official who was North's liaison to the treasury]" (Sutherland 1975, 526).

10. Sutherland (1975, 524).

11. For Macartney's friendship with Burke, see, for example, Barrow and Macartney (1807, 414*ff*). Burke also told Macartney that "no man wishes your success more cordially than I do" (Robbins 1908, 126).

12. See Sutherland (1975, 520). Sutherland (1975, 528) also notes that, for all his complaints about Indian corruption and oppression connected to the Nawab of Arcot's debts, Edmund Burke supported Claud Russell's candidacy, evidently because he had married one of Lord Pigot's daughters. Pigot's brother was Admiral Hugh Pigot, a prominent member of the Rockingham Whigs, with whom Burke was strongly associated.

13. As Macartney wrote to a friend prior to his departure, "Most of the [Anglo-]Indians declare against an interloper, as they term me, and are trying to form a strong opposition to my appointment" (quoted in Robbins 1908, 120).

14. Quoted in Sutherland (1975, 524–545).

15. Quoted in Barrow and Macartney (1807, 69). Both statements—as well as Barrow's own evaluation of Macartney as "totally unconnected with the contenting factions or interests of any part of Hindostan" (Barrow and Macartney 1807, 74)—are belied by how quickly Macartney became entangled with both Macpherson and Benfield, the latter of whom loaned him £6,000 in travel costs (Sutherland 1975, 527).

16. Barrow and Macartney (1807, 75–76).

17. Barrow and Macartney (1807, 46).

18. Barrow and Macartney (1807, 79–80).

19. Macartney (1950, 108).

20. Barrow and Macartney (1807, 106).

21. Barrow and Macartney (1807, 213*ff*).

22. Macartney (1950, 152).

23. Macartney (1950, 3).

24. Macartney (1950, 5).
25. Macartney (1950, 23).
26. Macartney (1950, 48–49).
27. Quoted in Barrow and Macartney (1807, 457).
28. Macartney (1950, 136).
29. Both quotes from Macartney (1950, 40).
30. To John Macpherson, in Macartney (1950, 52).
31. Macartney (1950, 10–11).
32. Macartney (1950, 52).
33. Macartney (1950, 207).
34. Barrow and Macartney (1807, 300).
35. Barrow and Macartney (1807, 582–583).
36. Love (1988, v. III, 253–257).
37. Barrow and Macartney (1807, 600).
38. Barrow and Macartney (1807, 604–605).
39. Thorne (2004).
40. Rosselli (1974); Stein (1989).
41. Wickwire and Wickwire (1980, 7).
42. Sutherland (1952, 365–414); Wickwire and Wickwire (1980, 8–11).
43. Cornwallis (1859, v. I, 543).
44. Cornwallis (1859, v. I, 290).
45. To his close friend Viscount Brome, in Cornwallis (1859, v. I, 247).
46. Cornwallis (1859, v. I, 280).
47. For example, he wrote to Charles Stuart in 1787 that "Your Friend—seems to me to have lost his own senses, or to suppose that I have completely lost the use of mine" for expecting relief Cornwallis (1859, v. I, 296).
48. Cornwallis (1859, v. I, 279).
49. Quoted in Aspinall (1931, 16, n. 1). In the same correspondence, Cornwallis described Peter Speke—"Poor Speke"—as "one of the honestest men living." This is the same Speke whom a later governor-general, Wellesley, would accuse of manipulating Wellesley's predecessor, John Shore.
50. Cornwallis (1859, v. I, 318).
51. Cornwallis (1859, v. I, 279).
52. *The Case of Sir John Macpherson, Baronet, Late Governor General of India: Containing a Summary Review of His Administration and Services* (1808).

53. Macpherson (1800).
54. British Library, IOR/F291.61.
55. Guha (198, 165).
56. Cornwallis (1859, 226).
57. Cornwallis (1859, 428).
58. Cornwallis (1859, 454).
59. deGategno (2004).
60. Macpherson (1800).
61. Travers (2007, 213).
62. deGategno (2004).
63. Misra (1959, 130).
64. Misra (1959, 130).
65. British Library, F 291.19, 1.
66. Furber (1948, 235–240).
67. Moon (1989, 232).
68. Wickwire and Wickwire (1980, 40).
69. Travers (2007, 212).
70. Misra (1959, 33).
71. Wickwire and Wickwire (1980, 43).
72. Quoted in Wickwire and Wickwire (1980, 42).
73. Marshall (1993, especially 119–120).
74. Cornwallis (1859, v. I, 243–244).
75. Cornwallis (1859, v. I, 282).
76. Bayly (1989, 148–149).
77. Travers (2007, 231).
78. Wilson (2007).
79. Quoted in Prior, Brennan, and Haines (2001, 105).

5. MODERN MORAL SPACES

1. Chatterjee (1993).
2. "The Great Disembedding" refers to Taylor (2004).
3. Marshall (1987, 75–78).
4. Marshall (1987, 85–87).
5. Bowen (2004).
6. Bolts (1772, 214).
7. Bolts (1772, v).

8. Verelst (1772, 42).
9. Verelst (1772, 56–57).
10. Bolts (1772, chap. XVI); Kuiters (2002, 261–268).
11. Bolts (1772, 191–192).
12. Bolts (1772, 217).
13. Bolts (1772, x).
14. Verelst (1772, 42).
15. Bolts (1772, viii).
16. Verelst (1772, 139).
17. Gurney (1968, 83).
18. Gurney (1968); Phillips (1985).
19. Gurney (1968, 57).
20. Goodrich (1852, 329–362).
21. Marshall (2004a); Moles (2000).
22. Philips (1961, 36–41).
23. Dalrymple (1776, 8).
24. Dalrymple (1776, 7).
25. Dalrymple (1776, 13).
26. Dalrymple (1776, 17).
27. Quoted in Dalrymple (1776, 9), emphasis in the original.
28. Quoted in Dalrymple (1776, 21).
29. Quoted in Love (1988, 93).
30. Dalrymple (1776, 25).
31. Nightingale (1985, 6–7).
32. The facts of this account, when undisputed by Boothby, are drawn from Foster (1910, 13–15).
33. Also sometimes spelled "Wylde."
34. Boothby (1644).
35. Boothby (1644).
36. Boothby (1644, 5).
37. Boothby (1644, 5–6).
38. The lack of an explicit, public, and quasi-constitutional articulation of the role of the president in factories was a sore point for many disgruntled servants; in the Declaration Boothby asks that the Commission "were at least once a year read at a publick Assembly" (Boothby 1644, 8).
39. Boothby (1644, 6–7).

5. MODERN MORAL SPACES ⚬⚬ 257

40. Boothby (1644, 2).
41. A *peshkash* was a present given to Mughal authorities by subordinates in thanks for an administrative assignment.
42. Boothby (1644, 3).
43. "Little dreaming that a brother of the Company . . . was in condition of a slave, or School-boy, that might not take lawfull recreation, or travell a little to better his experience, without leave obtained from such Imperiall Majesty" (Boothby 1644, 4–5).
44. Boothby (1644, 5).
45. Braddyll (1746).
46. In two respects, the text is also unremarkable for its time. First, like several of the vindications and apologies that would come toward the end of the eighteenth century (Brewer 1976), the actual "vindication" itself is quite short, and the bulk of the text is taken up by appendixes reprinting correspondence, council minutes, and various testimonials from participants. Second, as in other company affairs of the time (but very unlike what would happen as the eighteenth century continued), there was comparatively little distinction made between British servants of the company and Indian elites. Braddyll, for example, notes that the investigation into Lowther's wrongdoing was "corroborated too by the declaration of the Broker Jaggernaut Lolldass [*sic*]" (Braddyll 1746, 7) without any question of his veracity. The testimony of an Indian person contained in the appendix—one "Bomanjee Rustumjee"—about corrupt dealings on the Bombay council is disputed, but only in tone, with the company official in question reporting that he only "jestingly" discussed corruption with Bomanjee (Braddyll 1746, 188–190).
47. Braddyll (1746, 5).
48. Braddyll (1746, 5).
49. Braddyll (1746, 3–4).
50. Braddyll (1746, 13).
51. Braddyll (1746, 16–17).
52. Samuel Foote's *The Nabob* (Foote and Colman 1778) is one option, but it concentrates on a returned nabob's metropolitan activity (and missteps). George Paterson's diary (Nightingale 1985) also broadly corroborates the moral background portrayed in *Tom Raw*, but it was not published during Paterson's lifetime (1734–1817).
53. D'Oyly and Ackermann (1828).

54. D'Oyly and Ackermann (1828, 90).
55. D'Oyly and Ackermann (1828, 33–35).
56. D'Oyly and Ackermann (1828, 32).
57. D'Oyly and Ackermann (1828, 100).
58. Neild-Basu (1984).
59. D'Oyly and Ackermann (1828, 100–101).
60. D'Oyly and Ackermann (1828, 205).
61. D'Oyly and Ackermann (1828, 206).
62. Trevelyan (1864).
63. Trevelyan (1864, 147–150).
64. These proper names are fictional. "Moffussilpore," for example, means roughly "anywhere in the hinterland."
65. Trevelyan (1864, 130).

CONCLUSION

1. The customary division between a "first" settler-colonial British empire and a "second" empire of indirect territorial control was articulated by Seeley (1891). More recently, scholars still recognize the shift, although they articulate it with far more nuance (Marshall 2005).
2. Calhoun (1998).
3. This phrase comes from Stinchcome (1978, 19–29).
4. See, for example, Sampson (2010).
5. I have in mind, particularly, Harrison (1999), Pierce (2016), Koechlin (2013), and Muir and Gupta (2018).
6. These kinds of jurisdictional struggles are the meat of Abbott (1988a) and Bourdieu (e.g., 1998).
7. Two exemplary works along this line are McDonnell (2020) and Zaloznaya (2017).
8. Koechlin (2013).
9. De Sardan (1999).
10. This process of self-clarification was called "substantive rationalization" by Weber (1946). When the understandings are so self-evident they become the tacit logic of a domain, Bourdieu called them "doxa."
11. All of the classical sociologists recognized this dynamic, although they differentially stressed the functional reliance of these domains on one

CONCLUSION ∞ 259

another. Habermas (1991) supplies a classic study of the dynamics of the "public sphere." More recently, see Lamont and Molnár (2002) and Alexander (2006).

12. For the state, see Migdal (2001), Mitchell (1999), and Mayrl and Quinn (2016). For the economy, see, among others, Polanyi (1944), Zelizer (1994), and Quinn (2019).
13. This, of course, follows the insights of postcolonial theory, and particularly Go (2016) and Chakrabarty (2011).
14. See Adams, Clemens, and Orloff (2005) for an excellent inventory.
15. See Kroeze, Vitória, and Geltner (2018) for an excellent recent example along these lines.
16. I have been inspired here by Abbott (2001).
17. Particularly Schattschneider (1975) and Fligstein and McAdam (2012).
18. Abbott (2005).
19. Marvin Mandel, who was convicted of mail fraud and racketeering in 1977. Ronald Reagan commuted his sentence in 1981, and his conviction was overturned by the U.S. Supreme Court in 1987.
20. Season 3, Episode 2, "Mr. Lisa Goes to Washington."
21. In the 2006 and 2016 General Social Survey waves, 43 percent of respondents said that "quite a lot" or "almost all" U.S. politicians were corrupt.
22. Crane (1972).
23. Compare, by contrast, with the organized campaigns sponsored by conservative activist networks that are endured by climate scientists: https://www.scientificamerican.com/article/how-to-cope-when-activists-ask-for-climate-scientists-personal-emails/.
24. https://www.washingtonpost.com/national-security/trump-ordered-hold-on-military-aid-days-before-calling-ukrainian-president-officials-say/2019/09/23/df93a6ca-de38-11e9-8dc8-498eabc129a0_story.html.
25. Like many progressives of my generation, I thought the symbolism of Hillary Clinton's candidacy was incredibly important and that she was clearly superior to Trump simply by dint of long experience and basic competence.
26. The record of my activities is drawn from notes I took that afternoon because I was worried I would fall prey to the "Mandela effect."

27. This beautiful phrase is Sarah Quinn's, and it refers to a social upheaval so broad that it throws a host of subsidiary social settings and institutions into simultaneous crisis.
28. Teachout (2016).
29. I never thought I would have to distinguish between a first and a second impeachment for an American president!
30. Nancy Pelosi (September 25, 2019), quoted in https://www.politico.com/story/2019/09/25/trump-ukraine-memo-1510895.
31. https://www.npr.org/2020/01/31/799372257/republicans-ready-for-likely-acquittal-in-trump-impeachment-trial and https://www.cnn.com/2020/01/31/politics/mitch-mcconnell-donald-trump-senate-impeachment-trial/index.html.
32. https://www.cbsnews.com/news/trump-impeachment-trial-senators-fidget-spinners-relieve-boredom/.
33. https://www.theatlantic.com/ideas/archive/2019/09/hunter-bidens-legal-socially-acceptable-corruption/598804/.
34. https://www.cnn.com/2016/02/05/politics/hillary-clinton-bill-clinton-paid-speeches/index.html.
35. Brown, Touchton, and Whitford (2011).
36. For example, Grewal (2017).
37. https://www.nytimes.com/2021/07/01/us/politics/trump-lawsuits-investigations.html.
38. https://www.politico.com/story/2018/07/17/corruption-republicans-democrats-poll-728977.
39. https://www.politico.com/news/2020/11/09/republicans-free-fair-elections-435488?nname=politico-nightly&nid=00000170-c000-da87-af78-e185fa700000&nrid=0000014e-f10a-dd93-ad7f-f90f318e0001&nlid=2670445.

REFERENCES

Abbott, Andrew. 1988a. *The System of Professions: An Essay on the Division of Expert Labor.* Chicago: University of Chicago Press.
———. 1988b. "Transcending General Linear Reality." *Sociological Theory* 6: 169–186.
———. 1995. "Things of Boundaries." *Social Research* 62, no. 4 (1995): 857–882. https://doi.org/10.2307/40971127.
———. 2001. *Chaos of Disciplines.* Chicago: University of Chicago Press.
———. 2005. "Linked Ecologies: States and Universities as Environments for Professions." *Sociological Theory* 23, no. 3 (2005): 245–274. https://doi.org/10.2307/4148873.
Abend, Gabriel. 2014. *The Moral Background: An Inquiry into the History of Business Ethics.* Princeton, NJ: Princeton University Press.
Adams, Julia. 1994. "The Familial State: Elite Family Practices and State-Making in the Early Modern Netherlands." *Theory and Society* 23, no. 4 (1994): 505–539. https://doi.org/10.2307/657889.
———. 1999. "Culture in Rational-Choice Theories of State-Formation." In *State/Culture: State Formation After the Cultural Turn,* edited by George Steinmetz. Ithaca, NY: Cornell University Press.
———. 2007. *The Familial State.* Ithaca, NY: Cornell University Press.
Adams, Julia, and Maya Charrad. 2011. *Patrimonial Power in the Modern World.* Thousand Oaks, CA: Sage.
Adams, Julia, Elisabeth Clemens, and Ann Shola Orloff, eds. 2005. *Remaking Modernity: Politics, History, and Sociology.* Durham, NC: Duke University Press.

Adut, Ari. 2004. "Scandal as Norm Entrepreneurship Strategy: Corruption and the French Investigating Magistrates." *Theory and Society* 33, no. 5 (2004): 529–578.

———. 2008. *On Scandal: Moral Disturbances in Society, Politics and Art*. Cambridge: Cambridge University Press.

Alexander, Jeffrey C. 2006. *The Civil Sphere*. Oxford: Oxford University Press.

Arditi, Jorge. 1998. *A Genealogy of Manners: Transformations of Social Relations in France and England from the Fourteenth to the Eighteenth Century*. Chicago: University of Chicago Press.

Aristotle. 2009. *The Nicomachean Ethics*. Edited by Leslie Brown. Translated by David Ross. Oxford: Oxford University Press.

Aspinall, A. 1931. *Cornwallis in Bengal*. Manchester: Manchester University Press.

Austin, J. L. 1975. *How to Do Things with Words*. 2nd ed. Edited by J. O. Urmson and Marina Sbisà. Cambridge, MA: Harvard University Press.

Bailyn, Bernard. 1992. *The Ideological Origins of the American Revolution*. Cambridge, MA: Harvard University Press.

Bank of England Historical Inflation Calculator. https://www.bankofengland.co.uk/monetary-policy/inflation/inflation-calculator.

Bargheer, Stefan. 2018. *Moral Entanglements: Conserving Birds in Britain and Germany*. Chicago: University of Chicago Press.

Bargheer, Stefan, and Nicholas Hoover Wilson. 2018. "On the Historical Sociology of Morality: Introduction." *European Journal of Sociology /Archives Européennes de Sociologie* 59, no. 1 (2018): 1–12. https://doi.org/10.1017/S0003975618000012.

Barkey, Karen. 2008. *Empire of Difference*. Cambridge: Cambridge University Press.

Barrow, John, and George Macartney. 1807. *Some Account of the Public Life, and a Selection from the Unpublished Writings, of the Earl of Macartney*. London: T. Cadell and W. Davies.

Bayly, C. A. 1989. *Imperial Meridian: The British Empire and the World, 1780–1830*. London: Longman.

Becker, Howard Saul. 1973. *Outsiders: Studies in the Sociology of Deviance*. New York: Free Press.

Bence-Jones, Mark. 1974. *Clive of India*. London: Constable & Robinson.

Bhambra, Gurminder K. 2007. *Rethinking Modernity: Postcolonialism and the Sociological Imagination*. New York: Palgrave Macmillan.

———. 2011. "Historical Sociology, Modernity, and Postcolonial Critique." *American Historical Review* 116, no. 3 (2011): 653–662. https://doi.org/10.1086/ahr.116.3.653.

Black, Jeremy. 1990. *Robert Walpole and the Nature of Politics in Early Eighteenth-Century Britain*. Basingstoke: Macmillan Education.

Block, Fred, and Margaret R. Somers. 2016. *The Power of Market Fundamentalism: Karl Polanyi's Critique*. Reprint ed. Cambridge, MA: Harvard University Press.

Bobbin, Timothy. 1810. *The Passions, Humorously Delineated / By Timothy Bobbin, Esq., Author of the Lancashire Dialect: Containing Twenty-Five Plates, with His Portrait, Title Plate, and Poetical Descriptions*. London: J. Hayes.

Bobonich, Christopher, and Pierre Destrée, eds. 2007. *Akrasia in Greek Philosophy*. Leiden: Brill.

Bolts, William. 1772. *Considerations on India Affairs*. London: J. Almon.

Boothby, Richard. 1644. *A True Declaration of the intollerable wrongs done to Richard Boothby, Merchant of India, by two lewd servants to the honorable East India Company, Richard Wylde, and George Page. As also a remonstrance of the partiall, ingratefull and unjust proceeds of the India Court at home, against the said Richard Boothby, etc*. London: s. n.

Bourdieu, Pierre. 1998a. "Is a Disinterested Act Possible?" In *Practical Reason*, translated by Randal Johnson, 75–91. Stanford, CA: Stanford University Press.

———. 1998b. *The State Nobility: Elite Schools in the Field of Power*. Stanford, CA: Stanford University Press.

———. 2000. *Pascalian Meditations*. Translated by Richard Nice. Stanford, CA: Stanford University Press.

Bourdieu, Pierre, Loic J. D. Wacquant, and Samar Farage. 1994. "Rethinking the State: Genesis and Structure of the Bureaucratic Field." *Sociological Theory* 12, no. 1 (1994): 1–18.

Bourne, John. 1977. "The Civil and Military Patronage of the East India Company 1784–1858." PhD thesis, Leicester.

———. 1986. *Patronage and Society in Nineteenth-Century England*. London: E. Arnold.

Bowen, Huw V. 1988. "A Question of Sovereignty? The Bengal Land Revenue Issue, 1765." *Journal of Imperial and Commonwealth History* 16, no. 2 (1988): 155–176. https://doi.org/10.1080/03086538808582755.

———. 1989. "Investment and Empire in the Later Eighteenth Century: East India Stockholding, 1756–1791." *Economic History Review* 42, no. 2 (1989): 186–206. https://doi.org/10.1111/j.1468-0289.1989.tb00493.x.

———. 1991. *Revenue and Reform: The Indian Problem in British Politics, 1757–1773*. Cambridge: Cambridge University Press.

———. 1998. "British India 1765–1813: The Metropolitan Context." In *The Oxford History of the British Empire: The Eighteenth Century*, edited by Peter James Marshall, 530–531. Oxford: Oxford University Press.

———. 2004. "Bolts, William (1739–1808)." *Oxford Dictionary of National Biography*. Oxford: Oxford University Press.

———. 2006. *The Business of Empire: The East India Company and Imperial Britain, 1756–1833*. Cambridge: Cambridge University Press.

———. 2008. "Clive, Robert, First Baron Clive of Plassey (1725–1774)." *Oxford Dictionary of National Biography*. Oxford: Oxford University Press. https://doi.org/10.1093/ref:odnb/5697.

Bowyer, T. H. 1995. "Junius, Philip Francis and Parliamentary Reform." *Albion: A Quarterly Journal Concerned with British Studies* 27, no. 3 (1995): 397–418.

Braddyll, John. 1746. *The Vindication of Mr. John Braddyll, Against Mr. Henry Lowther. In a Letter Humbly Adress'd to the Honourable the Court of Directors for Affairs of the United Company of Merchants of England Trading to the East-Indies. With a Proper Appendix*. London.

Brewer, John. 1976. *Party Ideology and Popular Politics at the Accession of George III*. Cambridge: Cambridge University Press.

———. 1990. *The Sinews of Power*. Cambridge, MA: Harvard University Press.

British Library, Asia Pacific and Africa Collections, F 291.19, "Narrative of MacPherson's Reforms."

British Library, Asia Pacific and Africa Collections, IOR/F291.61, "MacPherson's Letters Relating to Fiscal Reform."

British Library, Asia Pacific and Africa Collections, IOR/MSS EUR/D 1087.

Brown, David S., Michael Touchton, and Andrew Whitford. 2011. "Political Polarization as a Constraint on Corruption: A Cross-National Comparison." *World Development* 39, no. 9 (2011): 1516–1529. https://doi.org/10.1016/j.worlddev.2011.02.006.

Buchan, B., and L. Hill. 2014. *An Intellectual History of Political Corruption. Political Corruption and Governance*. London: Palgrave Macmillan. https://doi.org/10.1057/9781137316615.

Burke, Edmund. 1981. *The Writings and Speeches of Edmund Burke: India: Madras and Bengal, 1774–1785*. Edited by P. J. Marshall. Oxford: Clarendon.

Calhoun, Craig. 1998. "Explanation in Historical Sociology: Narrative, General Theory, and Historically Specific Theory." *American Journal of Sociology* 104, no. 3 (1998): 846–871. https://doi.org/10.1086/210089.

Carter, Philip. 2001. *Men and the Emergence of Polite Society, Britain, 1660–1800*. Harlow, UK: Pearson Education.

——. 2002. "Polite 'Persons': Character, Biography and the Gentleman." *Transactions of the Royal Historical Society*, Sixth Series, no. 12 (January 2002): 333–354.

Chakrabarty, Dipesh. 2000. *Provincializing Europe: Postcolonial Thought and Historical Difference*. Princeton, NJ: Princeton University Press.

——. 2011. "The Muddle of Modernity." *American Historical Review* 116, no. 3 (2011): 663–675. https://doi.org/10.1086/ahr.116.3.663.

Chatterjee, Partha. 1993. *The Nation and Its Fragments*. Princeton, NJ: Princeton University Press.

Clark, J. 2000. *English Society, 1660–1832*. Cambridge: Cambridge University Press.

Cohn, Bernard S. 1962. "The British in Benares: A Nineteenth Century Colonial Society." *Comparative Studies in Society and History* 4, no. 2 (1962): 169–199.

——. 1987. "The Recruitment and Training of British Civil Servants in India, 1600–1860." In *An Anthropologist Among the Historians and Other Essays*, 500–553. New York: Oxford University Press.

Colley, Linda. 1992. *Britons: Forging the Nation, 1707–1837*. New Haven, CT: Yale University Press.

Cornwallis, Charles. 1859. *Correspondence of Charles, First Marquis Cornwallis*. Edited by Charles Derek Ross. London: J. Murray.

Corrigan, Philip, and Derek Sayer. 1985. *The Great Arch: English State Formation as Cultural Revolution*. Oxford: Blackwell.

Crane, Diana. 1972. *Invisible Colleges: Diffusion of Knowledge in Scientific Communities*. Chicago: University of Chicago Press.

Crooke, William, ed. 1915 [1733]. *A New Account of East India and Persia: Being Nine Years' Travels, 1672–1681. By John Fryer*. London: Hakluyt Society.

Dalrymple, Alexander. 1776. *Lord Pigot's Narrative of the Late Revolution in the Government of Madrass*. London: T. Cadell and W. Davies.

Davidoff, Leonore, and Catherine Hall. 1987. *Family Fortunes: Men and Women of the English Middle Class, 1780–1850.* Chicago: University of Chicago Press.

deGategno, Paul J. 2004. "Macpherson, Sir John, First Caronet (c. 1745–1821)." *Oxford Dictionary of National Biography.* Oxford: Oxford University Press.

De Sardan, J. P. Olivier. 1999. "A Moral Economy of Corruption in Africa?" *Journal of Modern African Studies* 37, no. 1 (1999): 25–52.

Descartes, René. 1985. "The Passions of the Soul." In *The Philosophical Writings of Descartes, Volume I,* edited by John Cottingham, Robert Stoothoff, and Dugald Murdoch, 325–404. Cambridge: Cambridge University Press. https://doi.org/10.1017/CBO9780511805042.010.

Dirks, Nicholas B. 2009. *The Scandal of Empire: India and the Creation of Imperial Britain.* Cambridge, MA: Harvard University Press.

Dixon, Thomas. 2003. *From Passions to Emotions: The Creation of a Secular Psychological Category.* Cambridge: Cambridge University Press.

Dodwell, Henry. 1920. *Dupleix and Clive: The Beginning of Empire.* London: Methuen.

———. 1925. "Warren Hastings and the Assignment of the Carnatic." *English Historical Review* 40, no. 159 (1925): 375–396.

———. 1926. *The Nabobs of Madras.* London: Williams and Norgate.

D'Oyly, Charles, and Rudolph Ackermann. 1828. *Tom Raw, the Griffin: A Burlesque Poem, in Twelve Cantos: Illustrated by Twenty-Five Engravings, Descriptive of the Adventures of a Cadet in the East India Company's Service, from the Period of His Quitting England to His Obtaining a Staff Situation in India.* London: R. Ackermann.

Elias, Norbert. 2000. *The Civilizing Process: Sociogenetic and Psychogenetic Investigations.* Rev. ed. Oxford: Blackwell.

Elliott, John H. 1992. "A Europe of Composite Monarchies." *Past & Present* 137 (1992): 48–71.

Emirbayer, Mustafa. 1997. "Manifesto for a Relational Sociology." *American Journal of Sociology* 103, no. 2 (1997): 281–317. https://doi.org/10.1086/231209.

Erikson, Emily. 2013. "Formalist and Relationalist Theory in Social Network Analysis." *Sociological Theory* 31, no. 3 (2013): 219–242. https://doi.org/10.1177/0735275113501998.

———. 2014. *Between Monopoly and Free Trade: The English East India Company, 1600–1757.* Princeton, NJ: Princeton University Press.

Fiddes, Richard. 1724. *A General Treatise of Morality, Form'd Upon the Principles of Natural Reason Only: With a Preface in Answer to Two Essays Lately Published in the Fable of the Bees* . . . London: S. Billingsley.

Fisman, Ray, and Miriam A. Golden. 2017. *Corruption: What Everyone Needs to Know*. New York: Oxford University Press.

Fligstein, Neil, and Doug McAdam. 2012. *A Theory of Fields*. Oxford: Oxford University Press.

Foote, Samuel, and George Colman. 1778. *The Nabob; a Comedy, in Three Acts. As It Is Performed at the Theatre-Royal in the Haymarket*. London: Cadell.

Forde, Steven. 2011. " 'Mixed Modes' in John Locke's Moral and Political Philosophy." *Review of Politics* 73, no. 4 (2011): 581–608.

Forrest, George. 1918. *The Life of Lord Clive*. London: Cassell.

Foster, William, ed. 1910. *The English Factories in India, 1630–1633*. Oxford: Clarendon.

Frickel, Scott, and Neil Gross. 2005. "A General Theory of Scientific/Intellectual Movements." *American Sociological Review* 70, no. 2 (2005): 204–232. https://doi.org/10.1177/000312240507000202.

Fukuyama, Francis. 1992. *The End of History and the Last Man*. New York: Free Press.

Furber, Holden. 1948. *John Company at Work: A Study of European Expansion in India in the Late Eighteenth Century*. Cambridge, MA: Harvard University Press.

———. 1997. *Private Fortunes and Company Profits in the India Trade in the 18th Century*. New York: Variorum.

Geertz, Clifford. 1983. *Local Knowledge*. New York: Basic Books.

George, Alexander, and Andrew Bennett. 2005. *Case Studies and Theory Development in the Social Sciences*. Cambridge, MA: MIT Press.

Gieryn, Thomas F. 1983. "Boundary-Work and the Demarcation of Science from Non-Science: Strains and Interests in Professional Ideologies of Scientists." *American Sociological Review* 48, no. 6 (1983): 781–795. https://doi.org/10.2307/2095325.

Gilding, Ben. 2022. " 'A New Tide of Corruption': Economical Reform and the Regulation of the East India Company, 1765–84." In *The Many Lives of Corruption*, edited by Ian Cawood and Tom Crook, 75–95. Manchester: Manchester University Press.

Go, Julian. 2013. "For a Postcolonial Sociology." *Theory and Society* 42, no. 1 (2013): 25–55. https://doi.org/10.1007/s11186-012-9184-6.

———. 2016. *Postcolonial Thought and Social Theory*. New York: Oxford University Press. https://doi.org/10.1093/acprof:oso/9780190625139.001.0001.

Goffman, Erving. 1974. *Frame Analysis: An Essay on the Organization of Experience*. New York: Harper & Row.

Goldthorpe, John H. 2000. *On Sociology: Numbers, Narratives, and the Integration of Research and Theory*. Oxford: Oxford University Press.

Gorski, Philip S. 2004. "The Poverty of Deductivism: A Constructive Realist Model of Sociological Explanation." *Sociological Methodology* 34, no. 1 (2004): 1–33. https://doi.org/10.1111/j.0081-1750.2004.00144.x.

Graham, Aaron. 2015. *Corruption, Party, and Government in Britain, 1702*. Oxford: Oxford University Press.

Granovetter, Mark. 2007. "The Social Construction of Corruption." In *On Capitalism*, edited by Victor Nee and Richard Swedberg, 152–172. Stanford, CA: Stanford University Press.

Greenblatt, Stephen. 1980. *Renaissance Self-Fashioning: From Moore to Shakespeare*. Chicago: University of Chicago Press.

Grewal, Amandeep S. 2017. "The Foreign Emoluments Clause and the Chief Executive." *Minnesota Law Review* 102 (2017): 639.

Guha, Ranajit. 1982. *A Rule of Property for Bengal*. Calcutta: Orient Blackswan.

Gupta, Akhil. 1995. "Blurred Boundaries: The Discourse of Corruption, the Culture of Politics, and the Imagined State." *American Ethnologist* 22, no. 2 (1995): 375–402.

———. 2012. *Red Tape: Bureaucracy, Structural Violence, and Poverty in India*. Durham, NC: Duke University Press.

Gurney, J. 1968. "The Debts of the Nawab of Arcot, 1763–1776." PhD thesis, Oxford University.

Habermas, Jürgen. 1991. *The Structural Transformation of the Public Sphere*. Cambridge, MA: MIT Press.

Hacking, Ian. 2004. *Historical Ontology*. Cambridge, MA: Harvard University Press.

Harling, Philip. 1996. *The Waning of 'Old Corruption': The Politics of Economical Reform in Britain, 1779–1846*. Oxford: Oxford University Press.

Harrison, Graham. 1999. "Corruption as 'Boundary Politics': The State, Democratisation, and Mozambique's Unstable Liberalisation." *Third World Quarterly* 20, no. 3 (1999): 537–550.

Harvey, Robert. 1998. *Clive: The Life and Death of a British Emperor*. New York: Macmillan.

Hastings, Warren. 1786. *Memoirs Relative to the State of India.* London: J. Murray.

Hastings, Warren, and John Macpherson. 1927. *Warren Hastings' Letters to Sir John Macpherson.* Edited by Henry Dodwell. London: Faber & Gwyer.

Hayton, David. 2002. "Contested Kingdoms, 1688–1756." In *The Eighteenth Century, 1688–1815,* edited by Paul Langford, 35–70. New York: Oxford University Press.

Hedges, William. 1887. *The Diary of William Hedges, Esq. (Afterwards Sir William Hedges), During His Agency in Bengal: As Well as on His Voyage Out and Return Overland (1681–1697).* London: Hakluyt Society.

Heidenheimer, Arnold Joseph, Michael Johnston, Victor T. Le Vine, and Victor Le Vine. 1989. *Political Corruption: A Handbook.* Piscataway, NJ: Transaction.

Hellmuth, Eckhart. 1999. "Why Does Corruption Matter? Reforms and Reform Movements in Britain and Germany in the Second Half of the Eighteenth Century." *Proceedings of the British Academy* 100 (1999): 5–24.

Hill, S. C., ed. 1905. *Bengal in 1756–1757.* Indian Records Series. London: J. Murray.

Hirschman, Albert O. 1997. *The Passions and the Interests.* Princeton, NJ: Princeton University Press.

Hirschman, Daniel, and Isaac Ariail Reed. 2014. "Formation Stories and Causality in Sociology." *Sociological Theory* 32, no. 4 (2014): 259–282. https://doi.org/10.1177/0735275114558632.

Hobbes, Thomas. 2009. *Leviathan.* Edited by J. C. A. Gaskin. Reissue ed. Oxford: Oxford University Press.

Holzman, James Mayer. 1926. *The Nabobs in England: A Study of the Returned Anglo-Indian, 1760–1785.* New York: Columbia University Press.

Hui, Victoria Tin-bor. 2005. *War and State Formation in Ancient China and Early Modern Europe.* New York: Cambridge University Press.

Hundert, E. J. 2005. *The Enlightenment's Fable: Bernard Mandeville and the Discovery of Society.* Cambridge: Cambridge University Press.

Huntington, Samuel P. 2002. "Modernization and Corruption." In *Political Corruption: Concepts & Contexts,* edited by Arnold J. Heidenheimer and Michael Johnston, 253–264. Piscataway, NJ: Transaction.

Impey, Elijah Barwell. 1846. *Memoirs of Sir Elijah Impey: Knt., First Chief Justice of the Supreme Court of Judicature, at Fort William, Bengal; with Anecdotes of Warren Hastings, Sir Philip Francis, Nathaniel Brassey Halhed, Esq., and Other Contemporaries; Comp. from Authentic Documents, in Refutation of the Calumnies of the Right Hon. Thomas Babington Macaulay.* London: Simpkin, Marshall.

James, Susan. 1997. *Passion and Action: The Emotions in Seventeenth-Century Philosophy.* Oxford: Clarendon.

Jancsics, David. 2014. "Interdisciplinary Perspectives on Corruption." *Sociology Compass* 8, no. 4 (2014): 358–372.

Johnson, Samuel. 1755. *A Dictionary of the English Language.* London: W. Strahan.

Johnston, Michael. 2005. *Syndromes of Corruption: Wealth, Power, and Democracy.* Cambridge: Cambridge University Press.

Kahn, Victoria, Neil Saccamano, and Daniela Coli, eds. (2006). *Politics and the Passions, 1500–1850.* Princeton, NJ: Princeton University Press.

Keane, Webb. 2015. *Ethical Life: Its Natural and Social Histories.* Princeton, NJ: Princeton University Press.

Klein, Lawrence E. 1984. "The Third Earl of Shaftesbury and the Progress of Politeness." *Eighteenth-Century Studies* 18, no. 2 (1984): 186–214. https://doi.org/10.2307/2738536.

———. 1989. "Liberty, Manners, and Politeness in Early Eighteenth-Century England." *Historical Journal* 32, no. 3 (1989): 583–605.

———. 1996. "Coffeehouse Civility, 1660–1714: An Aspect of Post-Courtly Culture in England." *Huntington Library Quarterly* 59, no. 1 (1996): 31–51.

Knights, Mark. 2014. "Samuel Pepys and Corruption." *Parliamentary History* 33, no. 1 (2014): 19–35. https://doi.org/10.1111/1750-0206.12087.

———. 2021. *Trust and Distrust: Corruption in Office in Britain and Its Empire, 1600–1850.* Oxford: Oxford University Press.

Koechlin, Lucy. 2013. *Corruption as an Empty Signifier: Politics and Political Order in Africa.* Leiden: Brill.

Kramnick, Isaac. 1968. *Bolingbroke and His Circle.* Cambridge, MA: Harvard University Press.

Krause, Monika. 2014. *The Good Project: Humanitarian Relief NGOs and the Fragmentation of Reason.* Chicago: University of Chicago Press.

Kroeze, Ronald, André Vitória, and Guy Geltner. 2018. *Anticorruption in History: From Antiquity to the Modern Era.* Oxford: Oxford University Press.

Kuiters, Willem G. J. 2002. *The British in Bengal, 1756–1773: A Society in Transition Seen Through the Biography of a Rebel: William Bolts (1739–1808).* Paris: Indes savantes.

———. 2004. "Rumbold, Sir Thomas, First Baronet (1736)." *Oxford Dictionary of National Biography*. Oxford: Oxford University Press.

Lamont, Michèle, and Virág Molnár. 2002. "The Study of Boundaries in the Social Sciences." *Annual Review of Sociology* 28, no. 1 (2002): 167–195. https://doi.org/10.1146/annurev.soc.28.110601.141107.

Langford, Paul. 1992. *A Polite and Commercial People: England, 1727–1783*. Oxford: Oxford University Press.

Lawson, Charles. 1895. *The Private Life of Warren Hastings: First Governor-General of India*. London: S. Sonnenschein.

———. 1905. *Memories of Madras*. London: S. Sonnenschein.

Lawson, Philip. 1993. *The East India Company: A History*. New York: Longman.

Lawson, Philip, and Jim Phillips. 1984. " 'Our Execrable Banditti': Perceptions of Nabobs in Mid-Eighteenth Century Britain." *Albion: A Quarterly Journal Concerned with British Studies* 16, no. 3 (1984): 225–241. https://doi.org/10.2307/4048755.

Lear, Jonathan. 1988. *Aristotle: The Desire to Understand*. Cambridge: Cambridge University Press.

Leighton, David. 1902. *Vicissitudes of Fort St. George*. Madras: A. Combridge.

Lenman, Bruce, and Philip Lawson. 1983. "Robert Clive, the 'Black Jagir', and British Politics." *Historical Journal* 26, no. 4 (1983): 801–829.

Leonard, Spencer. 2014. " 'A Theatre of Disputes': The East India Company Election of 1764 as the Founding of British India." *Journal of Imperial and Commonwealth History* 42, no. 4 (2014): 593–624.

Lieberson, Stanley. 1991. "Small N's and Big Conclusions: An Examination of the Reasoning in Comparative Studies Based on a Small Number of Cases." *Social Forces* 70, no. 2 (1991): 307–320. https://doi.org/10.1093/sf/70.2.307.

Locke, John. 2008. *An Essay Concerning Human Understanding*. Oxford: Oxford University Press.

Locke, John. 1693. *Some Thoughts Concerning Education*. London: A. and J. Churchill.

Love, Henry D. 1988. *Vestiges of Old Madras: Traced from the East India Company's Records Preserved at Fort St. George and the India Office, and from Other Sources*. Madras: Mittal.

Lukes, Steven. 2003. *Liberals and Cannibals: The Implications of Diversity*. London: Verso.

Macartney, George. 1950. *The Private Correspondence of Lord Macartney, Governor of Madras (1781–85)*. London: Offices of the Royal Historical Society.

Macaulay, Thomas Babington, and Vida Dutton Scudder. 1889. *Macaulay's Essay on Lord Clive*. The Students' Series of English Classics. Boston: Leach, Shewell, & Sanborn.

Machiavelli, Niccolò. 1984. *The Discourses*. London: Penguin Classics.

Machiavelli, Niccolò. 2005. *The Prince*. Oxford: Oxford University Press.

Macpherson, John. 1800. *Documents Explanatory of the Case of Sir John Macpherson, Baronet, as Governor General of Bengal*. London: W. Bulmer.

Mandeville, Bernard. 1970. *The Fable of the Bees*. New York: Penguin.

Marshall, P. J. 1965. *The Impeachment of Warren Hastings*. London: Oxford University Press.

———. 1976. *East Indian Fortunes*. Oxford: Clarendon.

———. 1987. *Bengal, the British Bridgehead: Eastern India, 1740–1828*. Cambridge: Cambridge University Press.

———. 1999. "The Making of an Imperial Icon: The Case of Warren Hastings." *Journal of Imperial and Commonwealth History* 27, no. 3 (1965): 1–16.

———. 2004a. "Benfield, Paul (1741–1810)." *Oxford Dictionary of National Biography*. Oxford: Oxford University Press.

———. 2004b. "Pigot, George, Baron Pigot (1719–1777)." *Oxford Dictionary of National Biography*. Oxford: Oxford University Press.

———. 2005. *The Making and Unmaking of Empires*. Oxford: Oxford University Press.

Master, Streynsham. 1911. *The Diaries of Streynsham Master, 1675–1680, and Other Contemporary Papers Relating Thereto*. Edited by Richard Carnac Temple. London: J. Murray.

Mauro, Paolo. 1995. "Corruption and Growth." *Quarterly Journal of Economics* 110, no. 3 (1995): 681–712.

Mayrl, Damon, and Sarah Quinn. 2016. "Defining the State from Within: Boundaries, Schemas, and Associational Policymaking." *Sociological Theory* 34, no. 1 (2016): 1–26. https://doi.org/10.1177/0735275116632557.

Mayrl, Damon, and Nicholas Hoover Wilson, eds. N.d. *Comparison After Positivism*. Manuscript.

McDonnell, Erin Metz. 2020. *Patchwork Leviathan: Pockets of Bureaucratic Effectiveness in Developing States*. Princeton, NJ: Princeton University Press.

McGilvary, George. 2008. *East India Patronage and the British State: The Scottish Elite and Politics in the Eighteenth Century*. London: Tauris Academic Studies.

McLean, Paul D. 2007. *The Art of the Network: Strategic Interaction and Patronage in Renaissance Florence*. Politics, History, and Culture. Durham, NC: Duke University Press.

Mehta, Uday Singh. 1999. *Liberalism and Empire: A Study in Nineteenth-Century British Liberal Thought*. Chicago: University of Chicago Press.

Migdal, Joel S. 2001. *State in Society*. Cambridge: Cambridge University Press.

Miner, Robert. 2009. *Thomas Aquinas on the Passions: A Study of Summa Theologiae*. Cambridge: Cambridge University Press.

Mische, Ann. 2011. "Relational Sociology, Culture and Agency." In *The SAGE Handbook of Social Network Analysis*, edited by John Scott and Peter J. Carrington, 80–97. London: Sage.

Misra, B. B. 1959. *The Central Administration of the East India Company, 1773–1834*. Manchester: Manchester University Press.

Mitchell, Timothy. 1999. "Society, Economy, and the State Effect." In *State/Culture: State Formation After the Cultural Turn*, edited by George Steinmetz, 76–97. Ithaca, NY: Cornell University Press.

Mohr, John W. 2013. "Bourdieu's Relational Method in Theory and in Practice: From Fields and Capitals to Networks and Institutions (and Back Again)." In *Applying Relational Sociology*, edited by Francois Depelteau and Christopher Powell, 101–135. New York: Palgrave Macmillan.

Moles, David. 2000. "An Able and Skilful Artist: The Career of Paul Benfield of the English East India Company." PhD thesis, Oxford University.

Muir, Sarah, and Akhil Gupta. 2018. "Rethinking the Anthropology of Corruption: An Introduction to Supplement 18." *Current Anthropology* 59, no. S18 (2018): S4–S15. https://doi.org/10.1086/696161.

Namier, L. 1957. *The Structure of Politics at the Accession of George III*. 2nd ed. London: Macmillan.

———. 1961. *England in the Age of the American Revolution*. 2nd ed. London: Macmillan.

National Archives of India. 1958. *Fort William-India House Correspondence and Other Contemporary Papers Relating Thereto*. Delhi: National Archives of India.

Nechtman, Tillman. 2010. *Nabobs: Empire and Identity in Eighteenth-Century Britain*. Cambridge: Cambridge University Press.

Neild-Basu, Susan. 1984. "The Dubashes of Madras." *Modern Asian Studies* 18, no. 1 (1984): 1–31. https://doi.org/10.1017/S0026749X00011203.

Nightingale, Pamela. 1970. *Trade and Empire in Western India 1784–1806*. Cambridge: Cambridge University Press.

———. 1985. *Fortune and Integrity*. Oxford: Oxford University Press.

Nye, J. S. 1967. "Corruption and Political Development: A Cost-Benefit Analysis." *American Political Science Review* 61, no. 2 (1967): 417–427.

Ogborn, Miles. 2006. "Streynsham Master's Office: Accounting for Collectivity, Order and Authority in 17th-Century India." *Cultural Geographies* 13, no. 1 (2006): 127–155.

O'Gorman, Frank. 1989. *Voters, Patrons, and Parties: The Unreformed Electoral System of Hanoverian England 1734–1832*. Oxford: Clarendon.

Osrecki, Fran. 2017. "A Short History of the Sociology of Corruption: The Demise of Counter-Intuitivity and the Rise of Numerical Comparisons." *American Sociologist* 48, no. 1 (2017): 103–125.

Ovington J. 1929. *A Voyage to Surat in the Year 1689*. London: Jacob Tonson.

Owen, John. 1976. *The Eighteenth Century, 1714–1815*. New York: Norton.

Oxford English Dictionary (OED). N.d. "Corruption," accessed December 16, 2020. https://www.oed.com/dictionary/corruption.

Padgett, John F., and Walter W. Powell. 2012. *The Emergence of Organizations and Markets*. Princeton, NJ: Princeton University Press.

Parkes, Joseph, and Herman Merivale. 1867. *Memoirs of Sir Philip Francis, K.C.B.: With Correspondence and Journals*. London: Longman.

Peers, Douglas M. 1995. *Between Mars and Mammon: Colonial Armies and the Garrison State in India, 1819–1835*. London: Tauris Academic Studies.

Penny, Fanny Emily. 1900. *Fort St. George, Madras*. Madras: S. Sonnenschein.

Perkin, Harold. 1969. *The Origins of Modern English Society 1780–1880*. London: Routledge & K. Paul.

Perlin, F. 1985. "State Formation Reconsidered." *Modern Asian Studies* 19, no. 3 (1985): 415–480.

Philips, Cyril Henry. 1961. *The East India Company: 1784–1834*. Manchester: Manchester University Press.

Phillips, Jim. 1983. "The Development of British Authority in Southern India: The Nawab of Arcot, the East India Company, and the British Government, 1775–1785." PhD thesis, Dalhousie University.

———. 1985. "A Successor to the Moguls: The Nawab of the Garnatic and the East India Company, 1763." *International History Review* 7, no. 3 (1985): 364–389. https://doi.org/10.1080/07075332.1985.9640384.

———. 1988. "Parliament and Southern India, 1781: The Secret Committee of Inquiry and the Prosecution of Sir Thomas Rumbold." *Parliamentary History* 7, no. 1 (1988): 81–97. https://doi.org/10.1111/j.1750-0206.1988.tb00542.x.

Phillipson, N. 1983. "Adam Smith as Civic Moralist." In *Wealth and Virtue: The Shaping of Political Economy in the Scottish Enlightenment*, edited by Istvan Hont and Michael Ignatieff, 179–202. Cambridge: Cambridge University Press.

———. 1989. *Hume*. New York: St. Martin's Press.

Pickett, Catherine. 2011. *Bibliography of the East India*. Annotated ed. London: British Library Publishing.

Pierce, Steven. 2016. *Moral Economies of Corruption: State Formation and Political Culture in Nigeria*. Durham, NC: Duke University Press.

Pincus, Steven. 2009. *1688: The First Modern Revolution*. New Haven, CT: Yale University Press.

Plumb, J. 1967. *The Growth of Political Stability in England: 1675–1725*. London: Macmillan.

Pocock, J. G. A. 1985. "The Varieties of Whiggism from Exclusion to Reform: A History of Ideology and Discourse." In *Virtue, Commerce, and History*, 215–310. Cambridge: Cambridge University Press.

———. 2003. *The Machiavellian Moment*. Princeton, NJ: Princeton University Press.

Polanyi, Karl. 1944. *The Great Transformation*. New York: Beacon.

Porter, Roy. 1990. *English Society in the Eighteenth Century*. Rev. ed. London: Penguin.

Prasad, Monica, Mariana Borges Martins da Silva, and Andre Nickow. 2019. "Approaches to Corruption: A Synthesis of the Scholarship." *Studies in Comparative International Development* 54, no. 1 (2019): 96–132.

Prior, Katherine, Lance Brennan, and Robin Haines. 2001. "Bad Language: The Role of English, Persian and Other Esoteric Tongues in the Dismissal of Sir Edward Colebrooke as Resident of Delhi in 1829." *Modern Asian Studies* 35, no. 1 (2001): 75–112. https://doi.org/doi:10.1017/S0026749X01003614.

Quinn, Sarah L. 2019. *American Bonds*. Princeton, NJ: Princeton University Press.

Ragin, Charles C. 1987. *The Comparative Method: Moving Beyond Qualitative and Quantitative Strategies*. Berkeley: University of California Press.

Raphael, David. 2007. *The Impartial Spectator: Adam Smith's Moral Philosophy*. Oxford: Clarendon.

Report from the Select Committee Appointed by the House of Commons . . . To Enquire into the Nature, State and Condition of the East India Company and of the British Affairs in the East Indies. 1773. London: T. Evans.

Robbins, Helen Henrietta Macartney. 1908. *Our First Ambassador to China: An Account of the Life of George, Earl of Macartney, with Extracts from His Letters, and the Narrative of His Experiences in China, as Told by Himself, 1737–1806, from Hitherto Unpublished Correspondence and Documents*. New York: E.P. Dutton.

Rorty, Richard. 1999. *Philosophy and Social Hope*. New York: Penguin.

Rose-Ackerman, Susan. 1978. *Corruption: A Study in Political Economy*. New York: Academic Press.

———. 1999. *Corruption and Government: Causes, Consequences, and Reform*. Cambridge: Cambridge University Press.

Rosselli, John. 1974. *Lord William Bentinck: The Making of a Liberal Imperialist, 1774–1839*. Berkeley: University of California Press.

Rossiter, Elliot. 2016. "Hedonism and Natural Law in Locke's Moral Philosophy." *Journal of the History of Philosophy* 54, no. 2 (2016): 203–225.

Rothschild, Emma. 2011. *The Inner Life of Empires: An Eighteenth-Century History*. Princeton, NJ: Princeton University Press.

Rothstein, Bo. 2011. *The Quality of Government: Corruption, Social Trust, and Inequality in International Perspective*. Chicago: University of Chicago Press.

Rothstein, B., and D. Torsello. 2014. "Bribery in Preindustrial Societies: Understanding the Universalism-Particularism Puzzle." *Journal of Anthropological Research* 70, no. 2 (2014): 263–284.

Rubinstein, W. D. 1983. "The End of 'Old Corruption' in Britain 1780–1860." *Past & Present*, no. 101 (1983): 55–86.

Rumbold, Elizabeth Ann. 1868. *A Vindication of the Character and Administration of Sir Thomas Rumbold, Bart., Governor of Madras . . . From the Misrepresentations of Colonel Wilks, Mr. Mill, and Other Historians . . . Including an Examination of Mr. Hastings Relations with Sir Thomas Rumbold*. London: Longmans, Green, Reader, and Dyer.

Ryan, Alan. 2013. "Conceptions of Corruption, Its Causes, and Its Cure." *Social Research* 80, no. 4 (2013): 977–992.

Sampson, Steven. 2010. "The Anti-Corruption Industry: From Movement to Institution." *Global Crime* 11, no. 2 (2010): 261–278.

Schattschneider, Elmer Eric. 1975. *The Semisovereign People*. New York: Dryden.
Schneewind, Jerome B. 1994. "Locke's Moral Philosophy." In *The Cambridge Companion to Locke*, edited by Vere Chappell, 199–225. Cambridge: Cambridge University Press.
———. 1998. *The Invention of Autonomy*. Cambridge: Cambridge University Press.
Schutz, Alfred. 1967. *Phenomenology of the Social World*. Translated by George Walsh and Fredrick Lehnert. Evanston, IL: Northwestern University Press.
Scott, James C. 1972. *Comparative Political Corruption*. Englewood Cliffs, NJ: Prentice-Hall.
———. 1998. *Seeing Like a State: How Certain Schemes to Improve the Human Condition Have Failed*. New Haven, CT: Yale University Press.
Seeley, Sir John Robert. 1891. *The Expansion of England: Two Courses of Lectures*. New York: Macmillan.
Semmel, Bernard. 1993. *The Liberal Ideal and the Demons of Empire: Theories of Imperialism from Adam Smith to Lenin*. Baltimore, MD: Johns Hopkins University Press.
Sewell, William H. Jr. 2005. *Logics of History: Social Theory and Social Transformation*. Chicago: University of Chicago Press.
———. 1996. "Three Temporalities: Towards an Eventful Sociology." In *The Historic Turn in the Human Sciences*, edited by Terrence J. McDonald, 245–280. Ann Arbor: University of Michigan Press.
Shaftesbury, Lord. 2012. *Characteristics of Men, Manners, Opinions, Times*. Cambridge: Cambridge University Press.
Simmel, Georg. 1971. *On Individuality and Social Forms*. Chicago: University of Chicago Press.
Smith, Adam. 2002. *The Theory of Moral Sentiments*. Cambridge: Cambridge University Press.
Spear, Percival. 1963. *The Nabobs*. Oxford: Oxford University Press.
Stanhope, Philip Dormer. 1992. *Lord Chesterfield's Letters*. Oxford: Oxford University Press.
Stein, B. 1985. "State Formation and Economy Reconsidered." *Modern Asian Studies* 19, no. 3 (1985): 387–413.
Stein, Burton. 1989. *Thomas Munro: The Origins of the Colonial State and His Vision of Empire*. New York: Oxford University Press.

Steinmetz, George. 2007. *The Devil's Handwriting*. Chicago: University of Chicago Press.

Stern, Philip J. 2009. "History and Historiography of the English East India Company: Past, Present, and Future!" *History Compass* 7, no. 4 (2009): 1146–1180. https://doi.org/10.1111/j.1478-0542.2009.00617.x.

———. 2011. *The Company-State: Corporate Sovereignty and the Early Modern Foundations of the British Empire in India*. Oxford: Oxford University Press.

Stinchcombe, Arthur L. 1978. *Theoretical Methods in Social History*. New York: Academic Press.

Sutherland, Lucy S. 1952. *The East India Company in Eighteenth-Century Politics*. London: Hyperion.

———. 1975. "Lord Macartney's Appointment as Governor of Madras, 1780: The Treasury in East India Company Elections." *English Historical Review* 90, no. 356 (1975): 523–535.

Tavory, Iddo. 2011. "The Question of Moral Action: A Formalist Position." *Sociological Theory* 29, no. 4 (2011): 272–293. https://doi.org/10.1111/j.1467-9558.2011.01400.x.

Taylor, Charles. 1985. *Human Agency and Language*. Cambridge: Cambridge University Press.

———. 1989. *Sources of the Self: The Making of the Modern Identity*. Cambridge, MA: Harvard University Press.

———. 2004. *Modern Social Imaginaries*. Durham, NC: Duke University Press.

Teachout, Zephyr. 2016. *Corruption in America: From Benjamin Franklin's Snuff Box to Citizens United*. Cambridge, MA: Harvard University Press.

The Case of Sir John Macpherson, Baronet, Late Governor General of India: Containing a Summary Review of His Administration and Services. 1808. London: W. Bulmer.

Thompson, Edward Palmer. 1978. "Eighteenth-Century English Society: Class Struggle Without Class?" *Social History* 3, no. 2 (1978): 133–165.

———. 1991. *Customs in Common*. New York: New Press.

Thorne, Roland. 2004. "Macartney, George, Earl Macartney (1737)." *Oxford Dictionary of National Biography*. Oxford: Oxford University Press.

Travers, Robert. 2005. "Ideology and British Expansion in Bengal, 1757–72." *Journal of Imperial & Commonwealth History* 33, no. 1 (2005): 7–27.

———. 2007. *Ideology and Empire in Eighteenth Century India: The British in Bengal*. New York: Cambridge University Press.

Trevelyan, Sir George Otto. 1864. *The Competition Wallah*. New York: Macmillan.

Vandenberghe, Frédéric. 1999. " 'The Real Is Relational': An Epistemological Analysis of Pierre Bourdieu's Generative Structuralism." *Sociological Theory* 17, no. 1 (1999): 32–67. https://doi.org/10.1111/0735-2751.00064.

Vaughn, James M. 2019. *The Politics of Empire at the Accession of George III*. New Haven, CT: Yale University Press.

Verelst, Harry. 1772. *A View of the Rise, Progress, and Present State of the English Government in Bengal: Including a Reply to the Misrepresentations of Mr. Bolts, and Other Writers*. London: J. Nourse.

Vernon, James. 2014. *Distant Strangers: How Britain Became Modern*. Berkeley: University of California Press.

Wahrman, Dror. 1992. "National Society, Communal Culture: An Argument About the Recent Historiography of Eighteenth-Century Britain." *Social History* 17, no. 1 (1992): 43–72. https://doi.org/10.1080/03071029208567822.

———. 2004. *The Making of the Modern Self: Identity and Culture in Eighteenth-Century England*. New Haven, CT: Yale University Press.

Walzer, Michael. 1983. *Spheres of Justice: A Defense of Pluralism and Equality*. New York: Basic Books.

———. 1984. "Liberalism and the Art of Separation." *Political Theory* 12, no. 3 (1984): 315–330.

Watson, I. B. 2004. "Winter, Sir Edward (1621/2)." *Oxford Dictionary of National Biography*. Oxford: Oxford University Press.

Watts, William. 1760. *Memoirs of the Revolution in Bengal Anno. Dom. 1757, By Which Meer Jaffeir Was Raised to the Government of That Province, Together with Those of Bahar and Orixa. Including the Motives to This Enterprize; the Method in Which It Was Accomplished; and the Benefits That Have Accrued from Thence to That Country, Our United Company Trading to the East Indies, and to the British Nation*. London: A. Millar.

Weber, Max. 1946. "Religious Rejections of the World and Their Directions." In *From Max Weber*, edited by H. H. Gerth and C. Wright Mills, 323–359. New York: Oxford University Press.

White, Harrison. 2008. *Identity and Control: How Social Formations Emerge*. 2nd ed. Princeton, NJ: Princeton University Press.

Wickwire, Franklin B., and Mary Wickwire. 1980. *Cornwallis, the Imperial Years*. Chapel Hill: University of North Carolina Press.

Wilson, Jon E. 2007. "Anxieties of Distance: Codification in Early Colonial Bengal." *Modern Intellectual History* 4, no. 1 (2007): 7–23. https://doi.org/10.1017/S1479244306001016.

———. 2011. *The Domination of Strangers*. London: Palgrave Macmillan.

———. 2016. *The Chaos of Empire: The British Raj and the Conquest of India*. New York: PublicAffairs.

Wilson, Kathleen. 1995. "Citizenship, Empire, and Modernity in the English Provinces, c. 1720–1790." *Eighteenth-Century Studies* 29, no. 1 (1995): 69–96.

Wilson, Nicholas Hoover. 2011. "From Reflection to Refraction: State Administration in British India, Circa 1770." *American Journal of Sociology* 116, no. 5 (2011): 1437–1477. https://doi.org/10.1086/657562.

Wood, Gordon S. 2009. *Empire of Liberty*. New York: Oxford University Press.

Wuthnow, Robert. 1987. *Meaning and Moral Order: Explorations in Cultural Analysis*. Berkeley: University of California Press.

Wyrtzen, Jonathan. 2016. *Making Morocco: Colonial Intervention and the Politics of Identity*. Ithaca, NY: Cornell University Press.

Yule, Henry. 1888. *The Diary of William Hedges*. 3 Volumes. London: Hakluyt Society.

Zaloznaya, Marina. 2017. *The Politics of Bureaucratic Corruption in Post-Transitional Eastern Europe*. Cambridge: Cambridge University Press.

Zelizer, Viviana A. 1994. *The Social Meaning of Money*. New York: Basic Books.

INDEX

Abend, Gabriel, 24, 239n11
abstraction: accusations involving, 25–26, 28; localization disembedded by, 5; situational moral order oriented by, 29
accusations, 4, 186, 201; abstraction involved in, 25–26, 28; among administrators, 5–6; audience presumed by, 7, 23–24, 27; behaviors contrasted with, 23; corruption as style of, 218, 222–223; escalation motivating, 27–28; moral backgrounds demonstrated by, 81; situational moral order deployed in, 98; universal moral order assumed by, 9
action, corruption defined by, 49
acts, corruption defined by, 9, 17
Adams, Julia, 45, 235n 41
Addison, Joseph, 68
administration, EIC, 29; in Bengal, 117, 126–127, 134–135, 162–163, 184; Bolts questioning, 180; Clive overseeing, 2; Cornwallis on, 163–164; corruption of, 191–192; Court of Directors appointing, 135–136, 140–141; economic exchange stabilizing, 172; governors balancing, 151; of Hastings, 128–130; India Act impacting, 142; Indians excluded from, 174; S. Khan consolidating, 107; in Madras, 96, 103, 146–159; "massacre of the Pelhamite innocents" purging, 65; moral backgrounds influencing, 212–213; moral orders influencing, 30; "Scottish school" of, 252n76; territorialization confusing, 181–182. *See also* councils; Court of Directors
administrators, EIC, 107, 189, 251n72; accusations among, 5–6; corruption contextualized by, 225; language of, 5, 36; moral backgrounds of, 35–36, 196–197; organizing of, 170–171; unitary moral biography relied on by, 5.

administrators (*continued*)
  See also governor-general;
  governors; officials; presidents;
  servants
Africa, charter referencing, 85, 244n3
Agnew, Spiro, 233n4
akrasia (lack of impulse control), 8, 234n22
Ali, Hyder, 147, 155
ambiguity, in defining corruption, 206–211
Amending Act (1786), 173
Anglo-Indians, ambiguity and, 207–208
Anglo-Mysore War (1780), 188
Aquinas, Thomas, 8, 57, 237n85
Arcot, Nawab of. *See* Khan al-Walajah, Muhammad Ali
Aristotle (philosopher), 8, 56–58, 234n22
army, EIC, 105–106; under Clive, 109, 177; country trade backed by, 118; Indian rulers influenced by, 101–102; *Tom Raw* depicting, 207
audience, 234n20; accusations presuming, 7, 23–24, 27; corruption before, 236n57; distance of, 30–31, 42; localization and, 224–225
Augustine (theologian), 57
Aurangzeb (emperor), 99, 107
"*Avarice & Dissipation*" (Bobbin), 71, 72

backgrounds, moral. *See* moral backgrounds
Bargheer, Stefan, 240n24

Barrow, John, 151, 253n15
Barwell, Richard, 127
Bay of Bengal. *See* Bengal, India
behavioral conformity, individual liberty contrasted with, 69
behaviors, 70, 75–76; accusations contrasted with, 23; corruption demonstrated through, 9–14, 16, 20–22, 220; judgments severed from, 13–14; Locke on, 52–53; moral regulation changing, 145; passions controlling, 154; universal moral order justifying, 43
Bence-Jones, Mark, 233n1–2
Benfield, Paul, 155–156, 189–190, 250n25; Burke against, 191; debts managed by, 102, 106
Bengal, India, 112–115, 128–129, 131–132, 160–161, 165–170; administration in, 117, 126–127, 134–135, 162–163, 184; Board of Trade of, 163; Bolts in, 176–187; Britain in, 109–110; Calcutta in, 84, 109, 116, 127, 130; Clavell in, 92; Madras contrasted with, 87, 164; Mughal Empire possessing, 107; social order of, 184–186; Supreme Council in, 130. *See also* Mir Jafar (Nawab of Bengal)
Bengal Council, EIC, 169; Clive contrasted with, 112–115; destabilization of, 111–112; Mir Jafar overthrown by, 110; presents dividing, 178; Verelst questioning, 180–181
Biden, Hunter, 230

INDEX 283

Biden, Joe, 228
Bill of Pains and Penalties, Parliament considering, 252n4
biography: accountability for, 56; accusation and, 26–27, 218; unitary moral, 5
"Black Hole of Calcutta" (prison), 109
Board of Control, EIC, 139, 141, 143, 162
"Board of Controul, or, the Blessings of a Scotch Dictator, The" (cartoon), 139, *140*
Board of Trade, Bengal, 163
Board of Trade, EIC, 173
Bobbin, Tim (pseudonym), 71, *71*
Bobonich, Christopher, 234n22
Bolst, Willem, 178
Bolts, William, 127, 165, 170–171, 185; administration questioned by, 180; in Bengal, 176–187; on EIC, 182–183; market prioritized by, 183–184; G. Pigot contrasted with, 192; servants exemplified by, 186–187; Verelst contrasted with, 126, 179–183
Bombay, India, 84, 87–88, 99, 203, 245n11
bonds, interest-bearing, 105–106
Boothby, Richard, 197, 200–202
Bourdieu, Pierre, 236n62, 239n9, 258n10
Bourne, John, 141
Braddyll, John, 202–206, 212, 257n46
bribery, 16; corruption reduced to, 15; in preindustrial societies, 19; presents contrasted with, 2

Britain, 33, 42, 166–167; in Bengal, 109–110; debts of, 125; *diwani* sought by, 125–126; EIC and, 32, 118–128, 137–138, 148, 251n58; Glorious Revolution in, 61–62, 85, 123, 245n6; House of Commons Select Committee of, 111; Indians interested in, 238n104; Khan al-Walajah assisted by, 103–105; Madras influencing, 190–191; moral backgrounds in, 41; moral orders impacting, 61; officials condemned in, 208–209. *See also* England; Parliament; Scotland
British, Indians contrasted with, 184–186, 210–211
British elites, 64, 69–70, 142; politeness emphasized by, 68; property of, 242n58; self-presentation of, 61–62, 66; social class and, 67
British Empire: EIC and, 3, 83, 217; eighteenth-century, 31–34; first contrasted with second, 32, 258n1. *See also* India
British studies, 33–34
Burke, Edmund, 139, 242n66, 253n11; against Benfield, 191; opposition party structure championed by, 66; Russell supporting, 253n12

Calcutta, Bengal, India, 84, 109, 116, 127, 130
Cape of Good Hope, Africa, 85, 244n3
Carnatic, India, 106, 187

Cartwright, Nancy, 39–40
Catholics, 62
causal inference, positivism emphasizing, 39
Charles II (King), 84
charter, EIC, 84, *138*, 251n58; Africa referenced by, 85, 244n3; Elizabeth granting, 83; renewal of, 85–86, 135, 146
Chatham, earl of, 125
Chennai, India, 84
Chesterfield (Lord), 70
Child, Josiah, 245n11
Child's War, 87, 99, 245n11
citizen, servants contrasted with, 195
Citizens United (U.S. Supreme Court case), 26
"civic republicanism," language of, 63
Civil War, in England, 62
Clavell, Walter, 92–93
Clavering, John, 127
Clinton, Hillary, 230, 259n25
Clive, Robert, 1, 3, 36, 233n1–2; administration overseen by, 2; army under, 109, 177; Bengal Council contrasted with, 112–115; on *diwani*, 116–117; Dudley instructing, 120; *jagir* possessed by, 2, 107, 111, 121–122; Macaulay on, 234n6
Cohn, Bernard S., 38, 141
Colebrooke, Edward, 175
Colebrooke, Henry, 175
Collier, John, 71, *71*
Committees, Court of (EIC), 93
company. *See* English East India Company

"Company's Commandments," of EIC, 94–95
Comparative Political Corruption (Scott), 12
Competition Wallah, The (Trevelyan), 37, 212
conflict, escalation of. *See* escalation, of conflict
conformity, liberty contrasted with, 69
consciousness, Locke on, 51–52, 240n19
Considerations on Indian Affairs (Bolts), 126, 179
Constitution (U.S.), Emoluments Clause of, 229
constitutionalist language, framing corruption, 193–194
Cooper, Anthony Ashley (earl of Shaftesbury), 59, 62, 68–69, 79, 243n86
Coote, Eyre, 152–155
Cornwallis, Charles, 143, 170–171, 175; on administration, 163–164; in England, 160; John Macpherson contrasted with, 37, 160–170, 173–174; servants resisting, 161–162; Speke described by, 254n49
corruption. *See specific topics*
Corruption (Rose-Ackerman), 15
Corruption and Government (Rose-Ackerman), 15–16
councils, EIC: of Bengal, 110–115, 169, 178, 180–181; of Madras, 189–190; Supreme, 127, 130; at Surat, 197–198
country trade, 172, 189; army backing, 118; bonds contrasted

INDEX ⚜ 285

with, 106; Court of Directors tolerating, 245n15; officials seeking, 89, 188
Court, General (EIC). *See* General Court
Court of Committees, EIC, 93
Court of Directors, EIC, 2, 116–117, 132, 157, 162, 245n16; administration appointed by, 135–136, 140–141; Braddyll appealing to, 202; country trade tolerated by, 245n15; debts concerning, 106; *diwani* influencing, 120; Master empowered by, 91–92; officials appealing to, 95–96; Parliament influencing, 123–125, *124*; presents known to, 112; situational moral order demonstrated by, 91
Court of Madras, 147
Court of Proprietors, EIC, 148
Cowan, Robert, 203
cultural conflict, corruption as source of, 67–72, *71*
culture, Rose-Ackerman on, 51–52

Daula, Siraj-ud-, 108–109, 177
debts, 111; Benfield managing, 102, 106; of Britain, 125; Court of Directors concerned with, 106; of Khan al-Walajah, 105–106, 170, 187–196; military paid for with, 101–103, 106, 108
Deccan Plateau, India, 99–101
Delhi, annual tribute to, 248n68
democracy, post-colonial states transitioning to, 10

Descartes, René, 57
desires, virtue as denial of, 240n26
Destrée, Pierre, 234n22
Dictionary of National Biography (Bence-Jones and Marhall), 233n2
Dictionary of the English Language, A (S. Johnson), 47, *48*
Directors, Court of. *See* Court of Directors
Discourses on Livy (Machiavelli), 58, 241n42
dividends, of EIC, *121*
Diwan (administrative post), 107
diwani (right to territorial revenues): Britain seeking, 125–126; Clive on, 116–117; Court of Directors influenced by, 120; EIC granted, 112
Dixon, Thomas, 234n22, 240n28
Dodwell, Henry, 252n8
"doxa," Bourdieu on, 258n10
D'Oyly, Charles, 37, 206–212, *207*
Dudley, George, 120
Durlabh, Rai, 110
Dundas, Henry, 139, 141, 163
"dynamic nominalism," Hacking on, 236n66

East India bill (proposed legislation), 160, 161
East India Company, English. *See* English East India Company
East India Company, Scottish, 245n8
"East India Reformers, or, New Ways & Means" (cartoon), *138*

286   INDEX

education: Locke centralizing, 55; passions regulated by, 58; in politeness, 70
EIC. *See* English East India Company
elections, U.S., 228, 231
elites. *See* British elites; Indian elites
Elizabeth (Queen), 83
embedded, corruption as, 4–5, 14, 23, 45–49, 204, 206, 220–221
Emoluments Clause, of U.S. Constitution, 229, 230
emotions, passions contrasted with, 240n28
England: Civil War in, 62; Cornwallis in, 160; fiscal crisis in, 126; India influenced by, 98; Macartney returning to, 159; Rumbold returning to, 147; Whigs controlling, 135
English, French in conflict with, 100–101
English East India Company (EIC), 33, 46, 168, 185, 221; archival record of, 38; Board of Control of, 139, 141, 143, 162; Board of Trade of, 173; Bolts on, 182–183; Britain and, 32, 118–128, 137–138, 148, 251n58; British Empire and, 3, 83, 217; "Company's Commandments," 94–95; corruption within, 34–35; Court of Committees of, 93; Court of Proprietors, 148; distance influencing, 37, 42; dividends of, *121*; *diwani* granted to, 112; General Court of, 119, 198–199, 251n63; historiography, 244n1; India pressuring, 42; Madras council of, 189–190; Mir J. paying, 109; moral order in, 86–98; moral regulation in, 83, 238n5; Mughal Empire impacting, 99–100, 245n11; "New," 86; oath of allegiance to, 90; organizational insulation of, 83–86; Parliament influencing, 125, 136–137; patronage of, 135–136, 139–143, 252n76; process tracing of, 36–37; publications discussing, 122–123, *123*; reforms in, 143–144; shareholders influencing, 121, 126; situational moral order influencing, 99, 118; stock transfers of, *122*; in Tanjore, 106, trade by, 84–85; transition impacting, 1–2, 34, 82, 99. *See also* administration; administrators; army; Bengal Council; charter; councils; Court of Directors; factories; governor-general; governors; officials; presidents; servants
English Supreme Court (Calcutta), governor-general compromised by, 130
Enlightenment (age), 73–74, 80
escalation, of conflict: accusations motivated by, 27–28; localization contrasted with, 223–224; by officials, 95
Essay Concerning Human Understanding (Locke), 51, 53–54

European merchant empires, Indian rulers chartering, 100
experiences: direct, 51, 74, 82–83; Hume emphasizing, 74–75; judgments influenced by, 51, 53; memories contrasted with, 52

Fable of the Bees (Mandeville), 59
factories, EIC: at Fort St. George, 89; presidents organizing, 87; servants restricted to, 130; social structure of, 87–88
family, individual contrasted with, 68
Farley, Joseph, 98
firmans. *See* imperial decrees
"first-order" effects, of corruption, 220
Foote, Samuel, 257n52
Fort St. George, India, 84, 89, 92
Foxcroft, George, 96–98, 247n34
Foxcroft, Nathaniel, 96, 98
Fox-North, Charles James, 137–139, *138*, 160
fractal, corruption as, 222–225
France, India contrasted with, 13
Francis, Philip, 127, 130–135
French, English in conflict with, 100–101
Fryer, John, 87

Gary, Henry, 98
Geertz, Clifford, 23
General Court, EIC, 119, 198–199, 251n63
generalizations, Pierce on, 20–21
General Social Survey, on corruption, 259n21

George III (King), 64–65, 160
Glorious Revolution (1688), 61–62, 85, 123, 245n6
Gorski, Philip S., 38
governor-general, EIC: authority of, 171; English Supreme Court compromising, 130; Hastings as, 127–128; John Macpherney as, 172; presidents controlled by, 251n69; Supreme Council overseen by, 127
governors, EIC: administration balanced by, 151; authority of, 192–195; Board of Control appointed by, 143; India Act and, *142*; of Madras, 187. *See also* presidents
Gupta, Akhil, 20, 236n57
Gurney, J., 249n22

Habermas, Jürgen, 258n11
Hacking, Ian, 236n66
Hall, Joseph, 92–93, 246n22
Hastings, Warren, 3, 134–135, 152, 190; administration of, 128–130; Francis opposing, 130–135; as governor-general, 127–128; judgments by, 129; Macartney questioning, 153–154; politeness of, 131–132
Hindu landholders (*Zamindars*), 108
Hindu vassals, Muslim rulers contrasted with, 100
Hirschman, Daniel, 241n35
Hobbes, Thomas, 50, 243n97
Horne, John, 203–204

House of Commons Select Committee, Britain, 111
Hume, David, 74–75, 79–80

impartiality, Rothstein on, 17–18
impartial spectator, 78; Macartney compared with, 150–151; politeness contrasted with, 80; Smith on, 75–76; universal moral order characterizing, 79
impeachments, of Trump, 229–230, 260n29
imperial decrees (*firmans*), 84
imperialism, modernity as concurrent with, 32
imperial official (*Mansabdar*), 111
impulse control, lack of, 8, 234n22
inams. See presents
India, 123–124, *124*; Bombay in, 84, 87–88, 99, 203, 245n11; Calcutta in, 84, 116, 127, 130; Carnatic in, 106, 187; Chennai in, 84; Deccan Plateau in, 99–101; EIC pressured by, 42; England influencing, 98; fiscal-military competition in, 100–103; Fort St. George in, 84; France contrasted with, 13; Gupta studying, 20; land revenues in, 102–103, 129–130, 188–189; Macartney not knowing, 150; situational moral order dominating, 82; social order in, 212–213. *See also* Bengal, India; English East India Company; Madras; Tanjore
India Act (1784), 119, 134–138, 140; administration impacted by, 142;

Board of Control established by, 139; governors and, *142*; Pitt tempering, 161
India Bill, by Fox-North, 138–139
"India Directors in the Suds, The" (cartoon), *137*
Indian elites, 108; D'Oyly characterizing, 210–211; servants contrasted with, 257n46; Trevelyan on, 214
Indian rulers: army influencing, 101–102; conflicts between, 103; European merchant empires chartered by, 100; succession of, 101, 105, 107–108, 110–111. *See also* Khan al-Walajah, Muhammad Ali; Mughal Empire
Indians: administration excluding, 174; Anglo-, 207–208; Britain interesting, 238n104; British contrasted with, 184–186, 210–211 individual, family contrasted with, 68 individual liberty, behavioral conformity contrasted with, 69 intellectual debate, influences on, 241n51

Jacobitism, 62–64, 74
jagir (annuity), Clive possessing, 2, 107, 111, 121–122
James, Susan, 240n28
James II (King), 62, 85
January 6, 2021 (insurrection), 228
Jearsey, William, 97
Johnson, Samuel, 47, *48*
judgments: behaviors severed from, 13–14; corruption enabling, 23;

experiences influencing, 51, 53; by Hastings, 129; on propriety of action, 77–78; sympathy and, 76. *See also* moral judgments
judicial precedent, structure of, 50
justice, Lukes on, 236n64

Khan, Alivardi, 108, 177, 248n68
Khan, Murshid Kuli, 107, 248n68
Khan, Shuja, 248n68
Khan al-Walajah, Muhammad Ali (Nawab of Arcot), 101, 104, 249n22; Britain assisting, 103–105; debts of, 105–106, 170, 187–196; Tanjore received by, 189–190; territorial revenues withheld by, 188–189
Knights, Mark, 233n1
Kramnick, Isaac, 242n58

land revenues, in India, 102–103, 129–130, 188–189
Langford, Paul, 242n58
Langhorne, William, 93
language, of corruption, 239n9; of administrators, 5, 36; of "civic republicanism," 63; as constitutionalist, 192–194; of liberty and property, 62; modernity demonstrated by, 5, 36, 217; passions referenced by, 98
Lawson, Charles, 244n1, 246n31
Lear, Jonathan, 241n40
Leighton, David, 247n34
Leviathan (Hobbes), 50
liberty, conformity contrasted with, 69

localization, 230; abstraction disembedding, 5; audience and, 224–225; corruption viewed through, 226–227; escalation contrasted with, 223–224
Locke, John, 243n97; on behaviors, 52–53; on consciousness, 51–52, 240n19; education centralized by, 55; Shaftesbury contrasted with, 243n86
Logics of History (Sewell), 238n100
Love, Henry D., 249n22
Lowther, Henry, 202–206
Lukes, Steven, 236n64
luxury, corruption associated with, 63

Macartney, George, 143, 146–148, 253n11, 253n13, 253n15; Coote and, 152–155; England returned to by, 159; Hastings questioned by, 153–154; impartial spectator compared with, 150–151; India not known to, 150; private and public roles distinguished by, 156–159; Rumbold compared with, 149; Stuart opposed by, 157
Macaulay, Thomas Babington, 234n6
Machiavelli, Niccolò, 8, 57–59, 241n42
Macpherson, James, 132, 253n9
Macpherson, John, 157, 171, 175, 189, 253n9; Cornwallis contrasted with, 37, 160–170, 173–174; as governor-general, 172; reforms proposed by, 165–168

Madras, India, 99–102, 104–107, 189, 193–196; administration in, 96, 103, 146–159; Bengal contrasted with, 87, 164; Britain influenced by, 190–191; Court of, 147; governors of, 187, 188; revolution in, 191–192; servants in, 102
Madras council, EIC, 189–190
Manafort, Paul, 231
Mandel, Marvin, 259n19
Mandeville, Bernard, 8, 59–60, 73, 79, 80, 241n46
Mansabdar. *See* imperial official
Maratha Empire, 99
Marhall, P.J., 233n2
market, state contrasted with, 183–184, 186
Marshall, P. J., 111
Martin, Claude, 102
Martin, Samuel, 251n72
Maryland (U.S. state), corruption in, 226
"massacre of the Pelhamite innocents" (administrative purge), 63, 242n67
Master, Streynsham: on "Company's Commandments," 94–95; Court of Committees endorsing, 93; Court of Directors empowering, 91–92; Yule on, 246n30
McConnell, Mitch, 229–230
Memoirs of the Revolution in Bengal (Watts), 113
memories, experiences contrasted with, 52
military, debts paying for, 101–103, 106, 108

Miner, Robert, 241n32
Mir Jafar (Nawab of Bengal), 177–178, 180–181; Bengal Council overthrowing, 110; EIC paid by, 109; presents from, 111, 114
Mir Qasim (Nawab of Bengal), 110, 112, 178, 180–181
Misra, B. B., 172
modernity. *See specific topics*
Mohr, John W., 236n62
moneylenders (*sarkars*), 105
Monson, George, 127
Montaigne, Michel de, 8
moral backgrounds, 257n52; Abend on, 24, 239n11; accusations demonstrating, 81; administration influenced by, 212–213; of administrators, 35–36, 196–197; in Britain, 41
moral character, unitary sense of, 245n20
moral judgments: civic republicanism influencing, 63; as contextual, 204–205; corruption invoking, 6–7; origin of, 51; Scott on, 14; standards of, 53–54
moral orders, 49–60; administration influenced by, 30; Britain impacted by, 61; in EIC, 86–98; Wuthnow defining, 239n11. *See also* situational moral order; universal moral order
moral regulation, 43, 45; behaviors changed by, 145; in EIC, 83; within EIC, 238n5; through politeness, 94

Mughal Empire, 84, 108, 128, 188; Bengal possessed by, 107; EIC impacted by, 99–100, 245n11; succession in, 118–119; Vijayanagar dynasty resisting, 187
Muir, Sarah, 236n57
Muslim rulers, Hindu vassals contrasted with, 100

nabob (perjorative), 119, 233n4, 251n61
Nabob, The (Foote), 257n52
Namjh, Siraj-ud-, 110
nawabs. *See specific nawabs*
Nepean, Evan, 143
Newcastle, duke of, 65, 242n67
New York (U.S. state), corruption regulated in, 226–227
Nicomachean Ethics (Aristotle), 57, 234n22
Nigeria, corruption in, 20–21
Nizam (administrative post), 107
nomological machine, Cartwright on, 39–40
North (Lord), 134–135, 148, 160, 191, 252n8
Nye, Joseph: corruption defined by, 10–11, 235n35; Rose-Ackerman compared with, 15–17; Scott contrasted with, 12–14

oath of allegiance, EIC, 90
OED. *See Oxford English Dictionary*
officials, EIC, 90, 111; agency of, 193; Britain condemning, 208–209; country trade sought by, 89, 188; Court of Directors appealed to by, 95; escalation by, 95; presents received by, 102, 106, 136; presidents struggled with by, 244n2; renumeration for, 88–89; rights of, 199; self-presentation of, 43; universal moral order separating, 214–215
oppositions, relations contrasted with, 236n62
orders, moral. *See* moral orders
Ovington, John, 93–94
Oxford English Dictionary (OED), corruption defined by, 239n8

Page, George, 197, 200–201
Parliament, British, 2, 85–86; Bill of Pains and Penalties considered by, 252n4; Court of Directors influenced by, 123–125, *124*; EIC influenced by, 125, 136–137; patronage beyond, 64; Rumbold prosecuted by, 148, 252n4; Scottish, 245n8; Select Committee of, 134; servants in, 250n24
passions, 7, 60, 133–134; behaviors controlled by, 154; education regulating, 58; emotions contrasted with, 240n28; Hirschman on, 241n35; language referencing, 98; Miner on, 241n32; the self overwhelmed by, 8; situational moral order guided by, 56–58
Passions, Humorously Delineated, The (Bobbin), *71*, 71–72

Paterson, George, 102, 257n52
patrimonial hierarchy, corruption as deviation from, 116
patronage, 21, 196; of EIC, 135–136, 139–143, *142*, 252n76; of Newcastle, 242n67; beyond Parliament, 64; of Pitt, 66–67; of Scotland, 139, 141; social order greasing, 73–74; Whigs lacking, 65–66
Pelham, Henry, 65
"Pelhamite innocents, massacre of the" (administrative purge), 63, 242n67
Penny, Fanny Emily, 246n33
peshkash (type of present), 257n41
Phillips, Jim, 249n22
Pierce, Steven, 20–21
Pigot, George, 170, 196, 250n33, 253n12; Bolts contrasted with, 192; Madras council against, 189–190; presents received by, 188; Stuart against, 192–195
Pigot, Hugh, 253n12
Pitt, William, 66–67, 119, 134–140, 160–161, 251n69
Plassey, battle of, 1, 109–111, 177–179
Polanyi, Karl, 237n86
politeness, 73, 243n87; British elites emphasizing, 68; Cooper on, 68–69; education in, 70; of Hastings, 131–132; impartial spectator contrasted with, 80; moral regulation through, 94
political conflict, corruption as source of, 61–67

politicians, corruption associated with, 259n21
positivism, causal inference emphasized by, 39
post-colonial states, democracy transitioned to by, 10
preindustrial societies, bribes in, 19
presents (*inams*), 110, 257n41; Bengal Council divided by, 178; bribery contrasted with, 2; Court of Directors knowing of, 112; from Mir J., 111, 114–115; officials receiving, 102, 106, 136; G. Pigot receiving, 188
presidents, EIC, 93, *142*; factories organized around, 87; governor-general controlling, 251n69; officials struggling with, 244n2; servants contrasted with, 256n38. *See also specific presidents*
Prince, The (Machiavelli), 58
principles, of state, 133
private interests, public duty contrasted with, 9
Proprietors, Court of (EIC), 148
the public, Macartney protecting, 157
publications, discussing EIC, 122–123, *123*
public duty, private interests contrasted with, 9
"public sphere," Habermas on, 258n11
public table, Ovington on, 93–94

Quality of Government (Rothstein), 17
Quinn, Sarah, 260n27

rational-choice theory, 14–15, 235n41
Reagan, Ronald, 259n19
Regulating Act (1773), 127, 128, 146, 191
regulation, moral. *See* moral regulation
relational theory, of corruption, 22–24
relations, oppositions contrasted with, 236n62
Reza Khan, Muhammad, 129
Rhetoric (Aristotle), 57
Robinson, John, 253n9
Rockingham, marquis of, 65–66, 125, 160, 252n4
Rorty, Richard, 236n62
Rose-Ackerman, Susan, 15–17
Rothstein, Bo, 17–18, 19
rulers, Indian. *See* Indian rulers
Rumbold, Thomas: England returned to by, 147; Macartney compared with, 149; Parliament prosecuting, 148, 252n4
Russell, Claud, 253n12
Rustumjee, Bomanjee, 257n46
Ryan, Alan, 9, 239n10

Sadlier, Anthony, 155, 157
St. Thome, battle of, 101
sarkars. *See* moneylenders
scalar, corruption as, 222–225
Schiff, Adam, 230
scholarship, corruption narrowed by, 4, 15
Scotland, 64, 74–75, 80, 139, 141, 245n8
Scott, David, 141, 251n72

Scott, James C., 12–14, 16, 237n75
Scottish enlightenment, 74–75, 80
Scottish Parliament, 245n8
Seeley, John Robert, 258n1
Select of State (*Zubdat ul Mulk*), 111
the self: consciousness contrasted with, 51–52; passions overwhelming, 8; Taylor emphasizing, 240n22
self-presentation, 68, 176; of British elites, 61–62, 66; governing and, 59; of officials, 43; universal moral order influencing, 145
Sepoy Rebellion (1857), 212
servants, EIC: Bolts exemplifying, 186–187; citizen contrasted with, 195; Cornwallis resisted by, 161–162; factories restricting, 130; General Court campaigned by, 251n63; gentry aspired to by, 141–142; Indian elites contrasted with, 257n46; Lowther misguiding, 205–206; in Madras, 102; motivation of, 213; in Parliament, 250n24; presidents contrasted with, 256n38; rights of, 166–167; situational moral order exemplified by, 198–199; in Tanjore, 192. *See also* officials
Seths, Jagat, 109
Seven Years' War, 64, 109
Sewell, William, 34, 238n100
Shaftesbury, earl of. *See* Cooper, Anthony Ashley
Shah Alam (emperor), 112, 125
shareholders, EIC influenced by, 121, 126

Shelburne (Lord), 160
situational moral order, *29*, 59, 93–95, 122, 203–206, 219–221; abstraction orienting, 29; accusations deploying, 98; Boothby demonstrating, 197, 200; Court of Directors demonstrated by, 91; EIC influenced by, 99, 118; India dominated by, 82; *The Passions, Humorously Delineated* suggesting, 72; passions guiding, 56–58; servants exemplifying, 198–199; universal contrasted with, 30, 57, 60, 71–72, 81–82, 201–202, 218, 224, 227, 239n12
Smith, Adam, 77, 150, 243n97; on the impartial spectator, 75–76; within Scottish enlightenment, 80; on socialization, 78–79
social change, corruption and, 10–22
social class, British elites and, 67
socialization, Smith on, 78–79
social order, 195; anxieties over, 62–63; of Bengal, 184–186; corruption supplying, 215; the Enlightenment impacting, 73–74; in India, 212–213; patronage greased by, 73–74; sources of, 182; state creating, 185; universal moral order influencing, 31
social sciences, 4, 10, 19, 34, 46–47, 219; historical, 2, 31–32, 37, 39–41; universal moral order influencing, 240n24
sociology, on corruption, 22, 237n86, 239n9

Some Thoughts Concerning Education (Locke), 55
spectator, impartial. *See* impartial spectator
Speke, Peter, 254n49
"Spheres of Justice" (Walzer), 18
standards, of moral judgments, 53–54
state: market contrasted with, 183–184, 186; principles of, 133; social orders created by, 185; Verelst emphasizing, 184–186, 191
Steele, Richard, 68
Stern, Philip J., 244n1
stock transfers, EIC, *122*
Stratton, George, 189
Stuart, James, 190; Coote replaced by, 155; Macartney opposing, 157; against G. Pigot, 192–195
"substantive rationalization," Weber on, 258n10
Sulivan, Laurence, 121, 124–125, 146, 148, 252n8
Sultan, Tipu, 101
Supreme Council, in Bengal, 130
Supreme Council, in Calcutta, 127
Supreme Court, English (Calcutta), 130
Supreme Court, U.S., 26, 229
Surat, Council at, 197–198
Sutherland, Lucy S., 253n9
sympathy, judgments and, 76–77

Tamil Nadu, India. *See* Carnatic, India
Tanjore, India: EIC in, 106; Khan al-Walajah receiving, 189–190; servants in, 192

taxes, consolidation caused by, 62–63
Taylor, Charles, 25, 240n22
territorialization, administration confused by, 181–182
territorial revenues, 188–189. *See also* diwani
Theory of Moral Sentiments (Smith), 75–76, 79
Timana, Bera, 246n33
timing, and modernity, 222
Tom Raw (D'Oyly), 37, 206–212, 207, 257n52
"Tom Raw Presents Letters of Introduction" (D'Oyly), 207
Tories (British political party), 62, 65
Torsello, Davide, 19
trade, country. *See* country trade
Travers, Robert, 175
Trevelyan, George, M., 37, 175, 212–215
"True Alarm, The" (pamphlet), 180
"True Declaration of the Intolerable Wrongs Done to Richard Boothby by Two Lewd Servants, A" (Boothby), 198
Trump, Donald, 228, 240n14; Clinton contrasted with, 259n25; on corruption, 227; impeachments of, 229–230, 260n29; universal moral order not restraining, 229, 231
Trumpism, corruption and, 227–231

unitary moral biography, administrators relying on, 5
United Company of Merchants Trading to the East Indies. *See* English East India Company
United States (U.S.): elections in, 228, 231; Maryland in, 226; New York in, 226–227; Supreme Court of, 26, 229
universal moral order, 11, 15, 29, 47, 55–56, 241n40; accusations assuming, 9; behaviors justified by, 43; corruption expressing, 239n6; impartial spectator characterized by, 79; modernity reflected in, 49–50, 219–221; officials separated by, 214–215; reforms embracing, 43–44; self-presentation influenced by, 145; situational contrasted with, 30, 57, 60, 71–72, 81–82, 201–202, 218, 221, 224, 227, 239n12; social sciences influenced by, 240n24; spaces detangled in, 176; Trump not restrained by, 229, 231
U.S. *See* United States

Vansittart, Henry, 112
Verelst, Harry, 116, 171; Bengal Council questioned by, 180–181; Bolts contrasted with, 126, 179–183; state emphasized by, 184–186, 191
View of the Rise, Progress, and Present State of the English Government in Bengal, A (Verelst), 126, 179
Vijayanagar dynasty, Mughal Empire resisted by, 187
"Vindication" (Braddyll), 202, 204–205, 212, 257n46
virtue, as denial of desires, 240n26

Walpole, Robert, 74
War of Austrian Succession
  (1740–1744), 100, 251n58
Watts, William, 110, 113
Wealth of Nations, The (Smith), 76
Weber, Max, 237n86, 258n10
Western standards, of corruption,
  11–12, 19–20
Whigs (British political party), 62,
  68; England controlled by, 135;
  patronage lacking, 65–66; political
  order controlled by, 63–64
Whitehill, John, 148
Wilde, Richard, 197, 200, 201

William of Orange (King), 85
Wilson, Nicholas Hoover, 240n24
Winter, Edward, 96–98, 246n31,
  246n33
Winter, Thomas, 246n31
writership (administrative position),
  189, 251n72
Wuthnow, Robert, 239n11
Wyrtzen, Jonathan, 237n75

Yule, Henry, 246n30

Zamindars. See Hindu landholders
Zubdat ul Mulk. See Select of State

GPSR Authorized Representative: Easy Access System Europe, Mustamäe tee
50, 10621 Tallinn, Estonia, gpsr.requests@easproject.com

GPSR Authorized Representative: Easy Access System Europe, Mustamäe tee 50, 10621 Tallinn, Estonia, gpsr.requests@easproject.com

www.ingramcontent.com/pod-product-compliance
Lightning Source LLC
Chambersburg PA
CBHW022036290426
44109CB00014B/875